Basics of Hospitality Information Technology

Basics of Hospitality Information Technology

Hotel IT, Guest Experience, Cybersecurity, AI
and Financial Decision-Making for Hospitality Executives

Eric Bouf

ÉK::LÏT Editions for Hospitality

Published by: BoD · Books on Demand, 31 avenue Saint-Rémy, 57600 Forbach, France, bod@bod.fr

----

Édition : BoD · Books on Demand, 31 avenue Saint-Rémy, 57600 Forbach, bod@bod.fr
Impression : Libri Plureos GmbH, Friedensallee 273, 22763 Hambourg (Allemagne)

Impression à la demande
ISBN : 978-2-3228-5967-2
Dépôt légal : Mai 2026

TABLE OF CONTENTS

Copyright / Usage Note 7
Author's Note 9
Preface 11
How to Use This Book 13
Course Overview 15
Chapter 1 — Introduction to Hospitality IT & Hotel IT Functions 19
Chapter 2 — Hotel IT Architecture & Network Design 53
Chapter 3 — Cybersecurity, Data Protection & Risk Management 89
Chapter 4 — GDPR & PCI-DSS in Hospitality 123
Chapter 5 — Artificial Intelligence in Hospitality 159
Chapter 6 — Hospitality IT Ecosystem: IPTV, WiFi & Telephony 193
Chapter 7 — IT Vocabulary, Governance & IT for Executives 229
Chapter 8 — IT Financial Management: OPEX, CAPEX & ROI 265
Conclusion — Technology Serves Hospitality 299
Final Executive Framework — The Hospitality IT Decision Checklist....................303
Final Capstone Case Study 307
Complete Glossary of Hospitality IT Terms 313
Final Reflection Questions 319
Final Consolidated References and Further Reading 321
About the Author 325

COPYRIGHT / USAGE NOTE

This book is intended as an educational and professional learning resource for students, hospitality managers, hotel executives, consultants and readers who wish to understand the role of Information Technology in modern hospitality.

This book is designed to support learning in hospitality management and technology-related decision-making. It is not a technical engineering manual, legal advisory document, cybersecurity audit guide or financial consulting report. Readers should seek qualified professional advice when making legal, financial, cybersecurity, compliance or major technology investment decisions.

The examples, scenarios and case studies included in this book are intended for educational purposes. They may be inspired by common hospitality situations but should not be interpreted as representing any specific hotel, company, brand or individual unless explicitly stated.

AUTHOR'S NOTE

This book is the result of the author's professional journey in international hospitality and his current work as a hospitality management educator.

For more than thirty years, he has worked in the hotel industry across different regions of the world, including Asia, America, Europe, Dubai and North Africa. Throughout this journey, he has experienced hospitality from the inside: operations, service delivery, guest expectations, leadership challenges, hotel performance, brand standards and the constant need to adapt to changing markets.

Today, he teaches hospitality management to postgraduate students at AIM and Ferrandi, in Paris and Bordeaux. As a professor, he stands at the crossroads between professional experience and academic transmission. His role is not only to explain concepts, but to help future hospitality leaders understand how decisions are made in real hotel environments.

This book was written with that objective in mind. It is not a technical manual for IT specialists, but a management book for hospitality students, future executives, General Managers, asset managers, consultants and professionals who need to understand how technology affects hotel operations, guest experience, cybersecurity, compliance, financial decisions and strategic leadership.

Hospitality has always been a human industry, and it will always remain so. However, the systems that support hospitality have become increasingly digital. A hotel manager does not need to become an engineer, but must understand the business consequences of technology decisions. Poor WiFi, a PMS failure, weak cybersecurity, uncontrolled data, badly evaluated AI or poorly governed IT investments are not only technical problems. They are service, revenue, trust and leadership issues.

The ambition of this book is simple: to make hospitality technology understandable, practical and executive-oriented. The reader should be able to speak more confidently with IT teams, vendors, owners, asset managers and operational leaders. More importantly, the reader should understand that technology only has value when it serves hospitality.

This book is written for students preparing to enter the industry, but also for professionals who wish to strengthen their understanding of hotel technology from a managerial perspective. It is a bridge between the classroom, the hotel floor and the executive meeting room.

PREFACE

Technology has become one of the most important forces shaping modern hospitality. Yet for many hospitality students and managers, Information Technology remains intimidating, technical or distant from the daily reality of service. It is often associated with systems, servers, passwords, networks, software and support tickets. In reality, IT is much more than that.

In a hotel, technology is connected to almost every aspect of the guest journey. It supports reservations, check-in, housekeeping, payment, restaurant transactions, WiFi, telephony, in-room entertainment, guest profiles, revenue management, data protection, cybersecurity, reporting, vendor management and financial decision-making. When technology works well, it often becomes invisible. When it fails, the guest immediately feels the consequences.

A hotel does not need technology for the sake of technology. It needs technology because hospitality has become more complex, more connected and more dependent on accurate information. Guests expect seamless experiences. Owners expect financial discipline. Regulators expect compliance. Employees need reliable tools. Brands must protect trust. Executives must make investment decisions in a world where digital systems are no longer optional.

This book was created to help hospitality students and professionals understand IT from a managerial perspective. It does not ask the reader to become a technician. Instead, it helps the reader develop the vocabulary, logic and confidence required to discuss technology as a business issue.

The central idea running through the book is that IT decisions are never only technical. A PMS replacement affects operations and finance. A WiFi upgrade affects guest satisfaction and revenue. A cybersecurity incident affects trust and leadership. A data breach affects compliance and reputation. An AI project affects ethics, data quality and investment priorities. A SaaS subscription affects OPEX, CAPEX and long-term vendor dependency.

The book therefore approaches hospitality IT through the lens of executive decision-making. Each chapter connects technology to hotel operations, guest experience, risk management, compliance, brand positioning and financial performance. The objective is to help readers understand not only what technology does, but why it matters.

This book can be used as a course reading book, a professional introduction to hospitality technology, or a revision tool for students preparing for executive-style discussions and presentations. It is designed to be practical, structured and accessible, while remaining serious enough for postgraduate hospitality education.

Above all, this book defends a simple conviction: technology should not replace hospitality. It should support it, protect it and help professionals deliver it with greater clarity, consistency and intelligence.

HOW TO USE THIS BOOK

This book has been designed as a structured learning journey through the main areas of hospitality Information Technology. It can be read from beginning to end, or chapter by chapter according to the reader's needs.

Each chapter introduces a major topic in hospitality IT and connects it to hotel management, guest experience, operational performance and executive decision-making. The chapters are written in a standalone format, meaning that each one can be understood without access to a classroom presentation or technical manual.

Readers are encouraged to use the book actively. The main text provides the conceptual and managerial foundation. The hospitality examples help connect the ideas to real hotel situations. The case studies encourage applied thinking. The final section of each chapter, entitled To Review This Chapter, allows the reader to consolidate learning through key terms, reflection questions, review questions and references.

Students can use the book before class to prepare for discussion, during class to follow the logic of the topic, and after class to revise. Hospitality professionals can use it as a reference when preparing technology discussions, vendor meetings, investment proposals or operational reviews.

The book is not designed for memorization only. It is designed to develop judgment. Readers should regularly ask themselves: What is the business issue behind this technology topic? What is the guest impact? What is the operational risk? What is the financial consequence? Who is accountable? What should a hospitality executive ask before making a decision?

The strongest way to use this book is to read it with a managerial mindset. Technology vocabulary is important, but vocabulary is only the beginning. The real objective is to understand how technology decisions affect people, service, trust, revenue and long-term performance.

COURSE OVERVIEW

Basics of Hospitality Information Technology introduces the role of IT in modern hotel management from an executive and hospitality-focused perspective. The book is structured around eight chapters, each addressing a key dimension of hospitality technology.

The course begins with a broad introduction to hospitality IT and the main hotel IT functions. It then moves into hotel IT architecture and network design, helping readers understand the infrastructure behind modern operations. The next chapters explore cybersecurity, data protection, GDPR, PCI-DSS and compliance, showing why risk and trust are central to hotel technology governance.

The book then examines artificial intelligence in hospitality, with a practical focus on distinguishing AI from automation and analytics, identifying realistic use cases and avoiding vendor hype. It continues with guest-facing technology, including IPTV, WiFi and telephony, showing how infrastructure directly shapes the guest experience and revenue performance.

The final part of the book focuses on executive communication, governance and financial decision-making. Readers learn how to speak about IT in business language, understand steering committees, evaluate vendors, interpret KPIs and defend technology investments. The final chapter introduces IT financial management through OPEX, CAPEX, ROI, hidden costs, SaaS models and investment arbitration.

Together, these chapters provide a complete managerial introduction to hospitality IT. The objective is not to make the reader a technical specialist, but to prepare the reader to think, speak and decide more confidently about technology in a hotel environment.

Chapter 1 — Introduction to Hospitality IT & Hotel IT Functions
This chapter introduces hospitality IT as a strategic management topic. It explains why hotel managers must understand technology, how IT supports the guest journey, and why infrastructure, applications, security, support and governance are essential hotel functions.

Chapter 2 — Hotel IT Architecture & Network Design
This chapter explains the digital architecture behind hotel operations. It introduces LAN, WAN, WiFi, cloud, on-premise and hybrid models, system integration, property-level IT and regional-office IT governance.

Chapter 3 — Cybersecurity, Data Protection & Risk Management
This chapter presents cybersecurity as a leadership and business continuity issue. It covers ransomware, phishing, data breaches, attack surfaces, crisis roles and the first managerial decisions during a cyber incident.

Chapter 4 — GDPR & PCI-DSS in Hospitality
This chapter explains why compliance is a business issue, not only a legal or IT issue. It focuses on hotel data, payment security, GDPR principles, PCI-DSS, cloud vendors, loyalty databases and common hospitality compliance mistakes.

Chapter 5 — Artificial Intelligence in Hospitality
This chapter demystifies AI and distinguishes it from automation and analytics. It explores practical AI use cases in revenue management, CRM, operations, finance, HR and guest experience, while emphasizing data quality, ethics and human oversight.

Chapter 6 — Hospitality IT Ecosystem: IPTV, WiFi & Telephony
This chapter connects guest-facing technology to brand positioning, satisfaction and revenue protection. It shows why WiFi is a promise,

IPTV is more than television, and telephony remains important for safety and service continuity.

Chapter 7 — IT Vocabulary, Governance & IT for Executives
This chapter helps readers speak about technology in executive language. It covers IT vocabulary, KPIs, dashboards, steering committees, vendor management, governance, decision framing and executive briefings.

Chapter 8 — IT Financial Management: OPEX, CAPEX & ROI
This chapter explains why technology decisions are financial and strategic decisions. It explores CAPEX, OPEX, SaaS, hidden costs, ROI, technical debt, PMS replacement and how to defend IT investments to owners or boards.

Chapter 1

Introduction to Hospitality IT & Hotel IT Functions

LEARNING OBJECTIVES

By the end of this chapter, readers should be able to explain what Information Technology means in a hotel context and understand why it has become a strategic management topic rather than a purely technical function. They should be able to distinguish between IT, Operations and Finance responsibilities, identify the difference between Central IT and Property IT, and recognize the main hotel IT functions: infrastructure, applications, security, support and governance. They should also understand why hotel executives remain accountable for IT performance, even when technical specialists manage the systems, and apply basic IT thinking to the opening, daily management and long-term performance of a hotel.

OPENING PERSPECTIVE

For many people, Information Technology still suggests computers, cables, servers, passwords, software updates and technical support. In hospitality, however, IT is much more than a technical department. It is one of the invisible systems that allows a hotel to function. The more sophisticated the hotel experience becomes, the more dependent it is on systems that guests rarely see and that managers sometimes underestimate until something stops working.

A modern hotel cannot operate properly without technology. Reservations, room allocation, check-in, housekeeping status, restaurant transactions, spa billing, guest profiles, WiFi, payment systems, revenue management, online distribution, accounting, reporting and post-stay communication all depend on IT systems working together. The hotel may appear to the guest as a place of welcome, comfort and service. Behind that visible service promise is a large operational ecosystem made of data, applications, networks, devices, interfaces, vendors and procedures.

This chapter introduces hospitality IT as a strategic management topic. Future General Managers, asset managers, consultants, hotel owners and executives do not need to become technical specialists. They do, however, need to understand how technology protects revenue, supports operations, shapes the guest experience, secures data and informs business decisions. In a hotel, technology is not an isolated tool. It is part of the operating model.

A hotel leader does not need to configure a network. But a hotel leader must understand what happens when the network fails. A hotel leader does not need to code a Property Management System, but must understand what the PMS does for the business. A hotel leader does not need to be a cybersecurity engineer, but must understand why guest data, payment data and system access are high-risk areas. This is the core mindset of hospitality IT management: the executive may not perform the technical task, but the executive remains responsible for the business consequences.

In hospitality, IT is no longer only a technical language. It is a management language. It allows managers to discuss reliability, service quality, data accuracy, compliance, guest expectations, vendor performance, return on investment and operational continuity. A manager who cannot speak this language risks being excluded from important decisions, or worse, making decisions without understanding their consequences.

WHY DO HOSPITALITY MANAGERS NEED TO UNDERSTAND IT

Hospitality is an operationally complex industry. A hotel combines accommodation, food and beverage, sales, revenue management, housekeeping, maintenance, finance, security, marketing, guest relations and sometimes spa, wellness, events, retail or residential services. Each department has its own priorities, but all departments depend on shared information. The guest does not experience the hotel as a collection of departments. The guest experiences one promise, one stay and one brand.

Technology connects these departments. When a guest books a room, the reservation must reach the hotel. When the guest arrives, the front desk must see the reservation, allocate a room, verify payment information and understand the guest profile. When the guest has breakfast, the charge may be posted to the room. When housekeeping cleans the room, the room status must be updated. When maintenance repairs an air-conditioning issue, the front office must know whether the room can be sold again. When the guest checks out, the invoice must be accurate. After departure, the guest may receive a satisfaction survey or a personalized offer.

None of this is only technical. It is operational, commercial and relational. The guest may judge the hotel on the warmth of the welcome, the beauty of the lobby, the comfort of the bed or the quality of breakfast, but behind each of these touchpoints there are systems. A receptionist cannot welcome efficiently if the reservation is missing. A housekeeper cannot prioritize rooms correctly if the room-status system is inaccurate. A restaurant manager cannot control revenue if the POS is poorly integrated. A revenue manager cannot forecast effectively if data is incomplete or inconsistent.

This is why hospitality managers must be IT-literate. IT literacy does not mean becoming an engineer. It means being able to ask the right questions: Which systems are essential for daily operations? Which systems directly affect the guest experience? What happens if a system fails? Who is responsible for solving the problem? What data is being collected? Is the data secure? Are systems properly integrated? Are vendors reliable? Is the technology investment justified? Does the solution support the hotel's positioning and brand promise?

A manager who cannot ask these questions becomes dependent on technical specialists and vendors. A manager who can ask them becomes a more credible decision-maker. This credibility matters because technology projects are rarely neutral. They involve cost, change, training, risk and sometimes resistance from employees. A new PMS, a new POS, a new CRM or a new mobile key solution does not simply change a screen. It changes habits, responsibilities, workflows and sometimes the balance of power between departments.

Hospitality managers also need IT understanding because technology decisions often have long-term consequences. A poor system choice can lock a hotel into an unsuitable vendor for years. A weak integration decision can generate daily manual work. A poorly designed network can limit future guest-facing innovation. A neglected cybersecurity culture can expose the hotel to reputational damage. In this sense, IT decisions are not just operational decisions. They are strategic commitments.

FROM HOSPITALITY EXPERIENCE TO DIGITAL EXPERIENCE

Hospitality has always been about welcome, service, comfort, recognition and trust. Technology does not replace these fundamentals. Instead, it increasingly shapes how they are delivered. A hotel can have a beautiful design, an elegant service culture and a strong brand identity, but if its digital touchpoints are confusing, slow or unreliable, the guest experience is weakened.

The modern guest journey can be understood through five major stages: pre-arrival, arrival, stay, departure and post-stay. At every stage, IT plays a role. Some technologies are visible to the guest, such as online booking, WiFi, mobile check-in, IPTV or digital payment. Other technologies are invisible, such as reservation distribution, interfaces between systems, network architecture, data security, access rights or reporting tools. Both categories matter.

A common managerial mistake is to separate "real hospitality" from "technology." In reality, the guest does not make this separation. If the booking process is frustrating, that is part of the experience. If the WiFi is poor, that is part of the experience. If the invoice is wrong, that is part of the experience. If the guest's allergy note is not transmitted to the restaurant, that is part of the experience. Technology influences the emotional perception of the hotel because it shapes ease, confidence, recognition and trust.

PRE-ARRIVAL

Before arriving at the hotel, the guest may interact with several systems: the brand website, an online travel agency, a central reservation system, a mobile application, a booking engine, a confirmation email or a pre-arrival questionnaire. At this stage, technology supports availability, pricing, room selection, payment guarantee, preference collection and communication.

Pre-arrival is not only a commercial stage. It is the beginning of the relationship. A smooth booking path creates confidence. A confirmation email that is clear, accurate and personalized reassures the guest. A pre-arrival form that asks meaningful questions may help the hotel prepare the stay. Conversely, if the website is slow, the rate information is unclear, the booking confirmation is incorrect or the hotel fails to recognize a loyalty member, the guest arrives with uncertainty.

In luxury and upscale hospitality, pre-arrival technology can support anticipation. A hotel may use guest history to prepare preferred amenities, pillow type, transfer arrangements or dietary requirements. In corporate hospitality, it may ensure that billing instructions, negotiated rates and traveler profiles are correct. In resort hospitality, it may support pre-booking of restaurants, spa treatments, excursions or airport transfers. In each case, technology helps the hotel move from reaction to preparation.

ARRIVAL

Arrival is one of the most sensitive moments in the guest journey. The guest has expectations, luggage, perhaps fatigue, and often limited tolerance for delay. Technology supports this moment through the PMS, identity verification, room assignment, payment authorization, digital registration, key encoding, mobile check-in or mobile key activation.

Even in a luxury environment where human welcome remains central, technology must support the emotional quality of the arrival. If the system is slow, if the reservation cannot be found, if payment authorization fails, or if the room status is incorrect, the first impression may be damaged. The guest may not care whether the problem comes from the PMS, the payment terminal, the network or a channel manager. For the guest, the hotel is simply not ready.

Technology should not make the welcome colder. It should make it smoother. A well-designed arrival process frees employees from unnecessary administrative friction and allows them to focus on eye contact, recognition, explanation and care. In this sense, IT can protect the human dimension of hospitality by reducing operational noise.

STAY

During the stay, guests interact with both visible and invisible technologies. Visible technologies include WiFi, IPTV, digital room controls, mobile requests, online restaurant booking, spa reservations, messaging tools, digital concierge services and payment devices. Invisible technologies include housekeeping systems, maintenance tickets, internal communication platforms, guest profiles, POS integration, revenue tracking, network infrastructure, security tools and data storage.

The guest may not see the full ecosystem, but the guest feels its effects. A room that is ready on time, a preference that is remembered, a restaurant bill correctly posted to the room, a maintenance issue resolved quickly, a spa appointment confirmed properly or a strong WiFi connection all depend on technology working properly. A hotel stay is a chain of small operational promises. IT helps connect those promises.

The stay phase is also where technology most directly meets service culture. A mobile request tool may allow a guest to ask for extra towels, but the quality of the experience still depends on response time, tone and execution. A CRM may display a guest preference, but an employee must interpret it intelligently. Technology can provide information; hospitality transforms information into care.

DEPARTURE

Departure requires accuracy and speed. The bill must be correct. Payments must be processed securely. Loyalty points may need to be updated. Corporate billing instructions may need to be followed.

Invoices may need to be sent electronically. The guest may be in a hurry, and a small error at this stage can create disproportionate frustration.

A poor departure experience can weaken an otherwise positive stay. Billing mistakes, queues at check-out, missing charges, duplicate charges or payment problems create irritation at the final moment of the journey. The emotional memory of the stay may be influenced by the last interaction. Technology should help the guest leave with clarity, not confusion.

From a management perspective, departure is also a financial control moment. Accurate billing, proper posting of charges, secure payment processing and reliable reporting protect revenue. A hotel that repeatedly loses revenue through incorrect postings or poor interfaces may not notice the problem immediately, but the accumulated loss can be significant.

POST-STAY

After departure, technology supports feedback collection, guest relationship management, loyalty communication, complaint follow-up, reputation management and future booking incentives. The post-stay stage is strategically important because it connects one stay to the next.

A hotel that manages post-stay communication intelligently can strengthen loyalty, increase direct bookings and improve its understanding of guest expectations. A well-timed feedback request can reveal operational weaknesses. A personalized message can reinforce recognition. A direct booking offer can reduce dependency on intermediaries. A rapid response to a negative review can protect reputation.

Post-stay technology must be used with judgment. Too many automated messages may feel intrusive. Poorly personalized communication may damage trust. Data that is collected but not used responsibly becomes a liability rather than an asset. The aim is not to communicate more, but to communicate better.

WHEN IT FAILS: THE HOTEL WITHOUT TECHNOLOGY

To understand the importance of IT, imagine a busy Monday morning in a 200-room city hotel. The PMS stops working at 9:00 AM. Guests are checking out. New arrivals are expected later in the day. The front desk cannot confirm room status. Housekeeping cannot update cleaned rooms. The restaurant cannot correctly post breakfast charges to guest rooms. The finance team cannot finalize invoices. The reservations team cannot verify arrivals. Managers begin asking for reports that cannot be generated. Guests queue in the lobby. Some are late for meetings. Others begin to complain online.

The problem is not simply that a computer stopped working. The real issue is business disruption. The consequences may include delayed check-ins and check-outs, billing errors, guest dissatisfaction, operational confusion, revenue loss, reputational damage, staff stress, possible data loss and weakened management control.

The operational consequences can multiply quickly. Front office employees may create manual lists, but those lists may not match housekeeping information. Housekeeping may clean rooms in the wrong order because arrival priorities are unclear. Food and beverage charges may be held separately and posted later, creating errors. Managers may not know how many rooms are actually available. If the outage continues, the hotel may lose the ability to accept certain payments, produce accurate invoices or communicate confidently with guests.

The reputational consequences can also be immediate. A guest who waits thirty minutes in the lobby may post a review before the system is restored. A corporate traveler who cannot receive an invoice may complain to the travel manager. A loyalty guest who is not recognized may feel ignored. The technical incident becomes a service story, and service stories travel quickly.

This example shows why hotel executives must avoid seeing IT as a back-office concern. In hospitality, an IT failure quickly becomes an operations problem, a guest problem, a finance problem and a brand problem. The real managerial question is not whether technology can fail. It can. The question is whether the hotel has anticipated failure, prepared procedures and trained teams to respond.

IT IS NOT ONLY ABOUT COMPUTERS

One of the most important shifts for hospitality managers is to stop reducing IT to hardware. Computers, cables, servers and devices are only part of the picture. In hotels, IT delivers five broader forms of value: processes, data and insights, security, guest experience and business continuity.

This broader understanding changes how managers make decisions. If IT is only seen as equipment, the discussion becomes limited to cost, installation and maintenance. If IT is understood as an operating capability, the discussion becomes richer: How does this system improve service? How does it reduce risk? How does it support employees? How does it protect revenue? How does it strengthen decision-making?

PROCESSES

IT supports standardized, repeatable and efficient operations. A PMS structures reservations, room assignment, check-in, billing and guest profiles. A POS records transactions in restaurants, bars, spas and retail outlets. A housekeeping system helps teams track room status. A maintenance platform helps organize technical interventions. Good technology does not eliminate hospitality work. It organizes it.

Processes matter because hotels operate under time pressure. A hotel cannot improvise every reservation, every invoice, every room status update or every payment. Technology reduces manual errors, accelerates coordination and creates operational discipline. For example, if a room is marked clean but has not been inspected, the front office may assign it too early. If a restaurant charge is not posted correctly, the hotel may lose revenue. If a maintenance issue is not logged, the same complaint may return.

Standardized processes are especially important in multi-property hotel groups. A group cannot compare performance, train employees or deploy systems efficiently if each property uses completely different procedures. At the same time, processes should not become rigid bureaucracy. The best technology supports discipline while leaving room for service judgment.

DATA AND INSIGHTS

Hotels generate large volumes of data: occupancy, revenue, average daily rate, booking channels, guest preferences, length of stay, spending patterns, complaints, service requests and loyalty behavior. This data has limited value if it remains fragmented or unreliable. IT systems make data usable. When properly structured, data helps managers understand performance, identify risks, anticipate demand and make better decisions.

A hotel without reliable data is managed by instinct only. Instinct matters in hospitality, especially for reading people and situations, but it should be supported by evidence. A General Manager may feel that the hotel is performing well, but the data may reveal declining direct bookings, increasing complaint rates, weak conversion from certain channels or revenue leakage in outlets. Data gives managers the ability to move from impressions to analysis.

Data quality is therefore a managerial issue. If employees enter guest names inconsistently, duplicate profiles multiply. If market segmentation is poorly maintained, revenue reports become less useful. If POS categories are badly configured, food and beverage analysis is distorted. If guest preferences are entered as free text without structure, they may be difficult to retrieve. Technology does not automatically produce insight. It produces insight only when data is accurate, consistent and meaningful.

SECURITY

Hotels process sensitive information: names, addresses, passport details, payment information, loyalty profiles, corporate client data, employee records and sometimes health or preference information. This makes security a strategic responsibility. A data breach can damage trust, trigger legal obligations, generate financial consequences and harm the brand.

Security is not only about preventing hackers from entering systems. It is also about controlling user access, training employees, securing payment flows, managing vendors, updating systems and preparing response procedures. A weak password culture, shared user accounts, untrained employees or poorly supervised vendors can create vulnerabilities even when the technical infrastructure appears strong.

Hospitality environments are particularly exposed because they are open by nature. Guests, contractors, staff, event organizers, suppliers and temporary workers may interact with the property. Hotels also operate many connected systems: PMS, POS, WiFi, door locks, cameras, payment terminals, office systems, guest applications and sometimes building management systems. The more connected the environment, the more important governance becomes.

GUEST EXPERIENCE

Guests experience technology both directly and indirectly. They experience it directly when they use WiFi, digital keys, mobile check-in, IPTV, online booking, digital concierge tools or payment terminals. They experience it indirectly when employees use systems to recognize preferences, solve problems, communicate internally, prepare rooms, post charges correctly or respond faster.

Technology should not replace hospitality. It should allow hospitality to be delivered with more accuracy, consistency and intelligence. For example, a CRM cannot create genuine recognition by itself, but it can remind employees that a returning guest prefers a quiet room, celebrates an anniversary or had a previous complaint. A mobile ordering system cannot create warmth, but it can reduce waiting time and help staff coordinate delivery.

The risk is to confuse digitalization with service improvement. Not every digital tool improves hospitality. A poorly designed kiosk may frustrate guests. A chatbot that cannot answer practical questions may damage trust. A mobile app that duplicates rather than simplifies the journey may be ignored. The managerial question should always be: Does this technology make the experience easier, more reliable, more personal or more meaningful?

BUSINESS CONTINUITY

Hotels operate 24 hours a day, seven days a week. Unlike many offices, a hotel cannot simply stop operating when systems fail.

Guests are present. Payments must be processed. Rooms must be allocated. Security must be maintained. Business continuity means ensuring that the hotel can continue operating during or after a disruption.

Business continuity may require backup systems, disaster recovery plans, vendor support contracts, redundant internet connections, backup power for critical systems, manual fallback procedures and crisis communication plans. It also requires training. A procedure that exists in a folder but is not understood by employees will not protect the hotel in a crisis.

In hospitality, continuity is part of trust. Guests expect the hotel to remain calm and functional even when problems occur. The quality of crisis response often reveals the maturity of the organization. A hotel that has prepared for disruption can protect guest confidence. A hotel that improvises under pressure may expose its weaknesses.

DEFINING HOSPITALITY INFORMATION TECHNOLOGY

Hospitality Information Technology can be defined as the combination of systems, infrastructure, data, applications, security, support processes and governance mechanisms that enable a hotel to operate, serve guests, protect information and make management decisions.

This definition is intentionally broad. It includes visible and invisible dimensions. Visible technology includes tools that guests directly touch or notice: WiFi, mobile check-in, digital keys, IPTV, payment terminals, guest applications or online booking engines. Invisible technology includes the systems that make the hotel run: PMS, CRS, POS, servers, cloud platforms, network infrastructure, cybersecurity tools, reporting systems, integrations, user access controls and data storage.

A hospitality manager must understand both. Visible systems shape the guest experience. Invisible systems often carry the greatest operational and strategic risk. Guests may complain about WiFi because they see and feel it directly. They may not complain about a weak integration between PMS and POS, but the hotel will feel it through billing errors, manual corrections and lost productivity.

The definition also highlights that IT is not only a set of tools. It is a system of responsibilities. Someone must choose the technology, configure it, secure it, fund it, update it, train users, monitor performance and decide when to replace it. The more complex the hotel, the more important this responsibility becomes.

IT, OPERATIONS AND FINANCE

A hotel operates through several different managerial logics. Three of the most important are Operations, Finance and IT. Operations focuses on guest experience and service delivery. This includes front office, housekeeping, food and beverage, maintenance, spa, events and guest relations. Finance focuses on cost control, revenue, reporting, accounting, budgeting and financial performance. IT focuses on systems, data integrity, infrastructure, security, analytics and technology support.

These three functions are different, but they cannot work in isolation. IT is the digital thread connecting them. For example, the front office team may focus on welcoming guests, but the quality of that welcome depends on accurate reservations, room status, payment information and guest preferences. Finance may focus on reporting and control, but reliable reporting depends on accurate data from the PMS, POS, payroll, purchasing and accounting systems.

Revenue management depends on data from reservations, market demand, historical performance, pricing systems and distribution channels. Housekeeping depends on room-status updates, maintenance alerts and internal communication tools. Food and beverage depends on POS accuracy, inventory links, revenue center configuration and sometimes reservations or table management systems. Sales depends on CRM, group booking tools, contracts, availability and reporting.

This creates a simple managerial principle: poor IT integration creates poor operational coordination. When systems do not communicate, teams compensate manually. Manual compensation increases the risk of errors, delays, frustration and poor service. It may also hide the real cost of poor technology because employees spend time correcting issues that should not exist.

A useful way to view IT is therefore not as a department beside operations and finance, but as an enabling layer beneath them. IT provides the data and systems through which operations and finance can perform. If that layer is weak, the entire hotel becomes less reliable.

CENTRAL IT AND PROPERTY IT

In hotel groups, IT responsibilities are often divided between Central IT and Property IT. Central IT usually operates at headquarters, corporate or regional level. Its role is to define technology strategy, select major systems, set standards, manage cybersecurity policies, negotiate contracts, support compliance, supervise integration and create long-term technology roadmaps.

Property IT operates at hotel level. Its role is to support daily operations, troubleshoot local issues, assist employees, manage on-site infrastructure, implement corporate standards and ensure that guest-facing technology works in the real operating environment. The property team is closer to daily operational pressure. It understands the building, the staff, the local vendors, the guest profile and the practical constraints.

This division creates a natural tension. Central IT wants standardization. Standardization improves security, efficiency, purchasing power, reporting consistency and brand control. Property IT needs flexibility. Each hotel has its own building, guest profile, market, operational constraints and service culture. A resort, an airport hotel, a palace, a lifestyle hotel and a regional office may not have exactly the same technology needs.

The management challenge is to balance both. Too much centralization can make local teams feel constrained and slow down practical problem-solving. Too much local freedom can create fragmented systems, security gaps, inconsistent data and higher costs. The question for executives is therefore not simply whether IT should be centralized or decentralized. The better question is: Which IT decisions must be standardized, and where should local flexibility be allowed?

For example, cybersecurity policy, data standards, payment security rules and core PMS architecture may need strong central control. Local WiFi coverage planning, meeting room technology, guest communication practices or operational support arrangements may require property-level adaptation. Effective governance clarifies these boundaries before conflicts arise.

WHO IS RESPONSIBLE FOR IT?

Several actors contribute to hotel IT performance. The CIO or Head of IT defines technology strategy, manages major vendors, allocates budgets, supervises cybersecurity priorities and supports digital transformation. The hotel IT Manager handles daily support, local infrastructure, troubleshooting, system reliability, employee assistance and implementation follow-up. Vendors and integrators provide specialized systems, technical expertise, implementation support, maintenance, updates and contractual service levels.

The General Manager, however, remains accountable for the hotel's overall performance. This includes the consequences of IT decisions. This does not mean the General Manager must solve technical problems personally. It means the General Manager must understand risks, ask relevant questions, allocate resources, support staff training, challenge vendors and ensure that technology decisions are aligned with the hotel's business priorities.

A General Manager cannot simply say, "This is an IT problem." If guests cannot check in, it is also a service problem. If invoices are wrong, it is also a finance problem. If payment data is exposed, it is also a legal and reputational problem. If WiFi damages guest satisfaction, it is also a brand problem. Technical responsibility may be delegated. Executive accountability cannot be fully delegated.

This accountability is especially important during openings, renovations, system migrations and crisis situations. When a hotel opens, technology readiness affects the ability to operate from day one. During a system migration, poor preparation can disrupt employees and guests. During a cyber incident, leadership must coordinate legal, operational, communication and technical responses. The executive role is to connect the technical issue to the business reality.

CORE IT FUNCTIONS IN HOTELS

Hotel IT can be understood through five core functions: infrastructure, applications, security and data, support, and governance. Together, these functions form the technology foundation of hotel operations. They are closely connected. Strong applications depend on reliable infrastructure. Useful data depends on good system configuration. Security depends on governance and training. Support depends on clear responsibilities and vendor agreements.

For managers, these five functions provide a practical reading grid. When evaluating a hotel's technology maturity, do not ask only whether the hotel has modern tools. Ask whether the infrastructure is reliable, whether applications are integrated, whether data is secure and usable, whether support is responsive, and whether governance is clear.

INFRASTRUCTURE

Infrastructure is the technical foundation on which all hotel systems depend. It includes wired networks, WiFi, servers, cloud services, computers, tablets, printers, switches, routers, payment terminals, connectivity and sometimes in-room technology equipment. Infrastructure is not glamorous, but it is essential. It is similar to plumbing or electricity: when it works, people rarely notice it; when it fails, everything stops.

From a managerial point of view, three ideas are essential: reliability, redundancy and scalability. Reliability means that systems must work consistently. A hotel cannot afford repeated failures of WiFi, payment systems, PMS access or internal communication tools. Redundancy means that backup solutions exist when something fails. A hotel may need backup internet connectivity, backup power for critical systems, cloud redundancy or emergency procedures. Scalability means that technology can grow with the hotel's needs.

A system that works for a 50-room independent hotel may not be appropriate for a 300-room resort with multiple restaurants, meeting spaces, spa operations and complex distribution channels. Similarly, a network designed for basic office use will not meet the expectations of guests who stream video, attend online meetings, connect several devices and expect seamless coverage in bedrooms, meeting rooms, public spaces and outdoor areas.

Infrastructure decisions must also consider the building. Historic hotels, resorts spread over large areas, high-rise buildings and properties with thick walls may require specific network planning. A poor infrastructure design may not be visible at opening, but it may become a daily source of complaints. In hospitality, infrastructure is a service enabler.

APPLICATIONS

Applications are the software systems used in daily hotel operations. The PMS, or Property Management System, is one of the most central hotel applications. It supports reservations, room assignment, check-in, check-out, guest profiles, billing and operational coordination. The POS, or Point of Sale system, manages transactions in restaurants, bars, spas, retail outlets and other revenue centers. The CRS, or Central Reservation System, helps manage reservations, inventory and distribution.

A Channel Manager distributes availability and rates across online booking platforms. CRM systems support guest relationship management, preferences, loyalty and personalized communication. HR and Finance systems support payroll, accounting, scheduling, reporting and internal management. Depending on the property, additional applications may include event management, spa management, housekeeping, maintenance, procurement, learning management, reputation management or revenue management systems.

The key issue is not only whether each application works individually. The real question is whether the systems work together. A hotel may have many digital tools, but if they are poorly integrated, the operational result may be confusion rather than efficiency. Integration is therefore one of the most important words in hotel technology.

For example, if the PMS and POS are integrated, restaurant charges can be posted to the guest room accurately. If the PMS and CRM are connected, guest preferences may be available for personalization. If the PMS and revenue management system exchange reliable data, pricing decisions can be more informed. If housekeeping updates are visible to the front office in real time, room allocation improves. Each integration reduces friction; each missing integration may create manual work.

Managers should also consider usability. A technically powerful system that employees cannot use properly may fail operationally. In hospitality, systems are used by people working under pressure, often during guest-facing moments. Screens must be understandable, workflows must be practical and training must be sufficient. Technology should fit the rhythm of hotel operations.

SECURITY AND DATA

Security and data management are critical because hospitality businesses handle sensitive information. Hotels collect and process guest names, contact details, payment information, passport information, preferences, travel patterns, corporate accounts, employee records and loyalty data. This information has operational value, but it also creates responsibility.

Cybersecurity is not only a technical matter. It is an executive risk topic. A cyber incident can interrupt operations, expose guest data, damage trust, create legal obligations and generate financial consequences. The risk is especially important in hospitality because hotels combine open guest environments, many users, multiple systems, payment flows, third-party vendors and continuous operations.

Data must therefore be protected, governed and used responsibly. Security begins with basic discipline: strong access management, individual user accounts, password policies, employee training, timely updates, secure payment processes, vendor controls and incident response procedures. Many incidents do not begin with highly sophisticated attacks. They begin with human error, weak processes or poorly controlled access.

Data also needs governance. Who can access guest profiles? How long is data stored? Is personal data collected for a clear purpose? Are employees trained to handle sensitive information? Are vendors processing data securely? Are reports accurate? These questions connect IT to legal, ethical and managerial responsibilities.

Security is not optional. It is part of the hotel's duty of care. A guest entrusts the hotel not only with luggage and comfort, but also with personal information, payment data and sometimes identity documents. Protecting this trust is part of hospitality.

SUPPORT

IT support includes help desk services, troubleshooting, system maintenance, user onboarding, updates, access management and employee training. Support is often underestimated because it appears less strategic than system selection or cybersecurity. Yet support determines whether technology actually works in daily operations.

A hotel may invest in excellent systems, but if employees do not know how to use them, the investment fails. If problems are not solved quickly, frustration increases. If access rights are poorly managed, security risks grow. If updates are not coordinated, operations may be disrupted. Technology adoption depends on training, communication and follow-up.

Support must also match the reality of hotel hours. A hotel operates at night, on weekends and during holidays. If critical support is available only during office hours, the hotel may be exposed. Managers must understand service-level agreements, escalation procedures and vendor response times. Support is not just a technical comfort; it is an operational protection.

Employee experience is another reason support matters. When systems are slow, confusing or unreliable, employees become frustrated. That frustration may appear in the guest experience. Good IT support helps employees feel capable, confident and assisted. In a service industry, supporting employees is a way of supporting guests.

GOVERNANCE

Governance refers to how IT decisions are planned, funded, controlled, monitored and aligned with business objectives. It includes technology strategy, roadmaps, budget allocation, vendor management, risk assessment, compliance, change management, service-level agreements and performance indicators.

Without governance, hotels may accumulate disconnected tools, duplicate costs, weak security, unclear responsibilities and inconsistent data. Governance turns IT from a collection of systems into a managed business function. It clarifies who decides, who pays, who owns the data, who supports the system and how value is measured.

For executives, governance means asking: Who owns the decision? Who pays for the system? Who uses it? Who supports it? Who manages the vendor? What risk does it create? What value does it generate? How will success be measured? These questions are not technical. They are managerial.

Governance is especially important when hotels face vendor proposals. Technology vendors often present solutions as simple, innovative and transformative. Some solutions may indeed create value. Others may be expensive, poorly integrated or unnecessary. Strong governance helps managers separate strategic value from technological enthusiasm.

Change management is part of governance. A system implementation is not complete when the software is installed. It is complete when employees understand it, managers use its data, processes are adapted and the expected value is achieved. The human side of technology adoption is often the difference between success and disappointment.

HOSPITALITY EXAMPLES: HOW IT SHAPES DAILY MANAGEMENT

In a full-service hotel, IT influences almost every operational decision even when managers do not label the decision as technological. Consider a breakfast operation. The POS must identify whether the guest has breakfast included, whether the charge should be posted to the room, whether the guest is part of a group, whether a corporate package applies, and whether revenue should be assigned to the correct outlet. If these settings are wrong, the guest may be charged incorrectly or the hotel may lose revenue. The service issue may appear at the restaurant door, but its cause may be system configuration.

Consider housekeeping. A room attendant may clean a room perfectly, but if the room status is not updated in the system, the front desk may keep the guest waiting unnecessarily. If the PMS is not aligned with housekeeping priorities, early arrivals may not be handled properly. If maintenance defects are not connected to room status, a room may be sold while an issue is still unresolved. Technology therefore affects not only speed, but also trust between departments.

Consider sales and events. A sales manager may confirm a meeting room, catering requirements and accommodation block. This decision touches availability, pricing, contracts, deposits, banquet event orders, room inventory, billing instructions and operational communication. If systems are disconnected, employees must re-enter the same information several times. Each re-entry creates a risk of error. A strong IT environment reduces duplication and gives teams a shared version of the truth.

Consider a luxury guest relations team. Personalization depends on memory. Yet in a hotel with many employees and many shifts, memory cannot rely only on individual employees. A guest preference must be captured, stored, interpreted and shared appropriately. If the CRM is well used, employees can recognize returning guests with precision. If the CRM is poorly used, personalization becomes inconsistent or even intrusive. The difference is not only the software; it is the discipline of data entry, the culture of service and the governance of guest information.

These examples show that hospitality IT is practical before it is technical. It appears in the breakfast charge, the room status, the event contract, the guest preference and the invoice. For this reason, future hotel executives should not wait for a crisis to become interested in technology. They should observe how systems shape the daily rhythm of the hotel.

The same logic applies to independent hotels and hotel groups. In an independent hotel, the owner or General Manager may be closer to every system decision, from WiFi investment to PMS selection. In a hotel group, the decision may be shared between property leadership, brand standards, regional IT, corporate procurement and ownership. In both cases, the manager must understand how the technology will affect service, cost, risk and long-term flexibility.

APPLIED CASE STUDY: OPENING A NEW HOTEL

Imagine you are the General Manager of a new 120-room, 4-star hotel opening in Europe in six months. You must make the key IT decisions before opening day. These decisions will affect guest satisfaction, operating costs, staff readiness, legal compliance, revenue control and brand reputation. Your challenge is to identify which IT functions are mandatory for opening and which can be implemented later.

A practical decision framework should include four criteria: guest impact, operational risk, compliance risk and budget value. These criteria help managers avoid two opposite mistakes. The first mistake is underinvesting in essential systems and exposing the hotel to operational chaos. The second mistake is buying too many tools too early without ensuring that the basics are stable.

GUEST IMPACT

The first question is whether the technology directly affects the guest experience. A PMS, payment system, room access system, WiFi network and communication tools are essential because they affect arrival, stay and departure. If these systems fail, the guest will feel the consequences immediately. Other systems may be useful but less urgent for day-one operations. A sophisticated marketing automation tool, for example, may create value later but is unlikely to be more urgent than a reliable PMS or secure payment flow.

Guest impact should be considered across the full journey. Before arrival, reservations and confirmation systems must work. At arrival, check-in, payment authorization and key creation must be reliable. During the stay, WiFi, room technology, service requests and POS posting affect satisfaction. At departure, billing and payment must be accurate. After departure, feedback and loyalty systems support continuity. A good opening plan protects each of these moments.

OPERATIONAL RISK

The second question is what happens if the system fails. If the PMS is not ready, the hotel cannot operate properly. If the POS is not integrated, restaurant charges may be incorrectly posted. If WiFi is unstable, guests may complain and staff may lose access to cloud systems. If staff are not trained, errors will multiply during opening. Operational risk helps managers prioritize.

Opening periods are especially fragile because teams are new, procedures are not yet stabilized and guests may be curious or demanding. A small system issue can become a large operational issue because employees have not yet built routines. Managers should therefore test critical systems before opening, run simulations and prepare manual fallback procedures.

COMPLIANCE RISK

The third question is whether the system involves personal data, payment data, security obligations or legal requirements. A hotel opening cannot treat data protection and payment security as future topics. Guest data, employee data and payment flows exist from day one. Compliance cannot be improvised after opening.

For example, payment terminals, online payment processes, PMS user access, guest identification documents and loyalty data all require careful handling. The hotel must also know which vendors process data, where data is stored, who can access it and how incidents would be reported. A compliance weakness during opening can create serious consequences later.

BUDGET AND VALUE

The fourth question is whether the system is essential, affordable and aligned with long-term value. Some technology investments may appear expensive at the beginning but protect the hotel from greater costs later. Others may be attractive but not essential. Managers must distinguish between "nice to have" and "must have."

For opening day, the top IT priorities would normally include PMS and reservation management, payment systems and POS integration, secure network and WiFi infrastructure, cybersecurity and user access controls, telephony and communication systems, accounting and reporting connections, backup and support procedures, and staff training before opening.

The most dangerous mistake would be to treat IT as something that can be finalized at the last minute. In a hotel opening, delayed IT decisions often create operational chaos. Technology must be tested before guests arrive, not discovered during the first check-in.

MANAGERIAL TAKEAWAYS

The first lesson is that IT is business. Technology choices directly influence revenue, guest satisfaction, cost control, employee efficiency, legal exposure and brand reputation. A system decision is therefore also a business decision.

The second lesson is that managers do not need to be technical experts, but they must be IT-literate. They must understand the vocabulary, the risks, the priorities and the business consequences of technology decisions. IT literacy allows managers to participate intelligently in discussions with CIOs, vendors, owners and department heads.

The third lesson is that IT responsibility remains at executive level. A General Manager, asset manager or corporate leader cannot simply classify IT as a technical matter. In hospitality, an IT problem quickly becomes an operations problem, a guest problem, a finance problem and a brand problem.

The fourth lesson is that invisible systems often carry the greatest risk. Guests may notice mobile keys, IPTV or digital check-in. They may not notice network redundancy, integrations, cybersecurity controls or backup procedures. But these invisible systems protect the hotel's ability to operate.

The fifth lesson is that technology must serve hospitality, not replace it. The purpose of IT is not to make the hotel feel more mechanical. Its purpose is to help the hotel become more reliable, responsive, secure, personalized and intelligent. The best technology does not remove the human dimension of hospitality. It gives employees better conditions to deliver it.

TO REVIEW THIS CHAPTER

KEY TERMS

Hospitality IT : The systems, infrastructure, data, applications, support processes and governance mechanisms that enable hotel operations, guest experience, security and management decisions.

PMS - Property Management System : A core hotel system used for reservations, room assignment, check-in, check-out, guest profiles and billing.

POS - Point of Sale : A system used to process and record transactions in restaurants, bars, spas, retail outlets and other hotel revenue centers.

CRS - Central Reservation System : A system used to manage reservations, availability and inventory across distribution channels.

CRM - Customer Relationship Management : A system or approach used to manage guest profiles, preferences, loyalty and communication.

Infrastructure : The technical foundation of hotel IT, including networks, WiFi, hardware, servers, cloud services and connectivity.

Integration : The ability of different systems to communicate and exchange data reliably.

Central IT : The corporate, headquarters or group-level IT function responsible for strategy, standards, security, governance and major systems.

Property IT : The local hotel IT function responsible for daily support, troubleshooting, implementation and guest-facing technology.

Governance : The way technology decisions are planned, funded, controlled, monitored and aligned with business objectives.

Business Continuity : The ability of the hotel to continue operating during or after a disruption.

Cybersecurity : The practices, tools and processes used to protect systems, networks and data from unauthorized access, disruption or misuse.

Vendor Management : The process of selecting, supervising and evaluating external technology providers.

Redundancy : The presence of backup systems or alternative solutions in case a primary system fails.

Scalability : The ability of a technology solution to grow with the needs of the business.

REFLECTION QUESTIONS

- Why is it dangerous for a hotel manager to think of IT only as a technical support function?
- Which technologies do guests directly see during their stay? Which technologies do they depend on without seeing them?
- In your opinion, which hotel department depends most on IT: Front Office, Housekeeping, Finance, Food and Beverage, Revenue Management or Sales? Explain your answer.
- Why can a PMS failure become a brand reputation issue?
- Should a hotel group centralize most IT decisions, or should each property have more local flexibility?
- Why does the General Manager remain accountable for IT outcomes even when the hotel has an IT Manager?

- If you were opening a 120-room hotel, which IT system would you prioritize first and why?
- What is the difference between buying a technology tool and managing a technology function?
- How can poor IT integration damage the guest experience?
- What does it mean to say that technology should serve hospitality rather than replace it?

REVIEW QUESTIONS

- Define Hospitality Information Technology in your own words.
- Explain the difference between visible and invisible hotel technology.
- Identify the five main stages of the guest journey and give one IT example for each stage.
- Explain the difference between IT, Operations and Finance in a hotel.
- What is the difference between Central IT and Property IT?
- Name the five core IT functions in hotels.
- Why is system integration important in hotel operations?
- What are the main risks of poor IT infrastructure?
- Why is cybersecurity a strategic issue for hotels?
- What are the top IT priorities before the opening of a new hotel?

REFERENCES AND FURTHER READING

Oracle Hospitality. "What Is a Hotel Property Management System?" This professional resource explains how a hotel PMS supports reservations, check-in, check-out, room assignment, rates and billing. https://www.oracle.com/africa/hospitality/what-is-hotel-pms/

Oracle Hospitality. “Hotel PMS and Hotel POS Solutions.” This resource is useful for understanding the connection between PMS, POS, staff performance, operational integration and guest-facing innovation. https://www.oracle.com/apac/hospitality/hotel-property-management/

Hospitality Financial and Technology Professionals. “About HFTP.” HFTP is an international nonprofit association serving hospitality finance and technology professionals. https://www.hftp.org/about

National Institute of Standards and Technology. “The NIST Cybersecurity Framework (CSF) 2.0.” This framework provides guidance to organizations for managing, assessing, prioritizing and communicating cybersecurity risk. https://www.nist.gov/publications/nist-cybersecurity-framework-csf-20

National Institute of Standards and Technology. “Cybersecurity Framework.” This page provides access to NIST cybersecurity framework resources and updates. https://www.nist.gov/cyberframework

Chapter 2

Hotel IT Architecture & Network Design

Property, Regional Office and the Infrastructure Behind Modern Hospitality

LEARNING OBJECTIVES

By the end of this chapter, you should be able to explain the basic structure of hotel IT architecture without excessive technical jargon, distinguish between LAN, WAN and WiFi from a hospitality management perspective, and understand how PMS, POS, CRS and ERP systems communicate across the hotel technology ecosystem. You should also be able to compare cloud-based, on-premise and hybrid technology models in a hotel environment, identify how network design affects guest experience, operational continuity, revenue and risk, and differentiate between hotel-level IT responsibilities and regional-office IT responsibilities. Finally, this chapter should enable you to evaluate centralized, decentralized and hybrid IT models for a multi-property hospitality organization, and to apply infrastructure thinking to a regional office overseeing hotels across several countries.

OPENING PERSPECTIVE

A hotel is often described through its visible spaces: the lobby, the rooms, the restaurant, the spa, the meeting rooms, the corridors, the kitchen and the back office. Guests remember the atmosphere, the service, the comfort of the bed, the speed of the welcome and the quality of the breakfast. Managers, however, must also understand a second hotel that guests rarely see: the digital hotel that runs underneath the physical hotel.

This digital hotel is made of networks, servers, cloud platforms, applications, interfaces, WiFi access points, payment terminals, security controls, data flows and support processes. It is not separate from hospitality. It makes hospitality possible at scale. When a room is sold online, assigned in the PMS, cleaned by housekeeping, opened by a key card, charged through the POS, reviewed after departure and reported in financial dashboards, the guest journey is passing through an architecture.

Architecture does not mean complexity for the sake of complexity. In management terms, hotel IT architecture is the way technology components are organized, connected and governed so that the property can operate reliably. Network design is the way the hotel connects people, devices, systems, data and external services. Together, architecture and network design shape whether hotel technology feels smooth or fragile.

The purpose of this chapter is not to train hospitality managers to configure routers, design firewall rules or install switches. Those tasks belong to technical specialists. The purpose is to help managers understand dependencies, vulnerabilities and strategic trade-offs. A General Manager, asset manager, consultant or regional leader must be able to ask intelligent questions about infrastructure because infrastructure choices directly influence guest satisfaction, employee productivity, revenue protection, cybersecurity and long-term investment decisions.

The key managerial message is simple: **you do not need to build IT, but you need to understand it**.

WHY ARCHITECTURE MATTERS FOR HOSPITALITY MANAGERS

In many hotels, infrastructure receives attention only when something fails. Guests complain that WiFi is unstable. The PMS becomes unreachable. Credit card authorization stops. The restaurant cannot post charges to rooms. A meeting planner reports that the conference network cannot support a presentation. Staff cannot access cloud applications. Suddenly, what seemed invisible becomes the most visible problem in the building.

This reactive view is dangerous. Infrastructure should not be managed only after failure. It should be understood as a business continuity foundation. A hotel sells time-sensitive experiences. A late check-in, a billing error, a lost booking, a failed payment or a disconnected meeting room immediately affects trust. Unlike many businesses, a hotel cannot simply pause its operations until the network is repaired. Guests are already present. Service must continue.

Architecture matters first because it shapes the **guest experience**. WiFi, mobile check-in, digital keys, casting to in-room television, online restaurant reservations, self-service kiosks and mobile guest requests all depend on stable connectivity and well-integrated systems. In many hotel segments, guests may not notice infrastructure when it works, but they notice it immediately when it does not. A luxury guest may forgive a small operational delay if the recovery is elegant, but repeated digital friction weakens the perception of competence.

Architecture also matters because it shapes **operational efficiency**. Front office, housekeeping, food and beverage, maintenance, finance, revenue management and sales rely on shared data. A room status update must move quickly from housekeeping to front desk. A dinner charge must move from POS to PMS. Revenue data must flow toward reporting tools. If systems are slow, disconnected or unreliable, employees create manual workarounds. Those workarounds may save the moment, but they also create errors, duplication and stress.

Architecture matters for **revenue protection**. Downtime is not neutral. If online booking flows stop, revenue opportunities are lost. If a cloud PMS is unavailable during peak check-in, service slows down. If payment systems cannot authorize transactions, the hotel may face both cash-flow and guest-recovery issues. If meeting-room connectivity fails during an event, the commercial damage may extend beyond one guest to a corporate account.

Finally, architecture matters because it shapes strategic decisions. Choosing cloud or on-premise systems, selecting vendors, allocating budget, negotiating service-level agreements, designing redundancy and organizing regional support are all managerial choices. They require business judgment, not only technical knowledge.

THE HOTEL IT ECOSYSTEM AS THREE INTERCONNECTED LAYERS

A practical way to understand hotel IT architecture is to see it as three interconnected layers: infrastructure, operational systems and guest-facing technology.

The **infrastructure layer** includes the network, internet connectivity, cloud access, servers, switches, WiFi access points, firewalls, backups and security components. This layer is the foundation. If it is weak, everything built on top of it becomes fragile.

The **operational systems layer** includes PMS, POS, housekeeping systems, maintenance systems, accounting tools, HR platforms, purchasing solutions, revenue management systems and reporting dashboards. These systems organize daily work. They translate hotel activity into structured data and workflows.

The **guest-facing technology layer** includes guest WiFi, digital check-in, mobile key, in-room entertainment, IPTV, casting, digital concierge, guest messaging, self-service kiosks, online booking interfaces and payment experiences. This is the part of technology that guests often notice most directly.

The three layers depend on one another. A guest-facing app may look modern, but it cannot deliver value if it does not connect to the PMS. A PMS may be powerful, but it cannot support operations if network access is unstable. A reporting dashboard may be elegant, but it becomes misleading if the underlying data flows are incomplete. In hospitality, technology quality depends less on isolated tools than on how the whole ecosystem works together.

This is why managers should avoid evaluating technology only by its interface. A product demonstration may show attractive screens, but the real question is whether the solution integrates reliably with existing systems, whether the infrastructure can support it, whether employees can use it, whether data remains secure and whether the vendor can support the hotel during incidents.

LAN, WAN AND WIFI EXPLAINED FOR HOTEL MANAGERS

Hospitality managers do not need to memorize technical network theory, but they must understand three fundamental terms: LAN, WAN and WiFi.

A **LAN**, or Local Area Network, is the internal network that connects devices within the hotel. Cisco describes a LAN as a collection of devices connected together in one physical location, such as a building or office. In a hotel, the LAN connects front-desk computers, back-office devices, printers, POS terminals, local servers, staff workstations and other internal systems. It is the hotel's internal digital circulation system.

A **WAN**, or Wide Area Network, connects the hotel to the outside world. It allows access to the internet, cloud services, central reservation systems, regional offices, corporate systems, vendor platforms and remote support. If the LAN is the internal circulation inside the property, the WAN is the connection from the hotel to external digital environments.

WiFi is wireless access. It allows guests and staff devices to connect without physical cables. WiFi may serve guest rooms, the lobby, meeting spaces, restaurants, offices and back-of-house zones. It is often perceived by guests as a simple amenity, but it is supported by careful design: access points, bandwidth allocation, coverage mapping, authentication, security rules and support procedures.

A simple managerial formula can help: **LAN is inside the hotel; WAN is beyond the hotel; WiFi is the wireless bridge for people and devices**.

This distinction matters during incidents. If the WiFi fails, guests and mobile staff devices may lose connectivity, but some wired internal systems might continue to operate. If the LAN fails, internal operations may freeze because systems inside the property cannot communicate. If the WAN fails, the hotel may become digitally isolated from cloud systems, central reservations, online payment authorization or regional reporting. Each failure has different consequences and requires different contingency planning.

In a hospitality context, the most important question is not, 'What is the technical definition?' The most important question is, 'Which services depend on this connection, and what happens if it fails?'

NETWORK FAILURE AS A BUSINESS CONTINUITY ISSUE

Infrastructure becomes strategic when managers understand the consequences of failure. A network failure is rarely limited to the IT office. It travels through the hotel operation.

If guest WiFi fails, the immediate effect may be complaints, negative reviews, front-desk pressure and guest dissatisfaction. In a leisure hotel, guests may be unable to stream, work remotely or communicate comfortably. In a business hotel, the impact may be more serious: meetings, video calls, presentations, virtual negotiations and corporate work may be disrupted. For long-stay guests, weak connectivity can become a reason not to return.

If the WAN fails, cloud systems may become unavailable. A cloud PMS may not load. Online bookings may not synchronize. Payment authorization may slow or stop. Corporate dashboards may no longer receive data. Vendor support may be more difficult. The hotel may still have lights, rooms and staff, but its digital access to the outside world is weakened.

If the LAN fails, internal operations can become paralyzed. Front-desk terminals may not connect to the PMS. POS systems may freeze. Back-office printers may stop responding. Staff communication tools may fail. Even if the internet is technically available, the internal system layer may no longer function.

This is why network design must include redundancy and contingency planning. Redundancy may involve backup internet lines, alternative payment procedures, local backups, emergency access to key systems, clearly documented manual processes and vendor escalation contacts. Contingency planning means that employees know what to do when technology fails. A backup system without a trained team remains theoretical.

In hospitality, business continuity is not only a technical discipline. It is a service promise. Guests do not usually care whether the issue comes from LAN, WAN, WiFi, a vendor, an interface or a firewall. They care whether the hotel can continue to serve them professionally.

CORE HOTEL SYSTEMS THAT DEPEND ON INFRASTRUCTURE

The main hotel systems all depend on infrastructure. The PMS, POS, CRS and ERP may have different purposes, but they require connectivity, data exchange and support.

The **PMS**, or Property Management System, is the operational heart of the hotel. It manages reservations, check-in, check-out, room assignment, guest profiles, billing and operational coordination. Whether cloud-based or on-premise, the PMS depends on reliable network access and integration with other systems.

The **POS**, or Point of Sale system, records and processes transactions in restaurants, bars, spas, retail outlets, minibars, banqueting and other revenue centers. When a guest charges dinner to the room, the POS must communicate with the PMS. If the connection fails, employees may need to write charges manually, which increases risk of loss, dispute or delay.

The **CRS**, or Central Reservation System, manages reservations, availability and distribution across properties and channels. It connects the hotel to direct booking engines, brand systems, travel agencies, online distribution and sometimes global distribution systems. If CRS and PMS communication fails, the hotel may face booking discrepancies, rate issues, inventory errors or overbooking risk.

The **ERP**, or Enterprise Resource Planning system, supports finance, procurement, HR, inventory, accounting and reporting. In large organizations, ERP systems help consolidate operational data into financial and managerial information. If PMS and POS data do not flow accurately into financial systems, reporting becomes less reliable.

Managers should therefore think in terms of dependency chains. A booking may begin in the CRS, flow into the PMS, generate service activity during the stay, create POS charges, appear on the guest folio and later feed accounting and reporting systems. A failure at one point in this chain affects the rest of the chain.

HOW HOTEL SYSTEMS COMMUNICATE

System communication is one of the most important concepts in hospitality IT. Hotels do not operate through one single system. They operate through multiple systems that must exchange information.

A typical data flow may begin when a guest books a room through a brand website or distribution channel. The reservation is created in the CRS and then synchronized with the PMS. The PMS stores the guest stay information, room allocation, rate details and profile data. During the stay, restaurant or bar charges are recorded in the POS and posted to the PMS folio. At departure, billing information is finalized and financial data may be exported to an ERP or accounting system.

This communication often depends on interfaces or APIs. An interface is a connection that allows two systems to exchange information. An API, or Application Programming Interface, is a structured way for systems to communicate. For managers, the technical mechanics matter less than the management implications: the interface must be reliable, secure, supported and monitored.

When systems communicate well, employees experience flow. The guest's reservation appears correctly. Room charges post automatically. Accounting receives accurate revenue data. Reports are consistent. Staff spend less time reconciling errors.

When systems communicate poorly, employees experience friction. Charges may not post. Guest profiles may be incomplete. Rate changes may not synchronize. Housekeeping status may be inaccurate. Finance may question data reliability. Managers may receive reports that conflict with each other.

Common causes of communication breakdown include network outages, API compatibility issues, software version mismatches, incorrect firewall configuration, vendor changes, weak testing procedures, poor documentation and lack of ownership. The managerial lesson is clear: integration cannot be treated as a secondary detail. In hotels, integration is operational reliability.

CLOUD-BASED, ON-PREMISE AND HYBRID MODELS

One of the most important infrastructure decisions concerns where systems and data are hosted. In broad terms, hotel systems can be cloud-based, on-premise or hybrid.

A **cloud-based system** is hosted by a vendor or service provider in remote data centers. The hotel accesses the system through the internet. NIST defines cloud computing as a model that enables convenient, on-demand network access to a shared pool of configurable computing resources, such as networks, servers, storage, applications and services. For hotels, cloud systems may include PMS, CRS, CRM, revenue management, HR, finance or collaboration tools.

Cloud models often offer lower upfront investment, faster deployment, automatic updates, remote access and easier scalability. They can support multi-property reporting and centralized management. They also reduce the need for local server maintenance. For growing hospitality groups, this flexibility can be attractive.

However, cloud systems create dependency on reliable internet connectivity and vendor performance. If the WAN is unstable, cloud access may suffer. Managers must also evaluate data protection, service-level agreements, support availability, data location, integration capabilities and exit conditions. Cloud does not eliminate responsibility; it changes the type of responsibility.

An **on-premise system** is hosted on servers physically located at the hotel or within the organization's own environment. This model may provide more local control, potential independence from internet access for certain core operations and greater customization in some contexts. It may be preferred in properties with specific legacy systems, local regulatory concerns, weak connectivity or particular operational constraints.

On-premise systems, however, usually require higher upfront capital expenditure, technical maintenance, hardware replacement, manual updates, local expertise, security management and disaster recovery planning. Control comes with responsibility.

Many hotels use a **hybrid model**. A property may use a cloud PMS, local POS resilience, cloud revenue management, on-premise network components, cloud backups and local contingency procedures. Hybrid models reflect the reality of hospitality: different systems have different risk profiles, financial models and operational requirements.

There is no universal answer. A boutique lodge with unreliable internet, a luxury urban hotel, a resort with complex outlets and a regional group supervising multiple countries may require different architecture decisions. Managers should avoid simplistic conclusions such as 'cloud is always better' or 'on-premise is always safer.' The right question is: **which model best balances reliability, control, cost, scalability, security and guest experience for this specific business context?**

THE MANAGERIAL TRADE-OFFS BEHIND CLOUD AND ON-PREMISE CHOICES

Choosing between cloud and on-premise systems is not only an IT decision. It is also a financial, operational and strategic decision.

From a financial perspective, cloud solutions often move costs toward subscription models. This may reduce initial capital expenditure but create recurring operating expenditure. On-premise systems often require greater upfront investment in servers, licenses and implementation, followed by maintenance and upgrade costs. The financial chapter of this book will explore OPEX, CAPEX and ROI in greater detail, but managers should already understand that architecture decisions affect the cost structure of the hotel.

From an operational perspective, cloud systems may simplify access across properties. A regional leader can consult dashboards remotely. Corporate teams can monitor performance. Support teams can troubleshoot without being physically present. On-premise systems may provide stronger local continuity if internet access is unreliable, but they may be harder to update and standardize.

From a security perspective, neither model is automatically secure. A reputable cloud provider may offer strong security resources, monitoring and resilience. But hotels must still manage access rights, employee training, vendor contracts, data governance and incident procedures. An on-premise environment may keep certain data local, but it can become vulnerable if patches, backups and access controls are poorly managed.

From a brand perspective, consistency matters. A hotel group may prefer cloud and centralized systems because they support standard reporting, guest profiles, loyalty recognition and cross-property visibility. However, a highly individualized luxury property may need flexibility to adapt technology to its service style.

A mature manager evaluates architecture through trade-offs rather than slogans. Every model creates benefits and dependencies. The objective is not to eliminate all risk, which is impossible, but to understand risk clearly enough to manage it.

TYPICAL HOTEL IT SETUP

A typical hotel IT setup includes several components that managers should recognize, even if they do not configure them personally.

A **firewall** acts as a security gateway. It helps control traffic between the hotel's internal network and external networks. It contributes to protecting systems from unauthorized access. Managers should understand that firewall rules can affect both security and operations. Poor configuration may block legitimate system communication; weak configuration may expose the hotel to risk.

Switches distribute wired network connections across the property. They connect devices such as front-desk computers, office workstations, POS terminals, printers, servers and other equipment. If switches fail or are poorly designed, internal connectivity may suffer.

WiFi access points provide wireless coverage. Their placement, density, configuration and bandwidth management determine whether guests and staff can connect reliably. A beautiful hotel with thick walls, complex layouts or large event spaces may require careful wireless design. Coverage should be tested in real conditions, not assumed from a floor plan.

Servers may host local applications if the hotel uses on-premise systems. Even in cloud-oriented environments, some local equipment may remain necessary for network management, security, backup, building systems or specific applications.

Managers should also be aware of cabling, equipment rooms, power supply, cooling, backup internet, monitoring tools and service contracts. These items may not appear glamorous, but they support the guest-facing experience. A luxury suite can be perfectly designed, but if the network behind it is poorly planned, the digital experience will feel weak.

The managerial role is not to master every component. It is to know what each component does, what happens when it fails, who supports it, how quickly it can be repaired and how it fits into the hotel's continuity plan.

NETWORK DESIGN AND THE GUEST EXPERIENCE

Guest connectivity has become part of hospitality value. In the past, WiFi was sometimes treated as an additional amenity. Today, for many guests, it is a basic expectation. Business travelers need it for work. Leisure guests use it for communication, streaming and travel planning. Event clients need it for presentations and hybrid meetings. International guests may rely on it to avoid roaming costs.

The quality of WiFi affects satisfaction because it affects autonomy. A guest who cannot connect may feel trapped, delayed or unsupported. A meeting planner whose attendees cannot access the network may perceive the hotel as unprofessional. A luxury guest who cannot cast content to the television may feel that the room is not aligned with contemporary expectations.

Network design also affects employees. Mobile housekeeping devices, service request tools, POS tablets, maintenance apps and management dashboards may depend on reliable wireless access. If back-of-house coverage is weak, staff may delay updates or return to manual communication. This weakens service speed and data accuracy.

Hotels must also separate guest and staff needs. Guest WiFi should not compromise operational systems. Staff devices, POS systems, administration tools and sensitive data require appropriate security and segmentation. Bandwidth must be managed so that guest streaming does not damage critical operations. Public access networks require different controls than internal business networks.

The experience dimension is therefore connected to design quality. A good network is not simply a strong internet line. It is coverage, capacity, security, segmentation, monitoring, support and recovery.

ARCHITECTURE, SECURITY AND RISK

Architecture is closely connected to cybersecurity. Poor network design can increase risk, while well-structured architecture can help contain incidents and protect operations.

Hotels are attractive targets because they process payment data, store personal information, operate many connected systems and welcome a large number of guests, vendors and employees. The environment is open by nature. Guests bring devices. Contractors connect equipment. Staff turnover may be high. Systems may include both modern cloud platforms and older legacy applications.

Network segmentation is one example of architecture serving security. Guest WiFi should be separated from internal business systems. Payment environments should be protected. Administrative access should be controlled. Vendors should not have uncontrolled access to the entire network. If one area is compromised, segmentation can help prevent the incident from spreading.

Access management is another architectural concern. Who can access the PMS? Who can modify rates? Who can export guest data? Who can manage network equipment? Who can create users? These are not merely technical questions. They are governance questions.

The NIST Cybersecurity Framework emphasizes that cybersecurity risk should be understood, assessed, prioritized and communicated across organizations. For hotels, this means architecture must support managerial visibility. Leaders should know the most critical systems, the most sensitive data flows, the main vendors, the recovery procedures and the escalation path during an incident.

Architecture does not guarantee security, but weak architecture makes security harder.

FROM PROPERTY IT TO REGIONAL OFFICE IT

A single hotel and a regional office do not have the same IT responsibilities. The property focuses on immediate operations. The regional office focuses on consistency, support, reporting, governance and long-term strategy.

At property level, IT must keep the hotel running. This includes guest-facing technology, local troubleshooting, employee support, network reliability, vendor coordination, system access and rapid problem resolution. The property environment is urgent. If the front desk cannot check in guests, the issue must be solved quickly.

At regional level, IT must look across multiple hotels. It may define standards, negotiate vendor contracts, select platforms, coordinate security policies, support compliance, aggregate data, supervise helpdesk structures, plan upgrades and evaluate investment priorities. The regional environment is comparative and strategic. It asks how multiple properties can operate with consistency while respecting local realities.

The difference creates tension. Hotels often want flexibility and responsiveness. Regional offices often want control and standardization. Both needs are legitimate. The challenge is to define which decisions belong locally and which decisions require group-level governance.

For example, a regional office may standardize cybersecurity policies, PMS strategy, reporting definitions, vendor evaluation and data governance. A property may retain flexibility on certain guest-facing tools, local support arrangements or operational workflows, provided they remain compatible with standards.

The best hospitality organizations do not treat property and regional IT as rivals. They create a governance model where strategic consistency and local operational intelligence reinforce one another.

THE ROLE OF THE REGIONAL OFFICE

A regional office supervising several hotels may perform three broad IT roles: centralized support and standards, data aggregation and reporting, and security and compliance.

Centralized support and standards means defining common technology principles across properties. This may include approved vendors, system configurations, support procedures, user access standards, hardware policies, backup requirements and upgrade timelines. Standardization reduces unnecessary variation and makes support easier.

Data aggregation and reporting means collecting operational and financial data from multiple hotels and transforming it into management information. Regional leaders need to compare occupancy, revenue, system performance, guest satisfaction, distribution costs, support incidents and technology spending across properties. Without common definitions and reliable data flows, regional reporting becomes inconsistent.

Security and compliance means ensuring that properties follow required controls for data protection, payment security, cybersecurity and regulatory obligations. A regional office may coordinate incident response, monitor threats, enforce patching policies and support audits. In a hotel group, one property's weak security can damage the reputation of the entire brand or management company.

The regional office also plays an important role in vendor management. A single hotel may have limited bargaining power and limited technical expertise. A regional office can negotiate better contracts, compare vendor performance across properties and reduce duplication. However, central vendor decisions must still consider the operational realities of each property. A solution that works well in one country or segment may not automatically fit every hotel.

CENTRALIZED, DECENTRALIZED AND HYBRID IT MODELS

Multi-property hospitality organizations must decide how IT decisions are distributed. Three broad models are possible: centralized, decentralized and hybrid.

In a **centralized IT model**, the regional office or headquarters makes most IT decisions, manages major vendors, controls budgets and standardizes technology across properties. This model can generate cost savings through bulk purchasing, improve consistency, strengthen compliance oversight and simplify reporting. It is particularly relevant for standardized brands, large chains and organizations that require strong control.

The challenge is that centralized models may respond more slowly to local needs. A hotel with a unique building, market or guest profile may feel constrained by solutions designed for the average property. A one-size-fits-all approach can become inefficient when the portfolio is diverse.

In a **decentralized IT model**, each hotel manages more of its own IT decisions, selects local vendors, controls local budgets and adapts technology to property needs. This model can improve responsiveness and allow customized solutions. It may fit independent hotels, highly differentiated boutique properties or organizations with strong local leadership.

The challenge is inconsistency. Decentralization may create higher costs, duplicated efforts, incompatible systems, uneven security standards and fragmented reporting. A group may discover that every hotel has solved the same problem differently, making regional oversight difficult.

A **hybrid IT model** combines central standards with local flexibility. The organization may centralize core systems, cybersecurity rules, data definitions, vendor frameworks and reporting structures, while allowing hotels flexibility for certain operational tools or guest-facing adaptations. In many hospitality organizations, the hybrid model is the most realistic because it acknowledges both the need for control and the need for local responsiveness.

The best model depends on portfolio structure. A budget chain with hundreds of similar properties may benefit from high centralization. A boutique collection with distinct guest experiences may need more local flexibility. A mixed portfolio may require hybrid governance, with clear categories of decisions: mandatory standards, approved options and local choices.

HOW TO CHOOSE THE RIGHT IT GOVERNANCE MODEL

Choosing a governance model requires analysis rather than ideology. Centralization is not automatically professional, and decentralization is not automatically chaotic. Each model creates advantages and risks.

Managers should begin with the brand promise. If the brand promises consistent, predictable service across all properties, IT standardization becomes more important. If the brand promises highly individualized local experiences, some flexibility may be necessary.

Portfolio complexity is the second factor. A group with 200 similar hotels in one country can centralize more easily than a group with resorts, city hotels, extended-stay properties and boutique assets across several countries. Diversity increases the need for adaptable governance.

Regulation is the third factor. Data privacy, payment security, tax reporting, labor rules and cybersecurity requirements may vary by jurisdiction. Regional control can help ensure compliance, but local expertise is also needed to interpret country-specific obligations.

Internet quality is the fourth factor. A cloud-first strategy may work well in markets with reliable connectivity. It may require stronger contingency planning in regions where internet reliability is uneven. Architecture must reflect infrastructure reality, not only corporate preference.

Hotel maturity is the fifth factor. New builds may adopt modern cloud and network standards from the beginning. Older hotels may operate with legacy systems, physical constraints, outdated cabling or fragmented vendor arrangements. A regional office must understand where each property stands before imposing a roadmap.

Cost is the sixth factor. Centralization may reduce purchasing costs and support duplication, but transitions can be expensive. Decentralization may allow local optimization, but it may also create hidden costs through inefficiency and lack of scale.

The best governance model is the one that clarifies responsibility. A poor hybrid model is one where everyone assumes someone else owns the decision. A strong hybrid model defines who decides, who funds, who implements, who supports and who measures results.

ARCHITECTURE THROUGH THE LENS OF HOTEL DEPARTMENTS

One reason hotel architecture is difficult to manage is that every department experiences the same infrastructure differently. A technical diagram may show lines, devices and systems, but a hotel manager should translate those lines into departmental consequences.

For the **front office**, architecture is the ability to see reservations, allocate rooms, encode keys, authorize payments, post charges, manage profiles and check guests out with confidence. A front desk team can remain warm and professional only if the systems behind the welcome are responsive. When screens freeze or data is missing, employees must use emotional intelligence to compensate for technical weakness. That may work once, but it cannot become the service model.

For **housekeeping**, architecture is the speed and reliability of room status information. A room that is clean but not updated in the system is, operationally, still unavailable. Mobile housekeeping tools can reduce calls, paper lists and confusion, but only if wireless coverage reaches service corridors, linen rooms and back-of-house areas. A hotel that designs WiFi only for guests and forgets employees creates a hidden operational weakness.

For **food and beverage**, architecture is the connection between POS, inventory, kitchen workflows, guest folios and finance. A restaurant outlet may appear independent, but it is part of the hotel revenue ecosystem. If POS terminals are slow, if handheld devices disconnect, or if room charges do not post correctly, the problem becomes both service and revenue leakage.

For **sales and events**, architecture is the ability to support client expectations. Meeting planners ask about bandwidth, hybrid event capacity, secure access, presentation support, streaming and technical assistance. A hotel that sells conferences without reliable infrastructure risks damaging corporate relationships. In this context, the network is part of the event product.

For **finance**, architecture is data reliability. Finance depends on accurate transfers from PMS, POS, purchasing, payroll and accounting systems. When interfaces fail, finance teams spend time reconciling, correcting and questioning data. This delays reporting and weakens trust in management information.

For **revenue management and distribution**, architecture is the ability to synchronize availability, rates, restrictions and reservations across systems and channels. A delay between CRS, channel manager and PMS can create pricing errors, inventory discrepancies or overbooking risk. Here again, infrastructure directly protects revenue.

Looking at architecture department by department helps managers avoid treating IT as a separate technical object. The network is not only a network. It is the nervous system of operational coordination.

INFRASTRUCTURE DURING HOTEL OPENING, RENOVATION AND REPOSITIONING

Architecture decisions are especially critical during hotel opening, renovation or repositioning. These moments create both risk and opportunity. Decisions made before opening may shape the hotel's technology performance for years. Decisions ignored before opening may become expensive problems after guests arrive.

During a new opening, managers must think early about cabling, equipment rooms, WiFi coverage, guest-room technology, back-office workstations, payment terminals, POS locations, PMS setup, cloud access, vendor lead times, training schedules and support availability. Infrastructure cannot be treated as a finishing detail. Walls, ceilings, furniture placement, materials and building layout can all affect network performance. A beautiful historic building, for example, may create wireless coverage challenges because of thick walls or complex circulation areas.

During renovation, the challenge is different. The hotel may need to continue operating while infrastructure is upgraded. This requires phasing, communication, temporary solutions and careful coordination with operations. A network upgrade that interrupts check-in during high occupancy is not only a technical project; it is a service risk. Managers must ask how work will be scheduled, which areas will be affected, how employees will be informed and what contingency procedures will be available.

During repositioning, infrastructure may need to match a new brand promise. A hotel moving from midscale to upscale cannot keep technology assumptions from its previous positioning. Higher guest expectations may require stronger WiFi, better in-room entertainment, more integrated CRM, smoother mobile services, improved reporting and stronger cybersecurity. Technology must support the new promise; otherwise, the repositioning remains cosmetic.

Asset managers should also consider infrastructure during acquisition due diligence. A hotel may look attractive commercially but hide outdated cabling, weak network closets, unsupported systems, fragmented contracts or poor documentation. These issues can create capital expenditure after acquisition. IT architecture should therefore be part of property evaluation, not only post-acquisition cleanup.

The managerial lesson is that architecture has a lifecycle. It must be planned before opening, protected during operation, reviewed during renovation and reassessed during strategic repositioning.

VENDOR MANAGEMENT, SERVICE LEVELS AND ACCOUNTABILITY

Most hotels do not build or maintain every technology component internally. They depend on vendors, integrators, internet service providers, software providers, payment partners, support companies and sometimes brand-level technology teams. Architecture therefore includes a contractual ecosystem as well as a technical ecosystem.

Vendor management begins with clarity. Managers should know which vendor supports which system, what the contract includes, what the response time is, who can escalate an incident, what happens outside office hours and how service quality is measured. A hotel operating twenty-four hours a day cannot rely on vague support promises.

Service-level agreements, often called SLAs, define expectations for support availability, response time, resolution targets, uptime, maintenance windows and escalation. A strong SLA does not guarantee that nothing will fail, but it clarifies responsibility when failure occurs. Without clear SLAs, hotels may lose precious time during incidents because teams do not know who owns the problem.

Accountability becomes more complex when several vendors are involved. A PMS vendor may blame the network. The network provider may blame the internet line. The internet provider may blame local infrastructure. The POS vendor may blame an interface. During service disruption, the guest does not care which vendor is responsible. The hotel must coordinate resolution. This is why documentation, escalation maps and incident procedures matter.

Managers should also be careful with vendor dependency. A solution may look attractive because it solves a short-term problem, but it may create lock-in, integration limits, hidden costs or difficult exit conditions. Before signing, executives should ask how data can be exported, whether APIs are available, what happens if the hotel changes PMS, how upgrades are handled and how the vendor supports multi-property governance.

Technology purchasing is therefore not only procurement. It is risk management, operational design and strategic alignment. A vendor is not simply selling software or hardware; the vendor becomes part of the hotel's ability to serve guests.

MONITORING, DOCUMENTATION AND THE DISCIPLINE OF SIMPLICITY

A well-designed architecture is not enough if nobody monitors it, documents it or understands how it changes over time. Hotels are living environments. New devices are added. Vendors change. Software is updated. Employees leave. Temporary solutions become permanent. Without discipline, architecture becomes progressively more complex and less visible.

Monitoring allows the hotel to detect issues before they become guest complaints. Network monitoring can identify bandwidth saturation, access point failures, unusual traffic, device outages or repeated disconnections. System monitoring can help identify slow performance, failed interfaces or backup problems. Monitoring does not eliminate incidents, but it improves response and reduces surprise.

Documentation is equally important. A hotel should know its critical systems, vendors, contracts, support contacts, network zones, data flows, key dependencies and recovery procedures. Documentation should be understandable enough for managers, not only technicians. During a crisis, a clear dependency map can save time.

Simplicity is a strategic discipline. Every additional system, interface, vendor, device and exception creates another point to manage. Complexity may be justified when it creates clear value, but unmanaged complexity increases cost and risk. Managers should regularly ask whether a tool is still needed, whether duplicate systems exist, whether integrations remain supported and whether employees understand the process.

Simplicity does not mean primitive technology. It means technology that is coherent, documented, supportable and aligned with business needs. A hotel can be technologically advanced and still simple in its architecture if decisions are governed carefully. Conversely, a hotel can have modest technology and still be dangerously complex if tools have accumulated without strategy.

The discipline of simplicity is particularly important for regional offices. Across multiple properties, small variations multiply quickly. If every hotel uses different tools, definitions and vendors, regional oversight becomes difficult. A clear architecture framework helps the organization remain adaptable without becoming chaotic.

THE HUMAN SIDE OF INFRASTRUCTURE DECISIONS

Infrastructure discussions can easily become abstract, but their consequences are human. Every technical weakness eventually reaches an employee or a guest. A receptionist apologizes because the system is slow. A waiter writes a room charge manually because the POS cannot connect. A housekeeper calls the desk because the mobile room-status tool is not updating. A manager spends the evening with an angry meeting planner because the conference WiFi failed. These are not only IT moments; they are hospitality moments under pressure.

Good architecture protects employees from avoidable friction. When systems are reliable and well integrated, teams can focus on service rather than workaround. They spend less time repeating information, correcting errors, calling other departments or explaining delays. This supports morale as well as efficiency. In high-pressure hotels, poor technology often becomes an invisible source of employee fatigue.

Good architecture also protects the emotional rhythm of service. Hospitality depends on presence. An employee who is fighting with systems has less attention available for the guest. A front desk agent who waits for screens to load may lose the natural flow of welcome. A restaurant team that struggles with unstable handheld devices may become less attentive to the dining room. Technology failure can therefore reduce the human quality of service, even when employees remain committed.

For managers, this means technology decisions should be evaluated not only through cost and features, but also through usability and operational fit. A technically powerful system that employees find difficult to use may create new problems. A highly integrated system that requires poor workflows may frustrate teams. Implementation should include training, testing, feedback and adjustment.

The best hotel technology is not the technology that attracts the most attention. It is often the technology that quietly allows people to do their work well. In that sense, infrastructure is part of leadership. It creates the conditions in which teams can deliver hospitality with confidence. This is why architecture should be discussed with department heads, not only with IT specialists. Front office, housekeeping, F&B, finance, sales, revenue management and engineering all understand different consequences of the same infrastructure. Their input helps identify blind spots before they become guest-facing problems. A strong infrastructure decision is therefore both technical and collaborative: it translates operational reality into a design that is reliable, supportable and aligned with the hotel promise.

APPLIED CASE STUDY: A NEW REGIONAL OFFICE

Imagine that a hospitality management company has created a new regional office. This office will supervise twelve hotels across four countries. The portfolio is diverse: some properties are boutique hotels with distinctive positioning, some are large resorts, some are full-service urban hotels and some are older assets with legacy systems. Internet quality differs by location. Local regulations vary. Technology maturity is uneven. The regional office has been asked to improve oversight, reduce risk and support better decision-making.

The central question is whether IT should be centralized, decentralized or hybrid.

A fully centralized model would allow the regional office to impose common standards, negotiate vendor contracts, control cybersecurity, consolidate reporting and reduce duplication. This could improve brand-level visibility and reduce long-term risk. However, it could also frustrate properties that need local responsiveness, especially those with unique guest experiences or infrastructure constraints.

A fully decentralized model would allow each hotel to choose tools and vendors based on local needs. This could support agility and property autonomy. However, it would make regional reporting difficult, increase security inconsistency, weaken purchasing power and complicate support across four countries.

A hybrid model would likely be the strongest starting point. The regional office could centralize cybersecurity standards, data definitions, vendor approval frameworks, reporting requirements, backup policies and major system architecture. Properties could retain limited flexibility for local guest-facing tools, operational workflows and market-specific solutions, provided they respect integration and security standards.

The immediate implications would be significant. The regional office would need to map the existing systems in all twelve hotels, identify critical risks, compare vendor contracts, assess internet resilience, review data flows, define a target architecture and create a phased roadmap. It would also need to communicate clearly with General Managers so that central governance is not perceived as bureaucratic interference but as a support mechanism.

The case illustrates an important principle: there is rarely a perfect IT model. Good decisions balance control, cost, risk and flexibility. A regional office should not centralize everything simply because it can, nor should it allow every hotel to operate independently without standards. The objective is disciplined adaptability.

MANAGERIAL TAKEAWAYS

The first takeaway is that infrastructure enables all hotel systems. PMS, POS, CRS, ERP, guest WiFi, mobile tools, reporting and cloud platforms depend on the quality of the underlying architecture. Infrastructure is invisible only when it works.

The second takeaway is that simplicity often reduces risk. Overly complex architectures create more points of failure, more vendor dependencies and more operational confusion. A hotel architecture should be as simple as possible while still meeting business requirements.

The third takeaway is that managers must understand dependencies. A system is not isolated. PMS depends on network access, POS integration, CRS communication, payment flows, user access and support procedures. One weak link can affect the whole operation.

The fourth takeaway is that cloud, on-premise and hybrid models should be evaluated through context. The right choice depends on reliability, cost, control, scalability, security, vendor capability and the hotel's operational reality.

The fifth takeaway is that regional IT governance must balance consistency and flexibility. Hotels need responsiveness; regional offices need control and visibility. Strong governance defines which decisions are central, which are local and which require shared approval.

The final takeaway is that architecture is a leadership topic. Technical specialists design and maintain the systems, but executives decide priorities, budgets, risk appetite and governance. A hospitality leader who understands architecture is better prepared to protect service quality, revenue and brand trust.

TO REVIEW THIS CHAPTER

KEY TERMS

Hotel IT Architecture : The organized structure of networks, systems, applications, data flows, security controls and governance mechanisms that allow a hotel or hotel group to operate reliably.

Network Design : The way devices, systems, users and external services are connected so that data can move securely and efficiently across the hotel environment.

LAN - Local Area Network : The internal network connecting devices within the hotel, such as front-desk computers, back-office workstations, POS terminals, printers and local servers.

WAN - Wide Area Network : The connection linking the hotel to external networks, including the internet, cloud platforms, regional offices, vendors and corporate systems.

WiFi : Wireless network access used by guests, staff devices and sometimes operational tools across the property.

PMS - Property Management System : The central hotel system supporting reservations, room assignment, check-in, check-out, guest profiles and billing.

POS - Point of Sale : The system used to record and process transactions in restaurants, bars, spas, retail outlets and other hotel revenue centers.

CRS - Central Reservation System : A system used to manage reservations, availability, rates and distribution across channels and properties.

ERP - Enterprise Resource Planning : A business management system that may support finance, HR, procurement, inventory, accounting and consolidated reporting.

API - Application Programming Interface : A structured method that allows different software systems to exchange data and communicate.

Interface : A connection between two systems that allows information to be exchanged, such as POS charges posting to a PMS folio.

Cloud-Based System : A system hosted remotely by a vendor or service provider and accessed through the internet.

On-Premise System : A system hosted locally on servers physically controlled by the hotel or organization.

Hybrid Model : A technology model combining cloud-based and on-premise components, often used to balance flexibility, control and resilience.

Firewall : A security gateway that helps control and protect traffic between internal networks and external networks.

Switch : A network component that distributes wired network connections to devices across the property.

Access Point : A device that provides wireless network coverage to a specific area of the hotel.

Redundancy : The use of backup systems, alternative connections or contingency procedures to reduce the impact of failure.

Single Point of Failure : A component or connection whose failure can disrupt an entire process, system or operation.

Centralized IT : A model in which a regional office or headquarters controls most technology decisions, standards, vendors and budgets.

Decentralized IT : A model in which individual properties manage many of their own technology decisions, vendors and budgets.

IT Governance : The management framework defining who makes IT decisions, how risks are controlled, how systems are funded and how technology aligns with business objectives.

REFLECTION QUESTIONS

1. Why should hotel managers understand IT architecture even if they are not responsible for technical configuration?
2. How can poor network design affect the guest experience in a luxury or full-service hotel?
3. What is the difference between a WiFi problem, a LAN problem and a WAN problem from an operational point of view?
4. Why is system integration more important than simply purchasing strong individual software tools?
5. In which situations might a cloud-based system create risk for a hotel?
6. In which situations might an on-premise system create unnecessary cost or complexity?
7. How should a hotel balance guest WiFi needs with operational network security?
8. Why does a regional office often prefer standardization across properties?
9. Why might an individual hotel resist a fully centralized IT model?

10. What would a good hybrid IT governance model look like for a portfolio of diverse hotels?

REVIEW QUESTIONS

1. Define hotel IT architecture in your own words.
2. Explain the difference between LAN, WAN and WiFi.
3. Identify three hotel systems that depend on reliable infrastructure.
4. Describe a typical data flow from CRS to PMS to POS to ERP.
5. What are the main advantages of cloud-based hotel systems?
6. What are the main advantages of on-premise hotel systems?
7. Why do many hotels use hybrid technology models?
8. What is a firewall and why does it matter in a hotel environment?
9. What is a single point of failure? Give one hospitality example.
10. Explain the difference between property-level IT and regional-office IT.
11. List two advantages and two risks of centralized IT.
12. List two advantages and two risks of decentralized IT.
13. What factors should be considered when choosing between centralized, decentralized and hybrid IT governance?
14. Why does infrastructure support business continuity?
15. What are the main IT recommendations you would make to a regional office supervising twelve hotels across four countries?

REFERENCES AND FURTHER READING

- Cisco. "What Is a LAN? Local Area Network." Cisco explains the basic concept of a local area network as a collection of devices connected in one physical location, which is useful for understanding hotel internal networks. https://www.cisco.com/site/us/en/learn/topics/networking/what-is-a-lan-local-area-network.html
- Cisco. "What Is a Wireless LAN (WLAN)?" Cisco provides a simple explanation of wireless local-area networks and radio-based connectivity, useful for understanding hotel WiFi access. https://www.cisco.com/site/us/en/learn/topics/networking/what-is-a-wireless-lan.html
- Mell, P., and Grance, T. "The NIST Definition of Cloud Computing." National Institute of Standards and Technology, Special Publication 800-145. This official definition explains cloud computing as on-demand network access to shared configurable computing resources. https://csrc.nist.gov/pubs/sp/800/145/final
- Oracle Hospitality. "Hospitality Integration Platform - PMS and POS." This professional resource explains how hospitality PMS and POS integrations can be centralized and streamlined through cloud-based integration and APIs. https://www.oracle.com/hospitality/integration-platform/
- Oracle Hospitality. "Hotel Property Management System." Oracle provides professional resources on hotel PMS platforms and their role in managing reservations, front-office operations, billing and guest experience. https://www.oracle.com/hospitality/what-is-hotel-pms/
- National Institute of Standards and Technology. "The NIST Cybersecurity Framework 2.0." This framework provides

guidance for organizations to understand, assess, prioritize and communicate cybersecurity risk. https://www.nist.gov/publications/nist-cybersecurity-framework-csf-20

- Hospitality Financial and Technology Professionals (HFTP). HFTP provides hospitality-focused resources connecting finance, technology, systems and professional practice in the hospitality industry. https://www.hftp.org/

Chapter 3

Cybersecurity, Data Protection & Risk Management

LEARNING OBJECTIVES

By the end of this chapter, readers should be able to understand cybersecurity as a strategic business risk in hospitality rather than a purely technical issue. They should be able to explain why hotels and hotel groups are attractive targets for cybercriminals, identify the main threats affecting the sector, including ransomware, phishing, data breaches, insider mistakes and vendor-related risks, and assess how a cyber incident can disrupt reservations, check-in, payments, guest care, reputation and business continuity. They should also be able to clarify the respective roles of the General Manager, IT, Legal, Finance, Operations, Communications and external partners during a cyber crisis, apply executive decision-making logic to the first hour of a confirmed data breach, and connect cybersecurity preparation to leadership maturity, brand protection and long-term guest trust.

OPENING PERSPECTIVE

Cybersecurity is often presented as a technical discipline. It involves networks, firewalls, encryption, malware, servers, identities, logs and specialist vocabulary. Yet in hospitality, cybersecurity quickly becomes something much wider: a leadership issue. When a hotel suffers a cyber incident, the visible problem may begin in a system, but the consequences move immediately into the lobby, the rooms, the restaurants, the call center, the finance office, the legal department and the brand reputation of the property or group.

A hotel is not a quiet office that can close its doors for a few days while specialists repair a technical problem. It is a living environment. Guests are already inside the building. New guests are arriving. Employees are trying to serve breakfast, prepare rooms, answer phones, process payments, manage complaints and keep the operation moving. In this environment, an IT failure is not abstract. It becomes a queue at the front desk, a locked room door that cannot be reissued, a payment that cannot be authorized, a reservation that cannot be found, a journalist asking for a statement, and an owner asking how much revenue has already been lost.

This chapter approaches cybersecurity from the perspective of hospitality executives. The objective is not to train technical specialists. The objective is to help future General Managers, asset managers, consultants and hotel leaders understand consequences, priorities, roles and decisions. A leader does not need to understand every line of malicious code. A leader must understand what the incident means for guests, staff, revenue, compliance, insurance, owners and long-term trust.

The central principle is simple: in hospitality, cyber risk is business risk. It is also service risk, legal risk, operational risk, reputational risk and leadership risk. A cyber crisis tests not only the quality of the hotel's systems, but also the quality of its governance, preparation and executive behavior under pressure.

WHY CYBERSECURITY MATTERS IN HOSPITALITY

Hospitality has several characteristics that make cybersecurity especially important. Hotels operate continuously. They collect valuable information. They depend on interconnected systems. They welcome large numbers of guests, employees, contractors and vendors into their environment. They often run multiple revenue centers and may belong to complex ownership or management structures. They also depend deeply on trust. A guest who shares identity documents, credit card information, travel plans and personal preferences with a hotel assumes that this information will be handled responsibly.

The 24/7 nature of hotels creates operational pressure. If a cyberattack affects a conventional office, the organization may postpone work, send employees home or temporarily suspend nonessential activity. A hotel has fewer options. Guests still need rooms. A family may be arriving after a long flight. A corporate guest may need an invoice before leaving for a meeting. A restaurant may be full. A spa may have treatments booked. A group may be checking in for a conference. The hotel must continue serving people even when digital systems are unstable.

Hotels also hold data that is valuable to criminals. This may include names, addresses, telephone numbers, email addresses, passport details, payment data, loyalty information, travel histories, corporate accounts, special requests, dietary information, VIP status, employee records and sometimes sensitive guest preferences. The attractiveness of hotel data increases when it is connected to payment flows, loyalty programs or high-net-worth individuals.

Another reason hospitality is vulnerable is system complexity. A full-service hotel may use a PMS, POS, CRS, channel manager, revenue management system, housekeeping platform, purchasing system, payroll system, door-lock system, CCTV, telephony, IPTV, WiFi, payment terminals, guest messaging tools, digital concierge solutions, marketing systems and corporate reporting platforms. Each system may have its own users, vendors, updates, access rights and interfaces. Every new convenience can create new exposure if it is not governed properly.

Hospitality culture itself can also create risk. Hotels are built around helpfulness. Employees are trained to solve problems, respond quickly, welcome guests and avoid saying no. Cybercriminals exploit this culture through social engineering. A convincing phone call to a help desk, a fake email from a vendor, a fraudulent urgent request from someone pretending to be a senior executive, or a message that appears to come from a booking partner can lead an employee to reveal credentials, click a malicious link or bypass procedure.

Cybersecurity therefore matters because hotels combine high-value data, high operational pressure, human service culture, complex technology and immediate reputational exposure. Attackers understand these pressures. Executives must understand them too.

THE HOTEL ATTACK SURFACE

An attack surface is the collection of points through which an attacker might try to enter, disrupt or exploit a digital environment. In hospitality, the attack surface is broad because hotels serve guests, staff, corporate teams, owners, partners and external vendors through many connected systems.

Guest WiFi is one visible part of this exposure. Guests expect easy, fast and reliable internet access. Yet guest WiFi must be designed so that it does not expose internal systems. A guest should not be able to reach operational networks used by the front desk, finance, payment terminals or management systems. The hospitality challenge is to provide convenience without weakening separation between public access and business-critical systems.

The Property Management System is another critical part of the attack surface because it is the operational heart of many hotels. It contains reservations, guest profiles, room status, billing information and operational data. If the PMS is compromised or unavailable, the hotel may struggle to check guests in, manage departures, issue keys, confirm rates or access guest histories.

Point-of-Sale systems are also sensitive. Restaurants, bars, spas, boutiques and other revenue centers process transactions and often post charges to rooms. POS environments connect guest service, revenue capture and payment security. Weaknesses in POS design, patching or access control can create exposure to payment data compromise and financial fraud.

Internet of Things devices create another layer of risk. Smart locks, thermostats, connected televisions, energy management systems, minibars, sensors and in-room controls can improve experience and efficiency. However, if such devices are poorly configured, rarely updated or connected too broadly to the network, they may become weak entry points. A device that seems operationally minor can become strategically serious if it allows movement into more sensitive systems.

Staff email is one of the most common entry points. Hospitality employees receive messages from guests, travel agents, suppliers, event planners, delivery companies, corporate offices and vendors. This creates fertile ground for phishing. A fake invoice, a malicious attachment disguised as a group booking list, or a link to a false login page can lead to credential theft.

Third-party vendors add further exposure. Hotels rely on booking engines, payment providers, outsourced IT support, maintenance companies, marketing platforms, payroll providers, cloud systems, consultants and franchise or management company platforms. Some vendors may require remote access or data exchange. If vendor access is poorly controlled, monitored or terminated, it can become a backdoor into the hotel environment.

The executive lesson is that cybersecurity is not only about protecting one server. It is about understanding how guest convenience, operational efficiency, vendor relationships and system integration create a web of exposure. Every new digital service should trigger a managerial question: what value does it create, and what new risk does it introduce?

CYBER RISK AS BUSINESS RISK

Cybersecurity becomes easier to discuss at executive level when it is translated into business consequences. Technical vocabulary may be necessary for specialists, but executives must speak in terms of impact. What happens to revenue? What happens to guests? What happens to reputation? What happens to compliance? What happens to owner confidence?

A reservation shutdown immediately affects revenue and customer confidence. If the hotel cannot receive new bookings, modify reservations or synchronize inventory, demand may be lost. Online channels may show incorrect availability. Guests may call and receive inconsistent answers. Group reservations may be disrupted. Revenue managers may lose visibility on pickup and demand.

A blocked check-in creates visible operational chaos. The front desk becomes the stage where digital failure becomes human frustration. Guests do not care whether the root cause is ransomware, interface failure, credential compromise or network outage. They experience waiting, confusion and uncertainty. In luxury hospitality, the gap between promise and reality can become especially damaging.

Payment disruption creates financial and trust issues. If payment terminals do not work, if preauthorizations cannot be completed, if room charges cannot be posted, or if invoices cannot be produced, the hotel loses control over revenue capture. Staff may attempt manual workarounds, but these create risk of errors, disputes and fraud.

Media exposure can escalate rapidly. A cyber incident involving a hotel is not only a technology story. It can become a consumer trust story, a brand story, a governance story or an owner-relations story. Social media may amplify guest frustration long before the organization has confirmed all facts. A hotel lobby full of delayed guests is a visible environment. Photos, videos and comments can circulate quickly.

Regulatory scrutiny adds another layer. If personal data is compromised, the organization may have notification obligations. If payment card data is involved, payment security requirements and card brand processes may apply. If the group operates across jurisdictions, the legal analysis may be complex. Delay, denial or poor documentation can worsen the problem.

Brand damage may last longer than the system outage. Guests may forgive inconvenience if they believe the hotel acted transparently, protected them and recovered professionally. They are less likely to forgive confusion, silence, denial or blame. Trust is part of hospitality capital. Cybersecurity protects that capital.

THE MAIN CYBER THREATS IN HOSPITALITY

Cyber threats change over time, but several categories are especially important for hospitality leaders: ransomware, phishing and social engineering, data breaches, insider mistakes, vendor compromise and weak legacy systems. Each threat has technical dimensions, but each also has managerial consequences.

Ransomware

Ransomware is malicious software or an attack method that prevents an organization from accessing its systems or data, often by encrypting files or disabling critical services. Attackers then demand payment in exchange for restoration or for not leaking stolen data. For a hotel, ransomware can be devastating because it directly attacks continuity.

Imagine that the PMS, POS, room key system, shared drives and reservation interfaces are unavailable. The hotel may still have staff, rooms, restaurants and guests, but the digital coordination layer has been frozen. Manual procedures may exist, but they may not be sufficient for a busy operation. Staff may not know which rooms are clean, which rates apply, which guests have prepaid, which charges have been posted or which arrivals are VIPs.

The executive dilemma around ransomware is difficult. Paying may appear to be a way to restore operations quickly, but it funds criminal activity and does not guarantee recovery. Not paying may extend downtime. There may also be legal, insurance, law enforcement and reputational considerations. The decision must never be made by IT alone. It requires executive leadership, legal counsel, insurers, cybersecurity specialists and, in some cases, law enforcement involvement.

The best ransomware decision is made before the attack, not during it. If the organization has tested backups, segmented networks, incident response plans, manual procedures, cyber insurance, decision protocols and trained teams, it has more options. If it has none of these, the crisis becomes far more dangerous.

Phishing and Social Engineering

Phishing is the use of fraudulent messages to trick people into clicking links, opening attachments, entering credentials or approving actions. Social engineering is broader: it manipulates human trust, urgency, authority or helpfulness to bypass security procedures. In hospitality, phishing and social engineering are particularly dangerous because employees handle constant communication from unknown or semi-known parties.

A reservations employee may receive a message that appears to contain a rooming list. A finance employee may receive a fake supplier invoice. A front desk agent may be called by someone pretending to be from corporate IT. A manager may receive a message appearing to come from an owner or executive requesting urgent action. These situations exploit normal hospitality behavior: speed, service and responsiveness.

Human risk does not mean employees are careless. It means employees operate in environments where pressure, distraction and goodwill can be exploited. Training must therefore be practical, repeated and specific to hotel scenarios. Staff should learn how to verify unusual requests, report suspicious messages, avoid credential sharing and pause when urgency is being used to force a decision.

Executives should avoid a culture of blame around phishing. Fear can suppress reporting. If employees believe they will be punished for admitting a click, they may hide the incident, allowing attackers more time. A strong security culture encourages rapid reporting, clear escalation and learning from mistakes.

Data Breaches

A data breach occurs when information is accessed, disclosed, stolen, altered or exposed in an unauthorized way. In hospitality, data breaches are especially serious because hotels hold information that relates to identity, travel, payment, preferences and relationships. Guests may be affected personally, financially and emotionally.

The consequences of a breach extend across stakeholders. Guests may face identity theft risk, fraud attempts or loss of privacy.

Corporate clients may question whether their travelers are safe. OTAs, franchise systems and vendors may reassess trust. Regulators may investigate. Owners may worry about litigation, fines and asset value. Employees may feel exposed if internal data is involved.

A data breach is therefore a trust crisis. The technical investigation matters, but the human and reputational response matters too. Guests need clarity: what happened, what information may be affected, what the hotel is doing, what they should do, and how they can get support. Silence creates anxiety. Overstatement creates credibility risk. Understatement creates legal and ethical risk.

Insider Mistakes

Not every cyber incident begins with a sophisticated external attacker. Many incidents are caused or worsened by internal mistakes. An employee may send a report to the wrong recipient, use weak passwords, share credentials, lose a device, print sensitive information, store payment details improperly, or keep access after changing roles. A manager may approve a vendor connection without security review. A property may delay updates because the operation is too busy.

Insider mistakes are often symptoms of weak processes. If employees do not know what data is sensitive, they cannot protect it consistently. If access rights are not reviewed, former employees or contractors may retain access. If managers reward speed but ignore procedure, staff may bypass controls. If the hotel has no simple reporting channel, small incidents may remain hidden until they become larger problems.

Good cybersecurity culture accepts that humans will make mistakes and designs controls accordingly. Access should be limited to what employees need. Important actions should require verification.

Training should be role-specific. Procedures should be realistic for hotel operations, not copied from an office environment without adaptation.

Vendor and Third-Party Risk

Hotels depend heavily on external partners. This is unavoidable and often beneficial. Vendors bring specialized expertise, cloud platforms, payment services, booking tools, maintenance solutions and guest technologies. However, third-party relationships create risk because data and access may extend beyond the hotel's direct control.

Vendor risk can appear in several ways. A vendor may suffer its own breach. A remote support account may be poorly protected. A contract may not clearly define security responsibilities. A system integration may expose more data than necessary. A vendor may store data in jurisdictions that create legal questions. A service may be discontinued, leaving the hotel with unsupported technology.

Executive management of vendor risk requires more than procurement. It requires questions about access, data, support, incident notification, security standards, subcontractors, recovery commitments, service-level agreements and exit plans. A cheaper vendor is not cheaper if it increases exposure or fails during a crisis.

CYBERSECURITY AND THE GUEST EXPERIENCE

Cybersecurity is sometimes viewed as the opposite of hospitality because security procedures can feel restrictive. Password rules, access controls, verification steps and data minimization may seem to slow down service. The executive challenge is to design security so that it protects the guest without destroying the warmth of the experience.

Consider identity verification. A luxury guest may expect recognition and discretion, but the hotel must also ensure that access to personal information, room keys, invoices and payment details is controlled. A front desk agent should not reveal a room number to an unauthorized caller. A concierge should not share itinerary information without proper verification. A reservations employee should not modify a booking based solely on a convincing email.

Cybersecurity is therefore part of the duty of care. Hotels protect guests physically through locks, staff presence, fire safety, emergency procedures and controlled access. They must also protect guests digitally through responsible data handling, secure payments, careful communication and controlled system access.

Good cybersecurity supports hospitality because it protects trust. Guests may not notice strong cybersecurity when everything works. But they will notice when trust is broken. A hotel that treats cybersecurity as part of service quality is better positioned to protect both experience and reputation.

EXECUTIVE RESPONSIBILITY IN A CYBER CRISIS

A cyber crisis tests executive behavior. Technical teams will investigate systems, isolate threats and coordinate specialist response. But the General Manager and executive team must lead the organization through uncertainty. The leader's role is not to become a technician. The leader's role is to maintain priorities, coordinate roles, communicate clearly and protect the business.

The first responsibility is to activate a command structure. The hotel needs a crisis cell or command center that includes the right people: General Manager, IT, Operations, Legal, Finance, Communications, Human Resources if needed, Security, and corporate or ownership representatives when appropriate. The group must define who is leading, who is documenting, who is communicating, who is making legal decisions and who is coordinating technical work.

The second responsibility is guest care. Guests on property must remain safe, informed and served. Even if systems are down, the hotel must manage arrivals, departures, room access, billing questions, complaints and basic services. Cyber response should not become so technical that the lobby is forgotten. In hospitality, the crisis is being lived by guests in real time.

The third responsibility is escalation. The executive team must contact corporate IT, ownership, legal counsel, insurers, cybersecurity response partners and possibly law enforcement or regulators depending on the incident. Escalation should be disciplined. Waiting too long can increase damage. Escalating without facts can create confusion. The goal is fast, structured coordination.

The fourth responsibility is documentation. Every major action, time, decision, instruction and communication should be logged. Documentation supports legal analysis, insurance claims, regulatory notifications, post-incident review and organizational learning. In a crisis, memory becomes unreliable. A clear log protects the organization.

The fifth responsibility is emotional leadership. Panic spreads quickly. If the General Manager appears confused, angry or defensive, the team may mirror that behavior. Calm does not mean passivity. It means disciplined urgency. Staff need to see that leaders are taking the incident seriously without losing control.

ROLES AND RESPONSIBILITIES DURING A CYBER INCIDENT

Confusion multiplies damage during a cyber incident. Effective response depends on knowing who does what. Roles may overlap, but responsibilities must be clear.

The General Manager

The General Manager leads the property response. The GM activates the crisis team, ensures guest care, maintains operational priorities, escalates to corporate or ownership, approves major decisions within authority, and coordinates with Legal and Communications. The GM does not diagnose malware or negotiate technical containment. The GM makes sure the right experts are engaged and that the business continues as safely as possible.

The GM must also protect the tone of the response. Blame, denial and improvisation can damage the organization. The GM should insist on facts, structured updates, clear roles and respectful communication. In a crisis, leadership behavior becomes part of the incident.

IT and Cybersecurity Teams

IT and cybersecurity teams focus on containment, diagnosis, preservation of evidence, recovery planning, vendor coordination and technical communication to leadership. They must determine which systems are affected, whether the threat is spreading, what data may be involved, which systems can be isolated, and how recovery should be sequenced.

IT should not make business decisions alone. It should not decide by itself whether to pay a ransom, communicate with the media, notify guests, delay reporting or reopen systems for operational convenience. These decisions require executive and legal involvement. Technical urgency must be balanced with business, legal and reputational judgment.

Legal and Compliance

Legal and compliance teams assess notification obligations, regulatory exposure, contractual responsibilities, insurance conditions, evidence preservation and liability. If personal data is involved, the organization may need to determine whether a breach is notifiable, when the organization became aware, which jurisdictions are involved, and whether affected individuals must be informed.

Under the GDPR, personal data breach notification to the supervisory authority is required without undue delay and, where feasible, not later than 72 hours after becoming aware of the breach, unless the breach is unlikely to result in risk to individuals. This makes early legal involvement essential for hotels handling EU guest or employee data.

Legal must work closely with IT. IT provides technical facts; Legal interprets obligations. If either function works in isolation, the organization may miss deadlines, overcommunicate, undercommunicate or fail to preserve evidence.

Communications and Public Relations

Communications teams manage internal and external messaging. They help prepare statements for guests, staff, media, corporate stakeholders and potentially owners or partners. Their role is not to hide the incident, but to communicate responsibly. Good communication is factual, calm, consistent and aligned with legal guidance.

A major mistake is communicating too early with false certainty. Another mistake is saying nothing when guests are already experiencing disruption. Communication must acknowledge what is known, what is being done, and where updates will come from. In hospitality, communication is not only reputation management; it is guest care.

Operations

Operations teams keep the hotel functioning. Front Office, Housekeeping, Food and Beverage, Engineering, Security and Guest Relations may need to activate manual procedures. They may use printed arrival lists, manual room status tracking, offline payment procedures, temporary communication channels or additional lobby staffing.

Operations must also report practical reality back to the crisis team. If manual check-in is failing, if guests are becoming angry, if elevators or room keys are affected, or if restaurants cannot post charges, leadership needs to know. Cyber response must be connected to what is happening on the floor.

Finance and Insurance

Finance assesses revenue impact, cost exposure, cash handling risks, payment disruption, invoice problems, refunds, compensation decisions and insurance documentation. Cyber incidents can generate immediate and hidden costs: lost revenue, consulting fees, legal fees, guest compensation, overtime, system restoration, forensic analysis, regulatory processes and possible litigation.

Cyber insurance may provide support, but only if conditions are respected. The insurer may require notification, approved vendors, documentation and coordination before certain decisions are made. Finance and Legal should work together early.

WHAT EXECUTIVES MUST NEVER DO

Cyber incidents are worsened by poor leadership decisions. Three mistakes are especially dangerous: hiding the incident, communicating prematurely without facts, and blaming IT publicly.

Hiding the incident is often the most damaging mistake. It may delay containment, violate reporting obligations, weaken insurance claims and destroy trust. Most cover-ups fail because guests, employees, vendors or media eventually reveal what happened. Transparency does not mean careless disclosure; it means responsible escalation and truthful management.

Communicating too early can also be dangerous. Executives may be tempted to reassure guests or owners before facts are known. If they later need to correct themselves, credibility suffers. A responsible statement can acknowledge disruption, confirm that specialists are investigating, explain immediate support for guests and promise updates without speculating on details.

Blaming IT publicly is another mistake. It creates internal fear, weakens coordination and may leak externally. Even if technical failures contributed to the incident, crisis response requires a united front. Accountability can be reviewed after containment and recovery. During the crisis, the priority is coordination.

Executives must also avoid unauthorized ransom discussions, uncontrolled media responses, deletion of evidence, reopening systems too quickly, ignoring legal advice, and allowing every department to communicate separately. In crisis, discipline matters.

THE FIRST HOUR OF A CONFIRMED DATA BREACH

The first hour of a confirmed data breach is critical because uncertainty is high and consequences are expanding. The goal is not to solve everything immediately. The goal is to establish control, protect guests, prevent further damage, activate expertise, preserve evidence and create a reliable decision rhythm.

Imagine that at 10:00 AM the hotel receives confirmation of a major cybersecurity incident. The PMS is unstable. Guests are checking in.

Journalists are calling. IT confirms that unauthorized access has occurred. The executive team must act.

The first decision is to activate the crisis team. The GM should bring together IT, Operations, Legal, Communications, Finance and relevant corporate or ownership contacts. The crisis team should agree on meeting rhythm, communication channels and decision authority.

The second decision is to protect guests and essential operations. Additional managers may be sent to the lobby. Manual procedures may be activated. Guest-facing teams need clear instructions on what to say and what not to say. Safety and dignity of service remain priorities.

The third decision is to contain the incident through IT leadership. Executives should authorize necessary containment steps, even if they temporarily disrupt operations. Keeping a compromised system online for convenience may increase damage. However, technical containment must be coordinated with operational needs so that teams understand what is happening.

The fourth decision is to contact corporate IT or external cybersecurity specialists. A serious incident requires expertise. If the hotel has an incident response provider or cyber insurance panel, this should be activated according to procedure.

The fifth decision is to engage legal counsel immediately. Legal must assess notification obligations, evidence preservation, privilege considerations, regulatory exposure and communication boundaries. The clock for potential reporting obligations may already be running.

The sixth decision is to create a decision log. Every major action should be documented: time, person, decision, reason and follow-up. This log will be essential later.

The seventh decision is to control communication. Only authorized spokespersons should speak externally. Employees should receive internal guidance. Media inquiries should be routed to Communications. Guests should receive clear and calm operational information, without speculation.

The eighth decision is to assess data exposure. IT and Legal must work together to determine what systems and data may be affected. The organization needs to know whether guest data, payment data, employee data or corporate client data may be involved.

The ninth decision is to manage financial and insurance implications. Finance should begin estimating operational impact, tracking costs, documenting losses, reviewing insurance notification requirements and coordinating payment workarounds.

The tenth decision is to set the next executive update. A cyber crisis cannot be managed by one meeting. The GM should establish a recurring update cycle, such as every 30 or 60 minutes during the initial phase, with clear inputs from IT, Operations, Legal, Communications and Finance.

These first decisions are managerial, not technical. They show that executive leadership is about creating structure under pressure. The exact sequence may vary by incident, but the logic remains consistent: command, care, containment, escalation, legal, documentation, communication, assessment, finance and rhythm.

FAST DECISIONS, SLOW DECISIONS AND LEADERSHIP QUALITY

Cyber incidents create a tension between speed and accuracy. Acting too slowly allows damage to spread. Acting too quickly without facts can create confusion or legal risk. The executive task is not to wait for perfect information. It is to make structured decisions under uncertainty.

Fast decisions are needed when delay increases harm. Activating the crisis team, isolating affected systems, engaging experts, protecting guests and documenting actions should not wait. These decisions establish control. They can be refined as information improves.

Slower decisions may be appropriate when facts are incomplete and consequences are significant. Public statements about the cause of the incident, statements about whether data was stolen, ransom decisions, regulatory notifications and individual guest notifications require careful coordination with IT and Legal. However, slow does not mean passive. It means deliberate.

Proactive leadership anticipates uncertainty and prepares before the crisis. A hotel with an incident response plan, trained managers, current contact lists, manual procedures, vendor agreements, cyber insurance and tested backups can move faster and more calmly. Defensive leadership reacts late, hides uncertainty, blames departments and improvises under pressure.

The difference between proactive and defensive leadership may determine whether the same cyber incident becomes a controlled disruption or a reputational collapse.

PREPARATION AS REPUTATION INSURANCE

Cybersecurity preparation is sometimes treated as a cost because its benefits are invisible when nothing happens. This is a dangerous view. Preparation is reputation insurance. It protects the hotel before an incident, during an incident and after an incident.

Before an incident, preparation reduces likelihood and impact. Staff training reduces phishing success. Access controls limit damage.

Backups support recovery. Network segmentation prevents attackers from moving freely. Vendor reviews reduce exposure. Clear policies prevent improvisation.

During an incident, preparation creates calm. A printed contact list, a tested crisis plan, pre-approved communication templates, manual check-in procedures, role clarity and external response partners all reduce panic. The hotel does not waste the first hour deciding who should be in the room.

After an incident, preparation supports recovery and credibility. Documentation helps explain what happened. Evidence supports insurance and legal processes. Training records show diligence. Tested plans demonstrate governance maturity. Post-incident reviews help improve the organization.

For hospitality leaders, cybersecurity maturity is not measured only by tools purchased. It is measured by the organization's ability to continue serving guests, protect data, communicate responsibly and learn from disruption.

CYBERSECURITY AS A GOVERNANCE DISCIPLINE

Cybersecurity must be governed. It cannot be delegated entirely to technical teams, because the risks affect the full organization. Governance means assigning accountability, setting priorities, defining policies, allocating budgets, monitoring performance and reviewing risk regularly.

A hotel or hotel group should know who owns cybersecurity at executive level, how often risks are reviewed, which systems are critical, which vendors have access, how incidents are escalated, how employees are trained, how backups are tested and how investments are prioritized.

The NIST Cybersecurity Framework 2.0 is useful for executives because it organizes cybersecurity outcomes around six functions: Govern, Identify, Protect, Detect, Respond and Recover. This structure helps leaders understand that cybersecurity is not only defense. It includes governance before the incident, knowledge of assets and risks, protection of systems and data, detection of abnormal activity, response to incidents and recovery after disruption.

In hospitality terms, governance asks: Do we know what we must protect? Do we know who can access it? Do we know which systems are essential to guest service? Do we know how fast we can recover? Do we know what we will tell guests? Do we know who makes decisions? Do we know which vendors must help us?

These questions should not be asked for the first time during a crisis. They should be part of the normal management rhythm.

RISK MANAGEMENT BEFORE THE INCIDENT

Cybersecurity risk management begins long before an attack is detected. A hotel that waits for a crisis before discussing cybersecurity has already lost valuable time. Risk management means identifying what could go wrong, estimating how serious the impact would be, deciding what must be protected first, and allocating resources accordingly. In hospitality, this work must be connected to the operating reality of the property. A risk register that ignores the lobby, the restaurant, the reservation office and the night audit process is incomplete.

The first step is to identify critical assets. For a hotel, critical assets are not only servers or databases. They include the PMS, POS, payment terminals, room key systems, internet connectivity, guest WiFi, internal communication tools, reservation interfaces, finance systems, payroll data, loyalty data and essential vendor connections. Some assets are critical because they hold sensitive data. Others are critical because the operation cannot continue without them.

The second step is to classify data. Guest personal data, passport information, payment information, employee records and corporate client contracts do not carry the same level of sensitivity as a general marketing brochure or a public menu. If teams do not know which data is sensitive, they cannot apply the right level of care. Data classification also helps managers decide which systems require stronger access control, encryption, monitoring, retention rules and deletion procedures.

The third step is to evaluate likelihood and impact. A minor system inconvenience may be likely but low impact. A ransomware incident may be less frequent but extremely high impact. A hotel that receives hundreds of supplier invoices each month may face a high phishing exposure. A resort with many connected room devices may face IoT exposure. A multi-country hotel group may face more complex regulatory and vendor risk.

The fourth step is to decide on treatment. Some risks are reduced through training, stronger authentication, network segmentation, vendor reviews, backups, patching, monitoring or revised procedures. Some risks are transferred through insurance, although insurance never replaces good management. Some risks may be accepted if the cost of mitigation is disproportionate, but this should be a conscious executive decision, not a hidden consequence of inaction.

The fifth step is review. Cyber risk is not static. A hotel opening, a PMS migration, a new payment provider, a new mobile app, a change in ownership, a new outsourced partner or a new regional reporting platform can change exposure. Risk management must therefore be part of the management rhythm, not a one-time document stored after an audit.

FROM PROPERTY RISK TO GROUP RISK

A single hotel and a hotel group experience cyber risk differently. At property level, the impact is immediate and operational. The GM sees the queue, the staff stress, the room key issue and the guest complaints. At group level, the concern expands to brand consistency, multi-property exposure, legal coordination, centralized systems, vendor contracts, insurance programs, reporting obligations and owner communication.

Group structures can reduce risk when they create standards, stronger vendor selection, centralized monitoring, negotiated response contracts and shared expertise. However, they can also concentrate risk. If many hotels depend on the same central platform, a failure or compromise can affect multiple properties at once. Standardization improves control, but it also means that one weakness may be repeated across the portfolio.

Property leaders must therefore understand both local and group responsibilities. A local hotel may not choose every system, but it remains responsible for applying policies, training employees, reporting incidents quickly, maintaining manual procedures and communicating operational realities to corporate teams. Corporate teams may own strategy, but they need accurate information from properties to understand exposure.

The best governance model creates a two-way relationship. Group IT defines standards and supports expertise. Property teams apply them and provide feedback. Legal and Finance connect compliance and insurance. Operations tests whether procedures are realistic. The aim is not to make cybersecurity a headquarters instruction. The aim is to make it a shared discipline across the hospitality ecosystem.

MEASURING CYBERSECURITY READINESS

Executives often ask how they can know whether the organization is ready. Cybersecurity cannot be measured only by the number of tools installed. Readiness should be measured through practical questions that connect systems, people and decisions.

A first indicator is whether the hotel has an incident response plan that is current, accessible and understood. A plan that nobody has read is not readiness. The plan should include contacts, roles, escalation paths, decision rights, communication rules, vendor details, insurance notification steps and manual procedures.

A second indicator is whether backups are tested. Having backups is not enough. The organization must know whether backups can actually be restored, how long restoration takes, which systems are prioritized and whether backups are protected from compromise. For hotels, recovery time must be translated into operational terms: how many arrivals will be affected, how many outlets will be unable to post charges, how long finance can operate manually, and what guest compensation may be required.

A third indicator is employee behavior. Do staff report suspicious emails? Do managers verify unusual payment or access requests? Are password resets controlled? Do employees know that sharing credentials is unacceptable? Can the night team reach support? Cybersecurity readiness is often weakest during evenings, nights, weekends and peak service periods, precisely when hospitality pressure is highest.

A fourth indicator is vendor clarity. The hotel should know which vendors have access to systems or data, how they authenticate, what service levels apply, how quickly they must notify the hotel of incidents, and what happens if the contract ends. Vendor lists should not live only in procurement files. They should be part of operational risk knowledge.

A fifth indicator is executive rehearsal. Tabletop exercises allow leaders to practice decisions before the pressure is real. A realistic exercise might simulate a PMS outage during a group arrival, a phishing-driven credential compromise, a ransomware message at night, or a confirmed breach involving guest passport data. The purpose is not to embarrass teams. It is to reveal gaps while there is still time to fix them.

A sixth indicator is the quality of leadership questions. Executives do not need to ask how to configure a firewall, but they should ask which systems are most critical, how quickly they can be restored, who has privileged access, how guests will be supported if systems fail, which vendors must be contacted first, and what decision cannot wait for perfect information. These questions move cybersecurity from a hidden technical concern to a visible management discipline.

Readiness is therefore not a certificate on the wall. It is the combined ability of people, processes, systems and leaders to reduce uncertainty when the hotel is under pressure. For hospitality organizations, that ability has direct commercial value because it preserves service, protects guests and limits reputational damage.

BUILDING A HOSPITALITY CYBERSECURITY CULTURE

Cybersecurity culture is the shared set of behaviors, habits and expectations that influence how people handle digital risk. In hotels, this culture must be practical and service-compatible. It must protect the guest without paralyzing the operation.

A strong culture begins with leadership language. If executives describe cybersecurity as a technical burden, teams will treat it as an obstacle. If executives describe cybersecurity as part of guest trust and brand protection, teams are more likely to take it seriously.

Training should use hotel scenarios. Employees should practice identifying suspicious booking attachments, fake supplier invoices, unusual password reset requests, fraudulent calls to the front desk, guest data disclosure risks and payment handling errors. Generic training is less effective than examples that reflect daily hospitality work.

Reporting should be easy and safe. Staff should know exactly who to contact when something seems wrong. They should be praised for reporting quickly, even if the event turns out to be harmless. Early reporting is one of the strongest defenses against escalation.

Managers should also reduce unnecessary pressure that creates risk. If employees are constantly rushed, understaffed or afraid to question authority, attackers can exploit that environment. Cybersecurity is therefore connected to operational culture, staffing, leadership and communication.

A hospitality cybersecurity culture does not ask employees to become technical experts. It asks them to pause, verify, protect, report and learn.

APPLIED HOSPITALITY CASE: CONFIRMED DATA BREACH AT 10:00 AM

A 180-room upscale hotel in a European capital is operating at 87 percent occupancy. The property includes two restaurants, a bar, meeting rooms, a spa and a strong corporate guest base. At 10:00 AM, the IT Manager informs the General Manager that the hotel has suffered a confirmed data breach. The PMS is unstable. Some front desk functions are slow or unavailable. Several guests are waiting to check out. A group arrival is expected at 1:00 PM. A journalist has called after receiving a tip from an external source. Corporate IT is not yet fully briefed.

The General Manager must lead without pretending to be a technical specialist. The first responsibility is to establish control. The GM activates the crisis team and names a single coordinator for documentation. IT is instructed to focus on containment and technical assessment. Operations is instructed to activate manual front desk procedures and deploy additional managers to the lobby. Legal counsel is contacted. Communications is asked to prepare holding lines for staff, guests and media, subject to legal review. Finance begins tracking disruption and potential claims. Corporate leadership and ownership are informed through a concise initial report.

The first message to staff is calm and practical: systems are being investigated, only designated people may communicate externally, guest care remains the priority, and all unusual system behavior or guest questions must be escalated. The front desk receives language that acknowledges technical disruption without speculating about cause or data exposure. Guests are offered assistance, documentation where possible and follow-up channels.

The GM refuses to make premature public claims. The hotel does not say "no data was stolen" until this has been verified. It does not blame a vendor. It does not allow departments to send separate explanations. It does not reopen unstable systems merely to reduce lobby pressure. The response is structured around people, operations, legal, communication and finance.

By the end of the first hour, the hotel has not solved the incident. But it has done something equally important: it has created disciplined leadership. The crisis team knows who is responsible for what. Guests are being supported. Legal and corporate teams are involved. The technical investigation is underway. A decision log exists. Communication is controlled. The hotel has moved from panic to managed uncertainty.

MANAGERIAL TAKEAWAYS

Cybersecurity is a leadership test. The quality of the response depends not only on technical defenses, but also on preparation, role clarity, communication and executive discipline.

Hotels are attractive targets because they combine valuable data, continuous operations, complex systems, many users, third-party dependencies and strong pressure to restore service quickly.

The attack surface of a hotel includes guest WiFi, PMS, POS, IoT devices, staff email, vendors, cloud systems and legacy infrastructure. Every convenience must be balanced with exposure.

Cyber risk must be translated into business impact. Executives should speak about revenue loss, service disruption, guest trust, legal exposure, operational continuity and brand value.

The General Manager does not need to understand hacking. The GM must understand consequences, activate the right people, protect guests, control communication and make decisions under pressure.

Silence is a decision. Delay, denial and unclear communication can damage trust and worsen legal or reputational consequences.

Preparation protects reputation. Incident response plans, manual procedures, training, vendor governance, backups, legal readiness and communication protocols are not administrative exercises. They are part of executive maturity.

TO REVIEW THIS CHAPTER

KEY TERMS

Cybersecurity: The practices, processes and controls used to protect systems, networks, devices and data from unauthorized access, disruption, misuse or damage.

Cyber Risk: The possibility that a digital threat will create operational, financial, legal, reputational or safety consequences for the organization.

Attack Surface: The collection of systems, devices, users, vendors and access points through which an attacker could attempt to compromise an organization.

Ransomware: A form of cyberattack in which systems or data are made unavailable, often through encryption, and attackers demand payment for restoration or non-disclosure.

Phishing: A fraudulent attempt to trick people into revealing credentials, opening malicious files, clicking harmful links or approving unauthorized actions.

Social Engineering: Manipulation of human trust, urgency, authority or helpfulness to bypass security procedures.

Data Breach: Unauthorized access, disclosure, alteration, loss or exposure of personal, payment, business or confidential information.

Incident Response: The structured process of preparing for, detecting, managing, communicating and recovering from cybersecurity incidents.

Containment: Actions taken to limit the spread or impact of a cyber incident, such as isolating affected systems or disabling compromised accounts.

Business Continuity: The ability of the hotel to continue essential operations during and after a disruption.

Manual Workaround: A temporary non-digital procedure used to maintain service when systems are unavailable or unreliable.

GDPR Breach Notification: The requirement under the GDPR to notify the supervisory authority without undue delay and, where feasible, within 72 hours after becoming aware of a notifiable personal data breach.

PCI-DSS: The Payment Card Industry Data Security Standard, a set of requirements for organizations that store, process or transmit cardholder data.

Cyber Insurance: Insurance coverage that may support costs related to cyber incidents, subject to policy conditions, notification duties and approved procedures.

Crisis Cell: A temporary leadership group activated to coordinate decisions, communication and recovery during a serious incident.

REFLECTION QUESTIONS

- Why is cybersecurity in hospitality more than a technical issue?
- How does the 24/7 nature of hotel operations change the consequences of a cyber incident?
- Which parts of the hotel attack surface are most visible to guests? Which are mostly invisible but highly risky?
- Why can a data breach become a trust crisis rather than only a compliance problem?
- How should a General Manager behave during the first hour of a cyber incident?
- Why is it dangerous for IT to make ransom payment decisions alone?

- How can hospitality culture, especially helpfulness and speed, be exploited by social engineering?
- What should a hotel communicate to guests when systems are down but the facts are not yet fully known?
- How can cybersecurity training be adapted to the daily reality of hotel employees?
- Why is preparation described as reputation insurance?

REVIEW QUESTIONS

- Define cyber risk in a hospitality context.
- List four reasons why hotels are attractive targets for cybercriminals.
- Identify six components of a typical hotel attack surface.
- Explain the difference between ransomware and phishing.
- What are the possible operational consequences of a PMS outage during a cyber incident?
- What are the main responsibilities of the General Manager during a cyber crisis?
- What should IT teams do during the early stage of an incident, and what should they not do alone?
- Why must Legal and Compliance be involved early in a confirmed data breach?
- What are three executive mistakes that should be avoided during a cyber incident?
- List ten managerial decisions that may be required in the first hour of a confirmed data breach.

REFERENCES AND FURTHER READING

CISA. StopRansomware Guide. Cybersecurity and Infrastructure Security Agency. https://www.cisa.gov/stopransomware/ransomware-guide

European Data Protection Board. Guidelines 9/2022 on personal data breach notification under GDPR. https://www.edpb.europa.eu/

European Union. General Data Protection Regulation, Article 33: Notification of a personal data breach to the supervisory authority. https://gdpr-info.eu/art-33-gdpr/

MGM Resorts International. Form 8-K and public statements related to the September 2023 cybersecurity issue. See also Reuters coverage of the estimated financial impact. https://www.reuters.com/business/mgm-expects-cybersecurity-issue-negatively-impact-third-quarter-earnings-2023-10-05/

National Institute of Standards and Technology. The NIST Cybersecurity Framework 2.0. https://www.nist.gov/cyberframework

National Institute of Standards and Technology. NIST Cybersecurity Framework 2.0: Resource & Overview Guide. https://nvlpubs.nist.gov/nistpubs/SpecialPublications/NIST.SP.1299.pdf

PCI Security Standards Council. PCI DSS Quick Reference Guide. https://www.pcisecuritystandards.org/document_library/

Verizon. 2024 Data Breach Investigations Report. https://www.verizon.com/business/resources/reports/dbir/

Chapter 4

GDPR & PCI-DSS in Hospitality

Why Compliance Is a Business Issue, Not Only an IT Issue

LEARNING OBJECTIVES

By the end of this chapter, you should be able to explain why GDPR and PCI-DSS are business, governance and trust issues in hospitality, not merely technical or legal concerns; identify the main types of personal data and payment data handled by hotels throughout the guest journey; distinguish the purpose and scope of GDPR and PCI-DSS in hotel operations; apply core GDPR principles such as lawfulness, transparency, purpose limitation, data minimization, security and accountability to practical hospitality decisions; understand how payment flows, POS, PMS, gateways and banks create PCI-DSS exposure and revenue-continuity risk; recognize common hospitality compliance mistakes, including shared passwords, uncontrolled Excel files, zombie accounts and unsafe paper trails; evaluate cloud vendors, international data transfers and loyalty databases through a managerial compliance lens; and make informed executive decisions when data protection, payment security, operational reality and commercial objectives create trade-offs.

OPENING PERSPECTIVE

Hotels are built on trust. Guests trust the property with their arrival time, identity documents, credit card, preferences, family details, corporate information, dietary needs, mobility requirements, loyalty history and sometimes very personal expectations. They trust the hotel to welcome them, serve them and protect them. In modern hospitality, that trust is not only delivered by warm service and elegant surroundings. It is also delivered by the way the hotel collects, stores, shares, protects and deletes data.

Compliance is therefore not a paperwork exercise. It is not a dusty legal file held somewhere at headquarters. It is not a technical certification delegated to an IT provider. It is a business discipline that connects guest confidence, payment continuity, legal exposure, operational discipline, vendor management and brand reputation. A hotel that fails to protect data does not only face penalties. It risks losing the confidence that makes hospitality possible.

Two frameworks are especially important for hotel executives. GDPR, the General Data Protection Regulation, governs how personal data related to individuals in the European Union is processed. PCI-DSS, the Payment Card Industry Data Security Standard, defines security requirements for organizations that store, process or transmit cardholder data. The first is a legal framework for personal data protection. The second is a payment-security standard connected to card schemes, banks and payment processors. Their logic is different, but their operational impact is similar: both require discipline, documentation, control and accountability.

For hotel managers, the essential lesson can be expressed simply: if you collect it, you must protect it; if you use it, you must justify it; if you share it, you must control it; if you keep it, you must know why. Compliance begins long before a regulator writes to the hotel. It begins at reception when a passport is scanned, in reservations when a guest email is stored, in marketing when a database is reused, in finance when a card deposit is processed, in food and beverage when a POS transaction is linked to a room, and in IT when a vendor is given access to a system.

This chapter explains GDPR and PCI-DSS from a hospitality management perspective. It does not turn managers into lawyers or payment-security auditors. Instead, it gives them the vocabulary, logic and reflexes needed to ask better questions, challenge unsafe habits and recognize when compliance has become a business risk.

DATA IS TRUST, PAYMENTS ARE REVENUE, NON-COMPLIANCE IS RISK

In hospitality, data and payment security are inseparable from the guest relationship. A hotel does not simply sell a room. It manages a sequence of promises: the room will be ready, the booking will be honored, the service will be personalized, the guest will be recognized, the payment will be secure, and the information shared by the guest will not be misused. When this promise is broken, the damage is wider than a technical incident.

Data is trust because guests provide information in situations where they expect discretion. A hotel may know where a guest sleeps, when they travel, whether they are traveling with a spouse, colleague or family, which company they work for, which rate they booked, what they ate, what they complained about, what language they prefer and what kind of room they like. Some of this data is necessary to perform the service. Some of it is useful for personalization. Some of it may be unnecessary or excessive. Managers must be able to distinguish the difference.

Payments are revenue because a hotel cannot function without secure transaction flows. Rooms, restaurants, bars, spas, events, deposits, pre-authorizations, no-show fees, gift cards, online bookings and corporate invoices all rely on payment systems. If a hotel loses the ability to accept cards, the effect is immediate. It can affect revenue collection, guest convenience, front-office operations, restaurant service and owner confidence.

Non-compliance is risk because failure creates consequences on several levels at the same time. There may be regulatory penalties, investigations, lawsuits, card-scheme fines, increased audit obligations, loss of merchant privileges, higher insurance costs, vendor disputes and reputational damage. The hotel may also face operational disruption while teams investigate what happened, notify affected individuals, repair controls and respond to stakeholders.

For executives, the practical message is clear: compliance must be understood as a form of operational governance. It is part of running the hotel responsibly. It protects the guest relationship, protects revenue channels and protects the asset from avoidable risk.

HOTELS AS DATA FACTORIES

Many hotels underestimate the quantity and sensitivity of the data they handle every day. Because data collection is embedded in familiar routines, it can become invisible. Reception asks for identification. Reservations stores emails. Marketing manages preferences. Finance processes deposits. Spa records treatment preferences. Events departments store guest lists. Human resources holds employee records. Loyalty programs collect stay history. Each action appears ordinary. Together, they create a complex data ecosystem.

Guest data commonly includes names, addresses, telephone numbers, emails, identification documents, passport or national identity details, nationality, date of birth, travel dates, room preferences, loyalty numbers, special requests, accessibility needs, dietary restrictions, complaint history, booking source and communication preferences. Some hotels also collect vehicle plates, photographs, scanned signatures, guest messages, CCTV footage or health-related information in spa and wellness contexts.

Payment data includes card numbers, expiry dates, cardholder names, authorization codes, payment tokens, deposits, refunds, pre-authorizations, billing addresses, invoices and transaction histories. Even when a hotel does not store full card details, it may still transmit or process payment-related information through POS, PMS, payment gateways and online booking channels.

Operational data can also become personal data when it relates to an identifiable person. A housekeeping note saying that a guest requested hypoallergenic pillows, a restaurant note about allergies, a complaint about noise, a VIP code in the PMS, or a record of late-night room service may all contribute to a profile. Managers often think only of passports and credit cards. In reality, hospitality data is much broader.

The phrase "data factory" is useful because it reminds managers that hotels do not merely receive data; they produce, transform, export, copy, analyze and retain it. The question is not whether a hotel handles data. The question is whether the hotel understands where the data comes from, where it goes, who uses it, why it is kept and how it is protected.

FOLLOWING DATA THROUGH THE GUEST JOURNEY

Data protection becomes easier to understand when managers follow data through the guest journey. Before arrival, personal data may enter through the hotel website, brand booking engine, online travel agency, travel management company, call center, central reservation system or group sales team. The guest may provide contact details, payment guarantee, stay dates, loyalty membership and preferences. At this stage, the hotel must know which entity collected the data, what privacy information was provided, and which systems received the data.

At arrival, the front office may verify identity, scan or record identification details, confirm payment, collect a signature, assign a room and update the PMS. The operational need is obvious: the hotel must know who is staying and must comply with local lodging-registration rules where applicable. The compliance question is whether the hotel collects only what is necessary, protects it properly and retains it only for the required period.

During the stay, data circulates across departments. Restaurant bills are posted to the room. Spa appointments may be added to the guest folio. Maintenance requests may be linked to a room number. Guest preferences may be updated. Internal notes may be created to improve service. The risk is that employees may add unnecessary, subjective or inappropriate comments. A hotel culture that values personalization must also teach employees how to record information respectfully and lawfully.

At departure, payment is finalized, invoices are issued, loyalty points may be updated and the guest profile may remain active for future stays. Post-stay, the hotel may send satisfaction surveys, targeted offers, rebooking incentives or loyalty communications. At this stage, the line between service communication and marketing communication becomes important. A hotel may need a different legal basis for each type of message.

Following data through the journey reveals that compliance is not a single department's responsibility. It touches sales, reservations, front office, housekeeping, F&B, spa, finance, marketing, revenue management, IT, legal and corporate teams. The more complex the journey, the more important it becomes to map data flows clearly.

GDPR AND PCI-DSS: DIFFERENT LOGIC, SIMILAR MANAGERIAL IMPACT

GDPR and PCI-DSS should not be confused. GDPR is a legal framework for personal data protection. It applies to the processing of personal data in contexts covered by the regulation, including data relating to individuals in the European Union. It is enforced by supervisory authorities and includes obligations around lawful processing, transparency, individual rights, security, accountability and data transfers.

PCI-DSS is not a law in the same sense. It is a global payment-card security standard maintained by the PCI Security Standards Council and required through contracts with card brands, acquiring banks and payment processors. It applies to organizations that store, process or transmit cardholder data, including hotels, restaurants, spas, online booking channels and any other payment environment connected to card transactions.

The difference matters because the accountability routes are different. GDPR exposure may involve data protection authorities, affected individuals, legal claims and public trust. PCI-DSS exposure may involve acquiring banks, card brands, forensic investigations, fines, increased validation requirements and potential restrictions on card acceptance. For a hotel, both can threaten business continuity.

The overlap is also important. A guest's payment card may be connected to a name, booking, stay record and invoice. A payment incident can therefore become both a PCI-DSS issue and a personal data breach. A loyalty database may not contain card data but can still create significant GDPR risk. A hotel executive must avoid thinking in separate silos. The practical question is: what data is involved, what systems touch it, who has access, which obligations apply and what could happen if control is lost?

For managers, both frameworks lead to the same executive behavior: ask questions, document decisions, reduce unnecessary exposure, control vendors, train staff and verify assumptions.

GDPR EXPLAINED FOR HOSPITALITY MANAGERS

GDPR can appear complex, but its managerial logic is direct. Before collecting or using personal data, a hotel should be able to answer three questions: What are we collecting? Why are we collecting it? How are we protecting it? If the hotel cannot answer these questions clearly, the processing activity is probably not sufficiently governed.

The first principle is lawfulness, fairness and transparency. Guests should not be surprised by what the hotel does with their data. If data is collected for booking and stay management, the guest should understand that purpose. If it is used for marketing, profiling or third-party sharing, the hotel must ensure that the legal basis and communication are appropriate. Transparency does not mean overwhelming guests with legal language. It means providing clear, accessible information about data use.

The second principle is purpose limitation. Data should be collected for specified, explicit and legitimate purposes. A hotel that collects an email address to confirm a reservation cannot automatically assume it may use that email for every future marketing campaign. A passport scan collected for legal registration should not become a general customer intelligence tool. The purpose defines the permissible use.

The third principle is data minimization. Hotels should collect only what is necessary. This principle is uncomfortable for hospitality because service culture often encourages collecting more information to personalize the experience. Yet more data means more risk. Managers must ask whether the extra data is truly needed, whether it improves the service in a justified way, and whether the guest would reasonably expect the hotel to keep it.

The fourth principle is security and confidentiality. Personal data should be protected against unauthorized access, loss, alteration and misuse. This includes technical measures such as access controls, encryption, backups and secure systems, but also organizational measures such as staff training, policies, role-based permissions, clean-desk practices and proper vendor contracts.

The fifth principle is accountability. The hotel must not only comply; it must be able to demonstrate compliance. This requires records, policies, contracts, logs, training evidence, retention rules and incident-response procedures. In practice, accountability is what turns good intention into governance.

LAWFUL BASIS, CONSENT AND LEGITIMATE INTEREST IN HOTEL OPERATIONS

One common misunderstanding is the belief that consent is always required for personal data processing. In reality, GDPR provides several lawful bases. In hospitality, contract is often relevant because certain data is necessary to create and perform the booking. Legal obligation may apply when local law requires registration data. Legitimate interest may apply in some situations, such as certain operational communications or fraud prevention, provided the hotel balances its interest against the guest's rights. Consent may be required for specific marketing activities, optional profiling or certain sensitive uses.

The managerial difficulty is that different uses of the same data may require different reasoning. A guest email used to send a booking confirmation is different from the same email used to send promotional offers six months later. A phone number used to coordinate an airport transfer is different from the same number shared with a third-party marketing partner. A preference recorded to prepare a stay is different from a preference used to build long-term behavioral profiles.

Consent must be specific, informed and freely given. It should not be hidden in vague terms. It should be possible to withdraw consent where consent is the lawful basis. In luxury hospitality, this is also a service issue. A guest who feels manipulated into marketing consent may lose trust. A clear choice can strengthen the relationship.

Legitimate interest requires careful judgment. It may be reasonable for a hotel to use limited data to manage service quality, prevent fraud, secure systems or analyze basic customer behavior. But the hotel should be able to explain the interest, show necessity and demonstrate that the individual's rights have been considered. This is why documentation matters.

For managers, the key reflex is not to choose legal bases casually. The operational question should be escalated to the appropriate legal or data protection resource when the use is new, sensitive, large-scale or connected to third-party sharing. Hospitality creativity must be supported by legal discipline.

PURPOSE LIMITATION AND DATA MINIMIZATION IN DAILY HOTEL DECISIONS

Purpose limitation and data minimization become practical when managers examine daily hotel habits. Can a hotel store passport scans forever? Usually, the answer should be no. If identity data is collected because local law requires verification or registration, it should be kept according to defined legal or operational retention rules, not indefinitely because the system makes it easy.

Can marketing reuse booking emails without consent or another appropriate lawful basis? Not automatically. The fact that a guest booked a room does not give the hotel unlimited permission to send promotional messages forever. Marketing must be aligned with privacy notices, lawful basis, opt-out rules and the guest's expectations.

Can staff export guest lists to personal Excel files? This is one of the most common and dangerous hospitality habits. Excel is convenient, flexible and familiar. It is also easy to copy, email, store locally, forget, lose or send to the wrong person. When guest lists are exported outside controlled systems, accountability and security weaken. Managers should treat uncontrolled spreadsheets as a serious governance risk.

Can a front desk agent write credit card details on paper for later processing? This may seem practical during a busy moment or system issue, but it creates payment-security risk and can violate internal policy and PCI-DSS expectations. The same applies to sticky notes, printed lists, shared notebooks and unsecured registration cards containing card information.

Data minimization is therefore not an abstract principle. It asks managers to reduce unnecessary collection, unnecessary copies, unnecessary retention and unnecessary access. In a hotel, convenience often creates risk. The role of management is to design processes that are convenient enough to work and controlled enough to be safe.

PCI-DSS AND THE HOSPITALITY PAYMENT ENVIRONMENT

PCI-DSS exists because payment card data is valuable and widely targeted. Any business accepting payment cards must protect cardholder data and maintain secure payment environments. Hotels are particularly exposed because payment can occur through multiple channels: online booking, central reservations, front desk, restaurant, bar, spa, retail, events, deposits, pre-authorizations, cancellation fees and corporate billing.

A simplified payment flow can be expressed as guest to POS or PMS, then to payment gateway, then to bank or processor. In reality, the flow may be more complex. A guest may book through an online travel agency, guarantee with a card, pay a deposit through a payment link, charge dinner through POS, post the charge to the PMS, settle at check-out and later receive a refund. Every point where card data is captured, transmitted, stored or processed affects the scope of risk.

The most important managerial principle is to reduce the number of systems and people that touch card data. The more touchpoints, the more controls are needed. If card data appears in email inboxes, paper forms, unprotected spreadsheets or PMS notes, the hotel has expanded its risk unnecessarily. If payment solutions tokenize card details and limit staff exposure, risk is reduced.

PCI-DSS is often perceived as technical because it includes security requirements around networks, access, vulnerability management, monitoring and testing. Yet the managerial implications are very practical. Hotels must know which systems are in scope, which vendors support payment flows, how staff process payments, how exceptions are handled, how card data is protected and whether procedures are followed during busy operations.

Payment security is revenue protection. A hotel that cannot accept card payments cannot operate normally. Guests may not have cash. Corporate guests expect card settlement. Online bookings require card guarantees. Restaurants and spas depend on fast and trusted payment. PCI-DSS compliance is therefore directly connected to commercial continuity.

PAYMENT FLOWS, PRE-AUTHORIZATIONS AND OPERATIONAL COMPLEXITY

Hotels face payment complexity that many other businesses do not. A retail shop usually completes a transaction at the time of sale. A hotel may authorize a card before arrival, adjust the folio during the stay, add minibar, breakfast, spa or restaurant charges, release or capture deposits, process no-show fees, split invoices, manage third-party payments, handle virtual cards from online travel agencies and issue refunds after departure.

Each of these practices requires control. Pre-authorizations must be handled through approved systems. Card details should not be requested through insecure email. Virtual cards must be processed according to agreed procedures. Refunds should require authorization and audit trails. Manual workarounds should be documented and limited. Staff should understand what they may and may not write down, store or share.

F&B operations add another layer. Restaurant and bar POS terminals may process cards from both hotel guests and external customers. If POS systems are poorly segmented from other networks, a payment incident in a restaurant environment may affect wider hotel systems.

If POS charges are posted to rooms, integration with PMS becomes operationally important but also creates dependency.

Events and groups create additional risk. A sales coordinator may receive card guarantees, deposits, attendee lists, rooming lists and billing instructions. If these are exchanged through unsecured email attachments or stored in shared folders without control, risk increases. Group business often involves many data subjects, making errors more consequential.

For executives, payment flow mapping is essential. The hotel should be able to describe how payment data enters, where it goes, which systems touch it, who can see it, how long it is kept, and what happens if a system fails. Without this map, payment compliance becomes guesswork.

LEGAL CONSEQUENCES AND OPERATIONAL CONSEQUENCES

Managers sometimes focus only on fines. Fines matter, but they are not the only consequence of non-compliance. Legal consequences may include regulatory investigations, administrative penalties, civil claims, contractual disputes, forensic audits and possible criminal exposure in severe cases. These consequences consume time, money and management attention.

Operational consequences may hurt even faster. A hotel could face interruption of payment processing, loss of merchant privileges, mandatory system reviews, forced changes to procedures, higher insurance premiums, vendor restrictions, temporary shutdown of compromised systems or reputational pressure that reduces bookings. An incident can also distract teams from service delivery, create anxiety among employees and damage relationships with owners or franchise partners.

In a hotel, regulatory and operational consequences often overlap. If a breach affects guest data, the hotel may need to investigate, notify authorities where required, communicate with guests, respond to media questions, manage legal advice, handle compensation requests and maintain operations at the same time. If payment systems are affected, the hotel must continue serving guests while protecting revenue and avoiding further exposure.

Trust erosion is one of the most difficult consequences to measure. Guests may not understand the technical details of a breach, but they understand whether the hotel appears responsible, transparent and competent. A poorly managed compliance incident can remain associated with the brand long after systems have been restored.

This is why prevention is cheaper than remediation. Training, access controls, vendor audits and data-retention rules may feel administrative, but they are far less costly than a major compliance failure.

WHO IS RESPONSIBLE?

Responsibility in compliance is shared, but accountability is not vague. The hotel legal entity is typically the accountable organization for the way guest data and payment processes are managed. IT may implement safeguards. Vendors may provide systems. Staff may handle daily processes. But senior management must ensure that the organization has the right governance, resources and controls.

The General Manager is not expected to interpret every article of GDPR or every PCI-DSS requirement personally. However, the GM is expected to create a culture where data protection and payment security are taken seriously. This includes supporting training, enforcing procedures, escalating risks, challenging unsafe practices and ensuring that departments do not prioritize convenience over control.

IT teams configure systems, manage access, support security controls, coordinate updates and respond to technical incidents. But IT should not be left alone to decide business uses of data, marketing purposes, retention periods or guest communication strategies. Those decisions involve legal, commercial and operational judgment.

Vendors play a major role because hotels rely on PMS providers, payment gateways, booking engines, CRM platforms, marketing agencies, cloud hosts, IT outsourcers and support providers. A vendor may act as a processor, service provider or technology partner, but the hotel must understand the contract, security commitments, data location, audit rights and incident notification obligations.

Staff members are daily compliance actors. A front desk agent sharing a password, a restaurant cashier writing card data on paper, a sales coordinator emailing a guest list, or a marketing assistant exporting a loyalty file can create serious exposure. Compliance succeeds only when everyday behavior aligns with policy.

TYPICAL HOSPITALITY MISTAKES

Shared passwords remain one of the most common weaknesses in hotels. A generic "frontdesk" account may seem efficient, especially with rotating shifts, but it destroys accountability. If everyone uses the same login, the hotel cannot know who accessed or changed a record. It also becomes harder to remove access when an employee leaves.

Zombie accounts are another frequent problem. These are accounts that remain active after employees leave, transfer departments or no longer need access. In hotels with high staff turnover or seasonal employment, access governance is critical. Every unnecessary account is a potential backdoor.

Excel everywhere is a practical but dangerous habit. Managers export arrivals lists, VIP lists, complaint logs, event participants, dietary restrictions, loyalty segments or payment follow-up files. These files may be saved locally, emailed, printed or forgotten. Once data leaves a controlled system, it becomes harder to protect, update or delete.

Paper trails are also risky. Hotels still use printed registration cards, banquet files, payment forms, rooming lists and handwritten notes. Paper is not automatically forbidden, but it must be controlled. Who can see it? Where is it stored? When is it destroyed? Does it contain card details or unnecessary personal information?

Another mistake is excessive internal visibility. Not every employee needs access to every guest profile, payment detail or loyalty note. Role-based access is a service-quality issue as well as a security issue. Employees should see what they need to serve the guest, not everything the hotel knows about the guest.

A final mistake is cultural: "we have always done it this way." Longstanding practice is not a compliance argument. In hospitality, many unsafe habits survive because they seem to make service faster. Leadership must redesign these habits before an incident exposes them.

CLOUD DOES NOT MEAN AUTOMATIC COMPLIANCE

Many hotel leaders assume that moving systems to the cloud automatically solves compliance. This is a dangerous misunderstanding. Cloud systems may improve security, scalability and resilience, but they do not remove the hotel's responsibility. A cloud provider may host or process data, but the hotel still needs governance.

The first question is where the data is hosted. Data location can affect jurisdiction, transfer rules, contractual requirements and risk assessment. A hotel group operating in Europe cannot ignore where guest data is stored and whether international transfer safeguards are required.

The second question is who can access the data. Does the vendor's support team have access? From which countries? Are accesses logged? Are support accounts temporary or permanent? Are administrators using strong authentication? Can the hotel review access activity?

The third question is how long data is kept. A cloud PMS, CRM or marketing platform may retain data by default. The hotel must define retention rules and ensure the system can support them. If the business no longer needs certain data, keeping it indefinitely only increases exposure.

The fourth question is what happens in case of breach. The contract should specify notification timelines, cooperation obligations, security responsibilities, audit rights and remediation support. Managers should not discover these clauses during a crisis.

Cloud compliance requires Data Processing Agreements, vendor due diligence, security documentation, audit rights, data-location awareness, access controls and incident procedures. Trusting a vendor is not the same as governing a vendor.

INTERNATIONAL DATA TRANSFERS AND LOYALTY DATABASES

Loyalty databases are among the most valuable and sensitive data assets in hospitality. They may include guest identity, contact details, stay history, spending patterns, preferences, complaints, service recovery gestures, marketing behavior and segmentation data. They are attractive because they support personalization and direct revenue. They are risky because they concentrate personal data over time.

Consider a hotel chain whose loyalty database is hosted outside the European Union and managed by a third-party marketing provider. The database powers personalized offers and targeted promotions. It includes guest preferences, booking history and contact information. Is this compliant? The correct managerial answer is not a simple yes or no. It depends on safeguards, legal basis, transparency, contracts, transfer mechanisms and governance.

International transfers under GDPR require careful assessment. If personal data is transferred outside the European Economic Area to a country without an adequacy decision, the organization may need safeguards such as Standard Contractual Clauses, Binding Corporate Rules or another valid transfer mechanism. The hotel must also assess whether the third-party provider offers sufficient protection in practice.

The Data Processing Agreement with the vendor is central. It should define the vendor's role, processing instructions, security measures, sub-processors, audit rights, breach notification requirements, return or deletion of data, and liability. Without a strong contract, the hotel may have little control over a critical asset.

Guest consent may be relevant for certain marketing uses, particularly where personalization goes beyond basic service delivery or where explicit marketing permission is required. But consent alone does not solve all transfer and security issues. A guest cannot meaningfully consent to a poorly governed vendor environment.

Management options may include keeping the provider but strengthening safeguards, moving hosting to an EU or adequate jurisdiction, reducing the data stored, redesigning the loyalty strategy, separating marketing data from operational data, improving consent management, or changing vendors. This is why compliance is a business trade-off, not a binary answer.

COMPLIANCE AS A BUSINESS TRADE-OFF

Compliance decisions often require balancing service ambition, operational reality, cost and risk. A luxury hotel may want deep personalization. A marketing team may want rich segmentation. A revenue team may want behavioral analytics. A regional office may want centralized reporting. A property may want practical flexibility. Compliance does not automatically forbid these ambitions, but it requires disciplined design.

The trade-off is not between compliance and business. Good compliance enables sustainable business. A hotel that governs data well can personalize with more confidence, negotiate better with vendors, respond faster to incidents and build guest trust. Poor compliance creates fragile growth because the business model depends on uncontrolled data practices.

One example is passport handling. Keeping passport scans indefinitely may seem useful in case of repeat stays or disputes, but it increases exposure. A better approach is to define what is legally required, what is operationally necessary, how long it must be retained, who can access it and how it is deleted.

Another example is marketing personalization. Using loyalty data to create targeted offers may be legitimate and commercially valuable, but the hotel must ensure transparency, lawful basis, preference management, secure processing and vendor control. Personalization should feel respectful, not intrusive.

A third example is payment convenience. Allowing card details by email may seem useful for guests or groups, but it creates unacceptable exposure. Better solutions may include secure payment links, tokenization and approved payment gateways. The business objective remains the same: collect payment efficiently. The process becomes safer.

Executives should therefore move away from asking, "Can we do this?" toward asking, "Under what conditions can we do this responsibly?" That question opens the door to better governance.

BUILDING A MANAGERIAL COMPLIANCE CHECKLIST

A practical compliance checklist for hospitality managers begins with data location. Where is the data hosted? Is it in the PMS, CRS, CRM, payment gateway, marketing platform, shared drive, cloud folder, vendor system or employee device? Without location awareness, there is no real control.

The second question is access. Who can see, change, export or delete the data? Are permissions based on job roles? Are accounts personal rather than shared? Are leavers removed quickly? Are privileged accounts monitored? Are vendors using controlled support access?

The third question is purpose. Why do we collect this data? Is it needed for contract performance, legal obligation, guest service, marketing, analytics, security or finance? Does the privacy notice reflect the purpose? Are employees using data only for that purpose?

The fourth question is retention. How long do we keep it? Is the period defined by law, accounting needs, operational necessity or habit? Can the system delete or anonymize data? Who reviews old data?

The fifth question is transfer. Is the data shared with corporate headquarters, regional offices, brands, franchise systems, marketing agencies, OTAs, payment processors, cloud vendors or support providers? Are the contracts and safeguards in place?

The sixth question is incident response. What happens in case of breach? Who is called? Who leads? Who investigates? Who communicates? How are authorities, guests, banks, insurers and partners notified where necessary? A checklist is useful only if it leads to rehearsed action.

MANAGERIAL SCENARIO: THE INTERNATIONAL LOYALTY DATABASE

Imagine that a hotel group operates twelve properties across Europe and uses a centralized loyalty database hosted outside the European Union. The platform is managed by a third-party marketing provider. It contains guest contact details, booking history, stay frequency, spending patterns, preferences, complaint notes and campaign responses. The marketing team wants to use it to send highly personalized offers before the summer season.

The commercial opportunity is real. Direct marketing can reduce dependency on online travel agencies, improve loyalty and increase repeat bookings. Personalized offers may also make guests feel recognized. However, the compliance risk is also real because the database contains personal data, is hosted internationally, is managed by a third party and is used for marketing beyond basic service delivery.

A responsible executive would not immediately shut the project down, nor approve it blindly. The first step would be to map the data. What categories are stored? Are any sensitive details included? How old is the data? Which guests are EU residents? Which properties contributed data? Which systems feed the database?

The second step would be to review the legal basis and transparency. Were guests informed that their data would be used for loyalty profiling and marketing? Did they consent where required? Can they opt out easily? Are preferences respected across all properties and channels?

The third step would be to examine the international transfer. Where exactly is the platform hosted? Does an adequacy decision apply? If not, are Standard Contractual Clauses or another transfer mechanism in place? Has the organization assessed the practical level of protection?

The fourth step would be to review the vendor. Is there a Data Processing Agreement? Are sub-processors identified? Are breach notification obligations clear? Are audit rights included? What security measures are documented? Can the vendor demonstrate compliance?

The fifth step would be to define management options. The group could proceed with stronger safeguards, reduce the data set, delay the campaign, migrate hosting, change vendor, request additional legal review, or redesign the loyalty approach. The best decision will balance risk, revenue, guest trust and operational feasibility.

This scenario illustrates the maturity expected from hospitality executives. Compliance is not about saying no to business. It is about making business decisions that can survive legal, operational and reputational scrutiny.

FROM COMPLIANCE PAPERWORK TO COMPLIANCE CULTURE

Policies are necessary, but they are not sufficient. A hotel can have a privacy policy, PCI-DSS documentation and vendor contracts, yet still fail because employees share passwords, export guest lists, write card numbers on paper or ignore suspicious requests. Compliance culture is what connects documents to daily behavior.

A compliance culture begins with leadership language. If managers describe data protection as bureaucracy, employees will treat it as an obstacle. If managers describe it as part of guest trust, employees are more likely to understand its purpose. The hospitality profession already values discretion. Data protection should be presented as the digital extension of discretion.

Training must be practical. Employees should not only hear legal definitions. They should practice real scenarios: a guest asks for another guest's room number; a colleague requests a password; a VIP list is needed for breakfast; a card number arrives by email; a former employee still appears in the PMS; a marketing agency requests an export; a laptop containing guest data is lost. These examples build reflexes.

Managers should also create safe escalation routes. Employees must know whom to call when they are unsure. If the only message is "never make mistakes," people may hide problems. A better message is "report quickly so we can protect the guest and the hotel."

Finally, compliance culture requires consistency. A hotel cannot demand strict behavior from line employees while executives bypass rules for convenience. If senior managers request uncontrolled Excel exports or ask staff to share credentials, the culture collapses. Accountability must be visible at every level.

VENDOR GOVERNANCE AND THIRD-PARTY RISK

Hotels rarely operate their digital environment alone. A single property may depend on a PMS provider, payment gateway, booking engine, channel manager, revenue management platform, CRM provider, email marketing tool, WiFi operator, outsourced IT help desk, cybersecurity provider, online reputation platform, payroll provider, CCTV maintenance company and several hardware suppliers. Each partner may touch systems, data or payment flows in different ways. This makes vendor governance one of the most important executive responsibilities in compliance.

Third-party risk begins before the contract is signed. Procurement should not consider price and functionality only. The hotel must understand what data the vendor will access, whether the vendor acts as processor or independent controller, where the data is hosted, whether sub-processors are used, what security controls are in place, how quickly the vendor must report incidents and what support is available during a crisis. A cheap vendor can become expensive if the contract leaves the hotel exposed.

The contract should translate compliance expectations into operational commitments. A Data Processing Agreement should not be treated as a formal attachment that no one reads. It should clarify instructions, confidentiality, security measures, international transfers, sub-processing, audit rights, deletion, assistance with data-subject requests and breach notification. Payment vendors should also define responsibilities around PCI-DSS scope, tokenization, terminal management, support and incident investigation.

Vendor governance also requires periodic review. A vendor that was appropriate five years ago may no longer match the hotel's risk profile, portfolio size or regulatory environment. Systems change, integrations multiply, new sub-processors appear, data volumes grow and service models evolve. A hotel group should therefore review critical vendors regularly, not only when something goes wrong.

Operational teams must know the vendor model as well. If a front office team calls a support provider and gives remote access to a terminal, is this access controlled and logged? If marketing sends a guest export to an agency, is this covered by contract? If a payment problem occurs at midnight, who has authority to call the gateway provider? Vendor governance is not a legal abstraction. It affects the speed and safety of daily operations.

DATA SUBJECT RIGHTS AND THE FRONT-LINE REALITY

GDPR gives individuals rights over their personal data, including rights of access, rectification, erasure, restriction, portability and objection in appropriate circumstances. In a hotel, these rights may appear first at the front desk, by email, through a loyalty account, via a call center or through a complaint. A guest may ask, "What information do you keep about me?" or "Please delete my profile." The employee receiving the request may not be a privacy specialist, but the response still matters.

Front-line teams should not improvise. They need a simple escalation process. If a guest requests a copy of their data, staff should know whom to contact and how to verify identity. If a guest asks for deletion, the hotel must consider whether data can be deleted immediately or whether legal, accounting or security obligations require retention for a defined period. If a guest objects to marketing, the preference must be respected across systems, not only in one local spreadsheet.

Data-subject rights are operationally difficult because hotel data is often fragmented. A guest profile may exist in the PMS, CRM, loyalty platform, marketing tool, reservation system, email archive, incident log and finance system. If the hotel cannot locate the data, it cannot respond properly. This is another reason why data mapping matters.

The service tone is important. A rights request should not be treated as an annoyance. It is an expression of guest control. A hotel that responds clearly and respectfully can strengthen trust even when the guest is concerned. A confused or defensive response can create the impression that the hotel does not understand its responsibilities.

For managers, data-subject rights create a useful test of governance maturity. If the hotel can quickly identify where guest data is stored, who owns each system, which data must be retained and which data can be removed, the compliance environment is probably well managed. If no one knows where to look, the problem is larger than the request itself.

DESIGNING SAFER HOSPITALITY PROCESSES

Compliance becomes sustainable when it is built into process design. A hotel should not rely only on employees remembering rules under pressure. The best processes make the safe action the easiest action. For example, a secure payment link is safer than asking staff to collect card details by email. Role-based PMS access is safer than shared accounts. Automated retention settings are safer than expecting managers to remember deletion dates manually.

Process design should begin with the guest journey and employee workflow. Where does the guest provide information? Which employee uses it? Which system stores it? Which step creates friction? Unsafe workarounds often appear when official processes are too slow or impractical. If the approved method for payment collection is inconvenient, staff may revert to email or paper. If the approved report is difficult to generate, managers may export data into spreadsheets. Compliance must therefore be designed with operational realism.

Hotels should also separate data according to sensitivity. Not every note belongs in a permanent profile. Not every department needs access to the same information. Not every marketing campaign requires detailed stay history. By reducing the volume and visibility of data, the hotel reduces both compliance risk and operational noise.

A safer process includes checks at key moments: employee onboarding, role changes, departure from the company, vendor onboarding, new campaign approval, system integration, payment exception handling and incident reporting. These checks should be simple enough to be used, but strong enough to prevent predictable failures.

Good process design supports hospitality rather than slowing it down. When employees trust the process, they can focus more confidently on service. When managers trust the controls, they can innovate without creating unnecessary exposure. Compliance maturity is reached when safe behavior becomes normal behavior.

MANAGERIAL TAKEAWAYS

GDPR protects personal data, but in hospitality it also protects trust. A guest who shares personal information expects care, discretion and control. Data protection is therefore part of the service promise.

PCI-DSS protects payment card data, but in hospitality it also protects revenue continuity. Secure payment flows are necessary for reservations, check-in, restaurants, spas, events and digital distribution.

Hotels are data factories. They collect far more information than many managers realize. The more data they collect, the more disciplined they must be about purpose, access, retention and security.

Cloud vendors and external providers do not remove accountability. They change the shape of accountability. Hotels must govern contracts, data location, access rights, security controls and incident obligations.

Compliance failures often begin with ordinary habits: shared passwords, old accounts, uncontrolled spreadsheets, paper forms, excessive access and vague retention. These habits must be redesigned before an incident occurs.

The executive role is to ask questions, not delegate blindly. Where is the data hosted? Who can access it? Why is it collected? How long is it kept? What happens if it is breached? These questions are not technical details. They are leadership responsibilities.

Compliance is not the enemy of hospitality. When properly managed, it strengthens the guest relationship by making personalization safer, payments more secure and trust more durable.

TO REVIEW THIS CHAPTER

KEY TERMS

GDPR: The General Data Protection Regulation, the European legal framework governing the processing of personal data in contexts covered by the regulation.

PCI-DSS: The Payment Card Industry Data Security Standard, a global security standard for organizations that store, process or transmit cardholder data.

Personal Data: Any information relating to an identified or identifiable individual, such as name, email, passport details, stay history or preferences.

Cardholder Data: Payment card information protected under PCI-DSS, including card numbers and related authentication or transaction data.

Data Controller: The organization that determines why and how personal data is processed. In many hotel contexts, the hotel or legal entity acts as controller.

Data Processor: An organization that processes personal data on behalf of a controller, such as a cloud PMS provider or marketing platform.

Data Processing Agreement (DPA): A contract defining how a processor handles personal data on behalf of the controller, including obligations around security, instructions and breach notification.

Lawful Basis: The legal justification required for processing personal data, such as contract, legal obligation, consent or legitimate interest.

Purpose Limitation: The GDPR principle that data should be used only for the specific purposes for which it was collected.

Data Minimization: The GDPR principle that organizations should collect only the data that is necessary for the intended purpose.

Accountability: The requirement to demonstrate responsible data governance through documentation, policies, controls and evidence.

Tokenization: A payment-security technique that replaces sensitive card data with a non-sensitive token that can be used for processing without exposing the original card number.

International Data Transfer: A transfer of personal data to a country or organization outside the relevant protected jurisdiction, requiring safeguards under GDPR when applicable.

Standard Contractual Clauses (SCCs): European Commission-approved contractual clauses used as a safeguard for certain international transfers of personal data.

Zombie Account: A user account that remains active after an employee leaves or no longer requires access, creating avoidable security risk.

Merchant Account: An account relationship that enables a business to accept card payments through acquiring banks and payment processors.

Retention Policy: A rule defining how long specific categories of data are kept and when they must be deleted or anonymized.

Access Control: The process of limiting system access according to user roles, business need and security requirements.

Data Breach: A security incident that leads to accidental or unlawful destruction, loss, alteration, unauthorized disclosure of, or access to personal data.

Compliance Culture: The shared behaviors, habits and leadership expectations that make data protection and payment security part of daily operations.

REFLECTION QUESTIONS

- Why should compliance be considered a business issue rather than only a legal or IT issue?
- What types of personal data does a hotel collect that employees may not immediately recognize as sensitive?
- How can personalization improve the guest experience while also increasing data protection risk?
- Why is it dangerous to assume that a cloud PMS or CRM automatically makes the hotel compliant?
- Which common hospitality habits create the greatest compliance risk in your opinion?
- How should a hotel balance marketing ambition with guest privacy and consent?
- Why can loss of card-payment capability be as serious as a regulatory fine?
- What should a General Manager ask before approving a new vendor that will process guest data?
- How can data minimization improve both compliance and operational discipline?
- In what ways does data protection reflect the traditional hospitality value of discretion?

REVIEW QUESTIONS

- Define GDPR and explain its relevance to hospitality.
- Define PCI-DSS and explain its relevance to hotel payment operations.
- List five types of personal data commonly handled by hotels.
- Explain the difference between personal data and cardholder data.
- What does the phrase "You collect it, you protect it, you justify it" mean for hotel managers?
- Name and briefly explain five core GDPR principles.
- Why is purpose limitation important in marketing and loyalty programs?
- Why should hotels reduce the number of systems and people that touch card data?
- What are four typical hospitality compliance mistakes?
- What is a Data Processing Agreement and why is it important?
- Why are international loyalty databases a compliance risk?
- What questions should an executive ask about data hosting, access, retention and breach response?
- Explain why shared passwords are dangerous in a hotel environment.
- What is the difference between a data controller and a data processor?
- How can compliance failures affect both brand trust and operational continuity?

REFERENCES AND FURTHER READING

- European Commission. "Principles of the GDPR." This official resource explains key data protection principles including data minimization, storage limitation, transparency and lawful processing.
- European Parliament and Council of the European Union. "Regulation (EU) 2016/679, General Data Protection Regulation." The official legal text of the GDPR and its core principles, including Article 5 on principles relating to processing of personal data.
- European Data Protection Board. "Guidelines 05/2021 on the Interplay between the application of Article 3 and the provisions on international transfers as per Chapter V of the GDPR." This guidance supports understanding of international transfer questions.
- Information Commissioner's Office. "A Guide to Lawful Basis." This practical guidance explains lawful bases such as consent, contract, legal obligation and legitimate interests.
- Information Commissioner's Office. "Legitimate Interests." This resource explains when legitimate interests may be used and how organizations should assess necessity and balance individual rights.
- PCI Security Standards Council. "PCI DSS v4.0.1." The official PCI DSS standard and supporting documentation for payment account data security.
- PCI Security Standards Council. "Just Published: PCI DSS v4.0.1." This announcement explains that v4.0.1 is a limited revision clarifying intent and guidance without adding or deleting requirements.

- Oracle Hospitality. "What Is a Hotel Property Management System?" This resource helps connect hotel systems, guest data and operational workflows.
- Hospitality Financial and Technology Professionals. HFTP provides professional resources at the intersection of hospitality finance, technology, payment security and governance.

Chapter 5

Artificial Intelligence in Hospitality

Opportunities, Limits and Executive Decision-Making

LEARNING OBJECTIVES

By the end of this chapter, readers should be able to distinguish clearly between automation, analytics and artificial intelligence in a hospitality context; identify realistic AI use cases across hotels, resorts and hospitality groups; explain why data quality, system integration and governance are essential prerequisites for useful AI; evaluate AI opportunities in revenue management, CRM, operations, finance, human resources and guest experience; recognize the ethical, operational and brand-related limits of AI; apply a decision matrix to prioritize AI investments under budget, data and capability constraints; and understand why AI should support human judgment rather than replace hospitality leadership.

OPENING PERSPECTIVE

Artificial intelligence is one of the most overused expressions in modern business. In hospitality, it can be used to describe almost anything: a chatbot, a dashboard, a pricing tool, a guest messaging platform, an automated email, a forecasting model, a robot in a lobby, or even a simple rule-based workflow. This creates confusion. When every vendor claims to sell AI, hospitality managers need the confidence to separate real intelligence from automation, analytics, marketing language and technological theatre.

For hotel executives, the most important question is not whether AI sounds innovative. The important question is whether it creates measurable value for the hotel, the guest, the employee, the owner and the brand. Artificial intelligence must therefore be treated as a management topic before it is treated as a technology topic. It raises questions of strategy, data, service design, revenue, staffing, risk, ethics, investment and organizational readiness.

The objective of this chapter is to demystify AI for hospitality managers. A future General Manager, asset manager, consultant or corporate leader does not need to build an AI model. However, they must know what AI can realistically do, what it cannot do, what data it needs, what risks it creates and how to decide whether an AI project deserves investment. The executive task is not to become fascinated by technology. The executive task is to make intelligent choices about technology.

In hospitality, AI is valuable when it helps people make better decisions, anticipate needs, protect revenue, reduce waste, improve service reliability and personalize experience without becoming intrusive. AI becomes dangerous when it is adopted because of fashion, implemented on poor data, sold as a magic solution, delegated blindly to vendors, or used in ways that damage trust.

ARTIFICIAL INTELLIGENCE WITHOUT THE HYPE

The first managerial challenge is linguistic. AI is often presented as if it were a single technology, but it is better understood as a family of techniques that allow systems to identify patterns, make predictions, generate outputs or recommend actions based on data. In practice, what matters for a hotel is not the technical category of the algorithm but the business behavior of the system: does it simply follow rules, summarize past performance, predict likely outcomes, or adapt its recommendations over time?

This distinction matters because it affects cost, risk and expectations. A hotel may not need AI when a simple automated rule would solve the problem. A luxury property may not need an expensive predictive personalization engine if its guest data is incomplete and its staff do not yet use the existing CRM consistently. A hotel group may buy an AI-branded platform and later discover that the tool is mostly a dashboard, a rules engine or a reporting interface. When managers cannot distinguish the categories, vendors control the conversation.

AI is not magic. It requires data, infrastructure, integration, governance, human oversight and a clear problem to solve. AI is also not limited to generative tools such as text or image systems. In hotels, many of the most valuable AI applications are predictive rather than generative: demand forecasting, pricing recommendations, maintenance prediction, segmentation, sentiment analysis, fraud detection, workload forecasting and attrition risk analysis.

AI is not a substitute for hospitality. It should not be imagined as a replacement for warmth, empathy, presence, discretion or judgment. The promise of AI in hospitality is not that it makes hotels less human. The promise is that it can remove friction, detect patterns, support faster decisions and give employees better information so that human service becomes more precise, timely and relevant.

AI, AUTOMATION AND ANALYTICS

Before evaluating any AI opportunity, hospitality managers must distinguish three related but different categories: automation, analytics and artificial intelligence.

Automation follows predefined rules. If a guest books a room, an automated confirmation email is sent. If an invoice is received, it is routed to a finance approval workflow. If a room is marked clean, the PMS may update the room status. Automation is useful, predictable and often highly profitable because it removes repetitive manual work. It does not necessarily learn. It performs a task because the rule has been defined.

Analytics explains data. A business intelligence dashboard may show occupancy, ADR, RevPAR, booking pace, channel mix, upsell conversion, guest satisfaction scores or labor cost ratios. Analytics helps managers understand what happened, where performance is changing, and which areas require attention. Analytics may include forecasting, but its main role is to support interpretation. It does not automatically replace the manager's decision.

AI goes further by using data to predict, classify, recommend, optimize or generate outputs in a way that is not simply a fixed rule. A dynamic pricing system may recommend rates based on demand, competitor pricing, booking pace, seasonality and historical behavior. A sentiment analysis system may classify reviews and detect hidden complaint patterns. A predictive maintenance system may estimate the likelihood of equipment failure. AI works with probabilities. It does not offer certainty.

This probability-based nature is essential. AI recommendations should be treated as informed signals, not as absolute truth. A revenue tool may recommend a price increase, but a manager still needs to consider a citywide event, a sudden travel disruption, a major group cancellation or a reputation issue. A guest personalization tool may recommend an upsell, but staff must judge whether the suggestion is appropriate for the guest's mood, profile and context.

AUTOMATION IN HOTELS

Automation is often the most practical first step for hotels because it addresses repetitive tasks with clear rules and measurable benefits. Many hotels would benefit more from strong automation than from premature AI investment. This is especially true when operations are still fragmented, data is inconsistent or employees spend too much time re-entering information across systems.

In the front office, automation can support confirmation emails, pre-arrival messages, online registration forms, payment links, room-ready notifications, digital check-in workflows and post-stay feedback requests. These processes reduce administrative work and allow staff to focus on guests who need human attention. However, automation must be designed carefully. A badly timed message or an impersonal tone can damage the sense of hospitality.

In finance, automation can support invoice routing, approval workflows, night audit checks, reconciliation, expense coding and recurring reporting. In HR, it can trigger onboarding tasks, document requests, training reminders and probation period follow-ups. In operations, it can create maintenance tickets, alert supervisors, update housekeeping status or route guest requests to the right department.

The managerial advantage of automation is that it is usually easier to explain, easier to control and easier to measure than advanced AI. The risk is that managers may call everything AI and overpay for solutions that are, in reality, automated workflows. A good executive question is simple: does this tool learn from data and adapt, or does it just follow rules? If it follows rules, it may still be valuable, but it should be evaluated as automation, not as AI.

ANALYTICS IN HOSPITALITY

Analytics is the bridge between digitized operations and intelligent decision-making. Hotels already produce large volumes of data through PMS, POS, CRS, CRM, RMS, staff scheduling tools, review platforms, guest surveys, maintenance systems and financial software. Analytics makes this data visible and usable.

A hotel without analytics may operate with isolated departmental opinions. The front office may feel that check-in is smooth, while guest comments suggest delays. F&B may believe a promotion is successful, while contribution margin shows weak profitability. Revenue management may focus on occupancy, while finance sees distribution costs rising. Analytics allows the leadership team to move from impressions to evidence.

In hospitality, analytics can support revenue dashboards, guest segmentation, booking pace monitoring, channel performance, upsell tracking, labor productivity, guest satisfaction trend analysis, complaint classification, cost control and sustainability reporting. It can also reveal patterns that would otherwise remain hidden: a repeated maintenance issue in certain room types, lower review scores after late check-in, higher cancellation rates from specific channels, or stronger spending patterns among certain guest segments.

Analytics still requires human interpretation. A dashboard may show that direct bookings declined, but it will not automatically explain whether the cause is pricing, website performance, brand awareness, loyalty benefits, OTA visibility, market demand or reputation. The human manager must connect data to context. The strongest hotels combine analytics with operational intelligence: the numbers show the pattern, and managers ask why it is happening.

WHAT MAKES AI DIFFERENT

Artificial intelligence differs from traditional reporting because it can use data to make predictions or recommendations. Instead of only showing what happened, AI can help estimate what is likely to happen next or which decision may produce a better outcome. This predictive capability explains why AI is especially attractive in revenue management, demand forecasting, personalization, fraud detection and operational planning.

AI learns from examples. If a model is trained on historical booking data, it may learn that certain booking patterns are associated with high demand, cancellations, group displacement, corporate compression or price sensitivity. If a model analyzes reviews, it may learn which words, tones or combinations of comments indicate guest dissatisfaction. If a maintenance model receives equipment data, it may learn which signals are associated with failure risk.

AI can also adapt over time when new data is included. This is both a strength and a risk. A system that adapts can become more useful as the hotel learns more about demand, guests and operations. However, if the underlying data is biased, incomplete or distorted by unusual events, the model may produce unreliable outputs. For example, demand data from a pandemic period, a temporary renovation, a brand repositioning or an exceptional event year may not represent normal future behavior.

AI therefore requires governance. Managers should ask how the model was trained, what data it uses, how often it is updated, who monitors its performance, what happens when predictions are wrong, and how employees can challenge recommendations. AI should not be a black box that the organization obeys without understanding. It should be a decision-support capability that remains accountable to human leadership.

WHERE AI HELPS HOTELS

AI creates value when it is connected to a clear operational or commercial objective. In hospitality, the most promising use cases tend to cluster around revenue management, CRM and personalization, operations, finance, human resources and guest experience. The right choice depends on the hotel's positioning, size, data maturity, systems, staff capability and investment capacity.

In sales and revenue, AI can support demand prediction, dynamic pricing, channel optimization, competitor tracking, segmentation and sales prioritization. These areas are attractive because hotels already have structured data and clear performance indicators. If the AI recommendation improves rate strategy, reduces distribution cost or increases conversion, the financial impact can be measured.

In operations, AI can support predictive maintenance, housekeeping optimization, energy consumption forecasting, inventory planning and workload allocation. These applications may not sound as glamorous as guest-facing AI, but they can be highly valuable. Preventing an elevator breakdown, optimizing room cleaning sequences or reducing energy waste can protect both guest experience and profitability.

In HR, AI may assist with CV screening, workforce planning, attrition prediction or training needs analysis. This area requires strong ethical governance because decisions affect employees' careers and rights. AI can help identify patterns, but final decisions about people must remain human, transparent and fair.

In guest experience, AI can support personalized offers, sentiment analysis, complaint prediction, response prioritization, pre-arrival upselling and guest communication. In luxury hospitality, however, personalization must be discreet. Guests may appreciate being recognized, but they may dislike feeling monitored. The manager's challenge is to use data to enhance care without creating discomfort.

DATA IS THE FOUNDATION

No clean data means no reliable AI. This may be the most important sentence in the chapter. Many AI projects fail not because the algorithm is weak, but because the organization does not have usable data. Hotels often underestimate this problem because data appears to exist everywhere: reservations, guest profiles, payments, reviews, surveys, loyalty records, POS transactions, HR systems and operational logs. But data volume is not the same as data quality.

Hospitality data is often fragmented. The PMS may contain guest stay records, the CRS may hold distribution data, the CRM may hold preferences, the POS may contain restaurant spending, the reputation platform may collect review data, the HR system may store employee information, and finance may work from a separate ERP. If these systems do not communicate properly, AI may receive an incomplete or inconsistent picture.

Data may also be duplicated, outdated or entered differently by different teams. One guest may appear under several profiles. Preferences may be recorded in free-text fields that are difficult to analyze. Corporate accounts may be coded inconsistently. Room types may be renamed during renovations. Historical data may include periods when the hotel was closed, partially renovated, repositioned or affected by exceptional market conditions. AI cannot automatically fix these issues.

Managers must therefore treat AI as a data governance project before treating it as a technology purchase. Before investing in AI, leaders should ask: which data sources will feed the model, who owns the data, how reliable is it, how is it cleaned, how is it protected, how is consent managed, and how will the output be monitored? A hotel that cannot answer these questions is probably not ready for advanced AI.

AI AS MORE THAN COST SAVINGS

A common mistake is to reduce AI to labor cost reduction. While AI can automate tasks and improve productivity, its most strategic value in hospitality often comes from revenue growth, experience quality, risk reduction and decision speed. Hotels should therefore evaluate AI not only by asking how much cost it removes, but by asking what value it enables.

AI can support revenue growth through dynamic pricing, better demand forecasting, improved channel mix, targeted upsells and personalized offers. It can help identify guests who may be interested in a suite upgrade, spa treatment, late check-out, transfer service or restaurant reservation. It can also help revenue teams detect changes in demand faster than manual analysis would allow.

AI can improve customer experience by identifying patterns in guest behavior and feedback. If a system detects that guests in a particular segment often request early breakfast, the hotel can adjust communication and operations. If reviews show recurring dissatisfaction with room temperature, noise or check-in delays, management can intervene earlier. If pre-arrival data shows a guest is celebrating an anniversary, staff can prepare a more thoughtful welcome.

AI can speed up decisions by summarizing large amounts of information. A manager may receive hundreds of reviews, dozens of performance indicators and multiple forecast scenarios. AI can help synthesize patterns and highlight anomalies. However, faster decision-making must not become careless decision-making. The human leader must still decide what matters, what is ethical, what fits the brand and what action should follow.

THE AI MATURITY CURVE

Hotels should not jump directly to advanced AI if they have not built the foundations. A practical maturity curve can be understood in four stages: digitization, automation, analytics and AI.

Digitization means that information is captured digitally rather than manually. Reservations, invoices, guest profiles, housekeeping status and maintenance tickets must exist in systems that can be accessed and analyzed. Without digitization, there is no reliable data foundation.

Automation means that routine workflows are performed according to rules. Confirmation emails, approval routing, room-status updates and task notifications can reduce friction and create consistency. Automation helps hotels become more disciplined and predictable.

Analytics means that the hotel can analyze past and current performance. Dashboards, segmentation, forecasting reports and operational metrics help managers understand trends and make better decisions. Analytics creates the managerial habit of using data rather than relying only on intuition.

AI becomes more meaningful when the previous stages are functioning. If a hotel lacks clean data, integrated systems and analytical discipline, AI will likely produce unreliable outputs or become another unused platform. Most hotels are still strengthening automation and analytics. There is nothing wrong with that. Strategic maturity means knowing what the organization is ready to absorb.

AI IN REVENUE MANAGEMENT

Revenue management is one of the most mature areas for AI in hospitality because it already depends on structured data, forecasting and optimization. Hotels have long used revenue management systems to support pricing decisions, and AI can strengthen this capability by processing large volumes of data and detecting patterns faster than humans can.

AI can support dynamic pricing by analyzing booking pace, historical demand, competitor rates, market events, lead time, cancellation behavior, channel performance and guest segments. The system may recommend rate adjustments for certain dates, room types or channels. In theory, this allows hotels to capture more revenue when demand is strong and stimulate demand when pace is weak.

Demand forecasting is another important use case. AI can help predict future occupancy and revenue by combining historical data with external indicators such as events, holidays, flight patterns, search behavior, economic conditions or competitor activity. Better forecasting supports staffing, purchasing, pricing, marketing and owner communication.

Channel optimization is also significant. A hotel may sell through direct channels, OTAs, corporate accounts, wholesalers, groups and brand platforms. Each channel has different cost, control and value implications. AI can help identify which channels are most profitable under certain conditions, but managers must avoid optimizing only short-term revenue while weakening brand strategy or direct relationships.

Human oversight remains essential. Revenue AI may struggle during abnormal periods such as strikes, geopolitical shocks, natural disasters, sudden travel restrictions, major events, brand crises or renovations. A system trained on past patterns may misread a new situation. The revenue leader must know when to trust the recommendation, when to override it and when to investigate the underlying assumptions.

AI IN CRM AND GUEST EXPERIENCE

CRM and guest experience are attractive AI areas because hospitality is deeply relational. Hotels want to understand guests, anticipate needs and personalize service. AI can help analyze behavior, preferences, spending patterns, feedback and communication history. However, this domain also carries high sensitivity because guest trust is at stake.

AI can support personalized offers before arrival. Based on booking profile, stay purpose, past behavior or segment patterns, the system may recommend an upgrade, breakfast package, airport transfer, spa treatment, restaurant booking or late check-out. If done well, this creates relevance and revenue. If done poorly, it feels like aggressive selling.

AI can also support sentiment analysis by reading reviews, surveys and guest comments to identify emotional tone and recurring issues. It may help managers detect whether complaints relate to cleanliness, noise, staff attitude, billing, breakfast, WiFi, room temperature or arrival delays. This can make reputation management more systematic.

In luxury hospitality, the most important principle is discretion. Personalization should not feel invasive. A guest may appreciate that the hotel remembers a pillow preference, but may feel uncomfortable if communication suggests excessive tracking. AI insights should often be delivered through human staff rather than through obvious automated messages. The guest should feel cared for, not profiled.

The best AI in guest experience supports human hospitality. It gives staff better memory, better timing and better context. It should not create robotic interactions or replace the intuition of experienced hospitality professionals. A concierge, receptionist or guest relations manager still needs to read the room, understand mood and apply judgment.

AI IN OPERATIONS

Operational AI can be less visible to guests but highly valuable for service reliability. Hotels are physical environments with rooms, equipment, energy systems, elevators, kitchens, laundry, meeting spaces, spas, pools and technical infrastructure. Operational failure directly affects guest satisfaction and cost control.

Predictive maintenance is a strong example. Instead of waiting for equipment to fail, AI can analyze patterns in maintenance logs, sensor data or operational history to predict which assets may need attention. This is especially relevant for HVAC systems, elevators, kitchen equipment, boilers, refrigeration, laundry equipment and room technology. Preventing breakdowns protects guest comfort and reduces emergency repair costs.

Housekeeping optimization is another practical use case. AI can help allocate room cleaning based on occupancy, arrival times, stayover patterns, guest priorities, room location and staff availability. It can reduce unnecessary walking, improve room readiness and support better labor planning. However, managers must ensure that optimization does not overload staff or reduce quality to a purely mathematical target.

Energy consumption prediction can support sustainability and cost control. AI may help optimize heating, ventilation, air conditioning and lighting based on occupancy, weather, room status and usage patterns. This can reduce waste while maintaining comfort. The challenge is to ensure that savings do not undermine the guest experience. A luxury guest should not feel that comfort is being sacrificed for efficiency.

Operations often provide clearer AI objectives than guest-facing projects because the desired outcome is measurable: fewer breakdowns, faster room readiness, lower energy consumption, better labor allocation, reduced waste. For many hotels, operational AI may be a wiser starting point than visible AI theatre.

AI IN HUMAN RESOURCES

Human resources is one of the most sensitive areas for AI. Hotels face recruitment pressure, turnover, labor cost constraints, seasonal demand, scheduling complexity and skills shortages. AI can help HR teams process information, forecast needs and identify patterns, but it must be governed carefully because it affects people directly.

AI can support CV screening by identifying candidates whose experience appears to match role requirements. It can help sort large applicant pools and reduce administrative workload. However, this use case carries a serious bias risk. If the model is trained on historical hiring patterns that favored certain profiles, it may reproduce or amplify unfairness. Hospitality employers must therefore ensure human review, transparency and regular bias checks.

Attrition prediction may help managers identify departments or profiles with higher risk of turnover. This can support proactive retention, better scheduling, targeted training or management intervention. The risk is that prediction becomes labeling. Employees should not be treated as problems because a system suggests they may leave. The purpose should be support, not suspicion.

Workforce planning can be a valuable AI use case. By combining occupancy forecasts, events, seasonality, historical workload and productivity data, AI may help estimate staffing needs across departments. This can improve service quality and cost control. However, hospitality labor is not simply a variable cost. Staff fatigue, morale, training and service culture matter. AI can inform staffing decisions, but it cannot replace responsible leadership.

AI in HR requires strict governance: privacy protection, explanation, human validation, challenge mechanisms, bias audits and compliance with applicable employment and data protection rules. In this area, efficiency must never be allowed to overrule fairness.

WHAT AI IS BAD AT

Understanding what AI cannot do is as important as understanding what it can do. AI is powerful at pattern recognition, prediction, classification, optimization and content generation. It is weak at empathy, moral judgment, cultural nuance, crisis leadership and brand intuition.

AI does not experience emotions. It can detect emotional language or classify sentiment, but it does not understand hurt, anxiety, embarrassment or disappointment as a human does. An upset guest may need to be heard, reassured and respected. A scripted automated response may make the situation worse if it feels cold or evasive.

AI does not possess hospitality intuition. It may recommend an upsell, but it cannot fully understand whether the timing is elegant. It may draft a response to a complaint, but it cannot take responsibility in the same way a manager can. It may detect a pattern in reviews, but it cannot walk through the lobby, feel the atmosphere and notice tension in the team.

AI is also weak in novel crises. During unprecedented situations, data from the past may not provide a reliable guide. A sudden security incident, weather event, health emergency, celebrity arrival, political disruption or brand controversy requires human judgment, coordination and courage. AI can support information gathering, but leadership remains human.

Finally, AI cannot define the soul of a brand. A hotel may use AI to support decisions, but the brand's promise, tone, service philosophy and emotional identity must be shaped by people. In luxury, this is especially important. Technology can help deliver excellence, but it cannot become the source of meaning.

THE ETHICS OF AI IN HOSPITALITY

AI ethics in hospitality is not an abstract academic topic. It concerns everyday questions about privacy, fairness, transparency, consent, employee dignity, guest trust and brand integrity. Because hotels collect rich personal and behavioral data, AI can easily cross the line from helpful personalization to uncomfortable surveillance.

Privacy is central. Guests may share information because it is necessary for service delivery, not because they expect every detail to be analyzed for commercial targeting. Hotels must be clear about what data is collected, why it is used, how long it is retained and who can access it. AI projects should be reviewed with GDPR and data protection obligations in mind, especially when profiling or automated decision-making is involved.

Bias is another risk. AI systems can reproduce patterns from past data. If historical data reflects unequal treatment, biased hiring, uneven service recovery or distorted pricing patterns, AI may reinforce those problems. Managers should not assume that a system is neutral because it is technical. Algorithms are shaped by data, design choices and objectives.

Transparency matters for employees as well as guests. Staff should know when AI is being used to evaluate performance, schedule shifts, screen applications or predict turnover. AI should not become an invisible management mechanism that employees cannot question. Trust inside the organization is as important as guest trust.

Ethical AI also requires proportionality. Not every possible use of data is desirable. A hotel may be able to infer guest preferences, mood, wealth or behavior, but that does not mean it should use every inference. The best hospitality leaders ask not only, 'Can we do this?' but also, 'Should we do this, and would it feel appropriate to the guest?'

CHOOSING AI INVESTMENTS UNDER CONSTRAINTS

Most hotels do not have unlimited budgets, large data science teams or fully integrated systems. AI strategy must therefore be realistic. A single independent luxury property with high guest expectations, limited IT budget and no data team should not begin with a complex enterprise AI transformation. It should begin with a focused use case that solves a real problem, uses available data and can be supported operationally.

A practical decision matrix should consider return on investment, complexity, data readiness, guest perception and ethical risk. ROI includes revenue generation, cost reduction, risk reduction or measurable service improvement. Complexity includes integration, vendor support, training, maintenance and internal capability. Data readiness asks whether the hotel has sufficient clean data. Guest perception asks whether the solution enhances or weakens hospitality. Ethical risk asks whether privacy, fairness or employment concerns are significant.

For a luxury property, AI revenue management may be attractive if the hotel already has reliable historical data and a revenue culture. Predictive maintenance may be attractive if equipment failures are affecting guest satisfaction and maintenance records are available. Guest chatbots may be useful for simple requests, but they must be carefully designed so that they do not cheapen the service atmosphere. AI HR recruitment may save time, but it requires strong governance and may not be the best first investment for a small property.

The best first AI project is usually not the most impressive one. It is the one that the organization can absorb, measure and govern. Starting small does not mean lacking ambition. It means building confidence, capability and evidence before scaling. A successful AI pilot should create a repeatable learning process: define the problem, test the solution, measure impact, manage risks, train users and decide whether to expand.

AI IN FINANCE AND FRAUD CONTROL

Finance may not be the first department associated with AI in hospitality, yet it offers several practical opportunities. Hotels generate constant financial signals through PMS postings, POS transactions, deposits, refunds, no-show charges, commissions, invoices, payroll, purchasing and inventory. AI can help detect anomalies, accelerate review and support more disciplined financial control.

Fraud detection is a useful example. A hotel may process thousands of payment transactions across rooms, restaurants, bars, spas, events and online channels. AI can help identify unusual refund patterns, suspicious transaction sequences, abnormal discounts, repeated voids, unexpected payment failures or inconsistencies between POS and PMS data. The objective is not to accuse employees or guests automatically, but to direct human attention toward transactions that deserve review.

Cash forecasting is another potential use case. By combining occupancy forecasts, booking pace, cancellation patterns, event calendars, payment terms, group deposits, supplier payment cycles and payroll timing, AI-supported tools may help finance teams anticipate liquidity needs more accurately. This can be useful for owners, asset managers and management companies that need better visibility on working capital.

AI can also support invoice classification and cost allocation. Supplier invoices may be coded automatically to the most likely cost center or account category, while unusual invoices are flagged for review. This can reduce administrative workload and improve reporting consistency. However, finance AI must be implemented with strong controls. Automated classification should not remove approval discipline, segregation of duties or audit trails.

For hospitality executives, the main lesson is that financial AI is not only about speed. It is about control, visibility and earlier detection. The value is created when finance teams can move from late correction to proactive monitoring. Still, final accountability remains human. A tool can flag risk, but management must decide whether the transaction is acceptable, suspicious, erroneous or strategically justified.

AI CHATBOTS AND GUEST COMMUNICATION

Chatbots are often the most visible AI application in hospitality, but they are also among the easiest to misunderstand. A chatbot can provide useful support when it answers simple, repetitive questions: check-in time, parking information, breakfast hours, spa opening times, airport transfer options, pet policies, cancellation rules or directions. In these cases, the guest receives quick information and employees avoid repetitive interruptions.

The risk appears when a chatbot is positioned as a substitute for service rather than a support layer. Hospitality is not only information delivery. A guest may ask about a late arrival because they are anxious about a delayed flight. A guest may ask about restaurant availability because they are planning an important celebration. A guest may complain about noise because they are tired and frustrated. In these situations, language, tone and escalation matter as much as factual accuracy.

A well-designed AI communication tool should know its limits. It should handle routine questions, collect useful context and escalate easily to a human when the request becomes emotional, complex, sensitive or high value. It should not trap the guest in endless automated loops. The guest should feel that technology creates convenience, not distance.

Luxury hotels should be especially careful. A guest paying a premium rate may accept digital convenience, but not digital indifference. AI communication should be discreet, elegant and optional. It can help staff by summarizing guest requests, translating simple messages, preparing response drafts or prioritizing urgent issues. But the final tone should remain aligned with the brand's service culture.

The success of guest communication AI should therefore be measured by more than response speed. Managers should track resolution quality, escalation rates, guest satisfaction, complaint reduction, staff workload and whether the tool preserves the desired atmosphere. Fast answers are useful only if they strengthen the relationship.

IMPLEMENTING AI IN A HOTEL ORGANIZATION

AI implementation should be managed as a change project, not as a software installation. A hotel can purchase a tool quickly, but adoption depends on people, processes, training, trust and leadership. Many technology projects fail because managers assume that buying the platform is the main work. In reality, the main work begins after purchase.

A practical implementation roadmap starts with problem definition. The hotel should identify a concrete issue: low upsell conversion, weak forecasting, recurring equipment failures, slow response to reviews, excessive invoice processing time or inconsistent staffing plans. A vague ambition to 'use AI' is not enough. The clearer the problem, the easier it becomes to select the right tool and measure success.

The second step is data assessment. The hotel must identify which systems contain the necessary data, whether the data is reliable, who owns it, how it can be accessed, whether guest or employee consent is relevant, and whether integration is technically and contractually possible. This step often reveals that the organization must clean its data before launching AI.

The third step is pilot design. A pilot should be limited enough to manage, but meaningful enough to test value. It should define baseline performance, expected benefits, users, risks, training needs, success indicators and review dates. A pilot without metrics becomes a demonstration, not a management test.

The fourth step is employee involvement. Staff must understand why the tool is being introduced, what it will do, what it will not do, and how it affects their work. If employees believe AI is designed to monitor or replace them, resistance will grow. If they see that AI removes repetitive tasks and supports better service, adoption becomes easier.

The final step is governance and scaling. If the pilot works, management should decide whether to expand, adjust or stop. Scaling requires documentation, training, budget, vendor management, cybersecurity review and performance monitoring. AI should never become an uncontrolled collection of experiments. It should become part of the hotel's management discipline.

EMPLOYEE ADOPTION AND THE HUMAN SIDE OF AI

AI adoption is not only a question of data and systems. It is also a question of culture. Hospitality employees often build their professional identity around service, intuition, craft and human contact. If AI is introduced clumsily, it may be perceived as a threat to competence or dignity. Managers must therefore explain AI in a way that respects the work of hospitality professionals.

Employees are more likely to accept AI when they understand the practical benefit. A housekeeper may value a tool that reduces unnecessary room changes and improves route planning. A maintenance technician may value early warning signals that prevent urgent failures. A revenue manager may value faster scenario analysis. A guest relations agent may value a clearer summary of past guest preferences. Adoption improves when AI solves real frustrations.

Training should focus not only on how to use the tool, but also on how to question it. Employees should know when to trust recommendations, when to escalate, and how to report outputs that seem wrong. This is particularly important because frontline staff often notice operational realities that models miss. A system may recommend a certain room assignment, but the receptionist may know that the guest has a special need or that a room has a subtle issue not yet recorded.

Managers should also avoid using AI as a symbol of control. If employees feel that every movement, decision or interaction is being scored by invisible algorithms, trust will decline. The goal should be augmentation, not surveillance. AI should help teams work better, not make them feel reduced to data points.

The human side of AI is therefore a leadership issue. A successful AI project requires communication, involvement, feedback loops and respect for operational knowledge. In hospitality, employees are not obstacles to digital transformation. They are the people who make digital transformation useful to guests.

MANAGING VENDORS AND AVOIDING AI HYPE

AI vendors can be valuable partners, but managers must remain critical. The AI market is full of strong solutions, weak solutions and exaggerated promises. Hospitality leaders must not allow vendor language to replace business analysis.

Before approving an AI tool, managers should ask what problem the tool solves, what data it needs, how it integrates with PMS, CRS, CRM, POS or ERP systems, what results have been proven in comparable hotels, how ROI will be measured, what human oversight is required, how the model handles errors, and what happens if the vendor relationship ends.

Managers should also ask whether the tool is truly AI or whether it is automation, analytics or a rules engine. There is nothing wrong with automation or analytics if they solve the problem. The danger is paying AI prices for non-AI functionality or adopting a complex tool when a simpler one would work better.

Contractual questions matter. Who owns the data? Where is it hosted? Can the vendor use hotel data to train models for other clients? What security certifications exist? How is guest data protected? What audit rights does the hotel have? How can data be exported? What service levels are promised? These questions connect AI to governance, cybersecurity and compliance.

A mature executive posture is curious but not naive. AI deserves attention, but it does not deserve blind enthusiasm. The right question is not, 'How can we use AI?' The better question is, 'Which hotel problem is important enough, measurable enough and data-ready enough for AI to be the right solution?'

AI, BRAND POSITIONING AND LUXURY CODES

AI does not affect every hospitality segment in the same way. A budget hotel, airport hotel, resort, palace and lifestyle property may use similar technology, but the meaning of that technology changes with brand positioning. In an economy hotel, AI may be valued primarily for speed, convenience and cost efficiency. In a luxury hotel, the same tool must be judged through discretion, emotional intelligence, privacy and symbolic value.

Luxury hospitality is built on recognition, anticipation and elegance. AI can support these qualities when it gives staff better memory and better timing. For example, a system may help identify a returning guest's preferred newspaper, room temperature, breakfast habit or arrival pattern. But the way this information is used matters. If a receptionist says too much about what the system knows, the guest may feel observed rather than recognized.

Brand positioning should therefore guide AI design. A lifestyle hotel may accept playful digital interaction. A business hotel may value speed and self-service. A resort may use AI to personalize itineraries. A palace may hide the technology almost completely and allow employees to translate data into graceful human gestures. The best AI strategy is not universal; it is brand-specific.

Managers should ask whether an AI tool reinforces or weakens the hotel promise. Does it make service more fluid? Does it protect privacy? Does it help employees deliver better attention? Does it reduce friction without reducing warmth? Does it support the desired atmosphere? In hospitality, the technology that is most advanced is not always the technology that is most appropriate.

This is why AI decisions should involve more than the IT department. Brand, operations, rooms division, revenue, marketing, HR, finance and the General Manager all see different consequences. A tool may appear efficient from a technical perspective and still feel wrong from a service perspective. Conversely, a modest AI feature may create exceptional value if it helps employees protect the emotional promise of the hotel.

APPLIED CASE STUDY: AI IN A LUXURY HOTEL

Imagine an independent luxury hotel with high guest expectations, limited IT budget and no internal data science team. The CEO asks a simple but difficult question: where should we start with AI?

The leadership team considers four possibilities. The first is AI revenue management, designed to optimize rates and forecast demand. The second is a guest chatbot, designed to answer routine questions and support 24/7 communication. The third is predictive maintenance, designed to prevent room equipment failures and protect comfort. The fourth is AI-supported recruitment, designed to screen applicants and accelerate hiring.

The revenue management option may offer strong financial return, especially if the hotel has several years of clean booking data, a clear rate strategy and integration with distribution systems. However, it requires trust from the revenue team and careful oversight during unusual market conditions. It may be a strong candidate if the hotel already has good data discipline.

The chatbot option may appear attractive because it is visible and modern. It can answer frequently asked questions, provide basic information and reduce repetitive calls. Yet in a luxury hotel, guest perception is critical. A poorly designed chatbot may feel impersonal. It should handle simple requests while making it easy to reach a human. The objective should be service convenience, not staff replacement.

The predictive maintenance option may be less glamorous but highly relevant. If guest complaints frequently involve air conditioning, elevators, lighting, plumbing or room technology, preventing failures can protect the luxury promise. This option may require reliable maintenance records or sensor data, but it can be measured through fewer breakdowns, fewer complaints and lower emergency repair costs.

The AI recruitment option may reduce HR workload, but it carries ethical and legal sensitivity. If the hotel has limited governance capability, it may not be the safest first AI project. Recruitment decisions affect people directly, and bias risk must be controlled.

A balanced recommendation might be to begin with predictive maintenance or revenue management, depending on the hotel's data readiness and pain points. If the hotel's most urgent issue is profitability and it has clean historical data, revenue AI may be the strongest first step. If the hotel's most urgent issue is guest comfort and operational reliability, predictive maintenance may be wiser. In either case, the hotel should avoid launching multiple AI initiatives at once. It should prove value, build capability and then scale.

MANAGERIAL TAKEAWAYS

Artificial intelligence is a tool, not a strategy. A hotel should not adopt AI because competitors are talking about it or because a vendor presentation is impressive. AI must serve a strategic purpose: better revenue decisions, stronger guest experience, more reliable operations, improved risk control or more effective management.

Data quality is more important than tools. Without clean, integrated and governed data, AI will produce weak recommendations and employees will lose trust. Before investing in AI, managers should evaluate data readiness honestly.

Start small and scale strategically. The best AI project is not necessarily the most advanced one. It is the project with a clear problem, measurable value, available data, manageable complexity, acceptable risk and organizational support.

Human oversight is mandatory. AI predictions are probabilistic. They can support decisions but should not replace accountability. Managers must remain responsible for final decisions, especially when guests, employees, pricing, privacy or brand reputation are affected.

Hospitality remains human. AI can help a hotel see patterns, anticipate needs and improve consistency. But empathy, discretion, creativity, crisis judgment and brand intuition remain human responsibilities. The future of hospitality technology is not a hotel without people. It is a hotel where technology gives people better information, more time and stronger capacity to deliver meaningful service.

TO REVIEW THIS CHAPTER

KEY TERMS

Artificial Intelligence (AI) : A family of technologies that can identify patterns, make predictions, generate outputs or recommend actions based on data.

Automation : A rules-based process that performs predefined tasks without necessarily learning from data.

Analytics : The analysis of past or current data to explain performance, reveal patterns and support decision-making.

Generative AI : AI systems that create new content such as text, images, summaries, responses or code based on prompts and training data.

Predictive AI : AI used to estimate likely future outcomes, such as demand, cancellations, equipment failures or guest behavior.

Dynamic Pricing : A pricing approach that adjusts rates based on demand, competition, booking pace, seasonality and other factors.

Sentiment Analysis : The use of AI or analytics to classify guest feedback by emotional tone or topic.

Data Readiness : The degree to which an organization has clean, reliable, accessible and integrated data for analysis or AI use.

AI Governance : The policies, controls, responsibilities and monitoring processes used to ensure that AI is safe, ethical, reliable and aligned with business goals.

Human Oversight : The requirement that people monitor, validate and remain accountable for AI-supported decisions.

Bias : A systematic distortion in data or model outputs that may produce unfair or inaccurate results.

AI Maturity Curve : A staged view of technology development: digitization, automation, analytics and AI.

Black Box : A system whose internal logic is difficult for users or managers to understand or explain.

Decision Matrix : A structured tool used to evaluate options against multiple criteria such as ROI, complexity, data readiness, guest perception and ethical risk.

Vendor Hype : Exaggerated technology claims that may make a tool appear more advanced or valuable than it actually is.

REFLECTION QUESTIONS

- Why can the word AI create confusion for hospitality managers?
- In your opinion, which hotel function offers the strongest opportunity for AI investment: revenue, operations, guest experience, finance or HR? Explain your reasoning.
- How can a luxury hotel use AI for personalization without becoming intrusive?
- Why is data quality more important than the sophistication of the AI tool?
- Which AI use cases should always require strong human oversight?
- What risks arise when AI is used in recruitment or workforce planning?
- How can a hotel distinguish between a real AI solution and vendor hype?

- Why might predictive maintenance be a better first AI project than a guest-facing chatbot?
- How should a manager respond when an AI recommendation conflicts with human intuition?
- What does it mean to say that AI should support hospitality rather than replace it?

REVIEW QUESTIONS

- Define artificial intelligence in a hospitality management context.
- Explain the difference between automation, analytics and AI.
- Give two examples of automation in hotel operations.
- Give two examples of analytics in hospitality decision-making.
- Why are AI predictions probabilistic rather than certain?
- List five hotel data sources that may support AI projects.
- Explain why poor data quality can damage AI performance.
- Identify three AI use cases in revenue management.
- Identify three AI use cases in hotel operations.
- What are the main ethical risks of AI in HR?
- Why is human oversight necessary in AI-supported decision-making?
- What criteria should be included in an AI investment decision matrix?
- Why should hotels start small before scaling AI initiatives?
- What questions should managers ask AI vendors before approving a project?
- Why is AI a tool rather than a strategy?

REFERENCES AND FURTHER READING

European Commission. "AI Act." The European Commission describes the AI Act as the first comprehensive legal framework on AI, built around risk-based regulation and trustworthy AI. https://digital-strategy.ec.europa.eu/en/policies/regulatory-framework-ai

National Institute of Standards and Technology. "Artificial Intelligence Risk Management Framework (AI RMF 1.0)." NIST provides guidance for organizations designing, developing, deploying or using AI systems to manage risks and improve trustworthiness. https://www.nist.gov/itl/ai-risk-management-framework`

OECD. "OECD AI Principles." The OECD principles promote AI that is innovative and trustworthy and that respects human rights and democratic values. https://oecd.ai/en/ai-principles

McKinsey & Company. "The State of AI: Global Survey 2025." This survey explores AI adoption, value capture and management practices related to scaling AI in organizations. https://www.mckinsey.com/capabilities/quantumblack/our-insights/the-state-of-ai

Oracle Hospitality. "What Is a Hotel Property Management System?" This resource helps connect hotel data foundations to PMS operations, reservations, guest profiles and billing. https://www.oracle.com/hospitality/what-is-hotel-pms/

Hospitality Financial and Technology Professionals (HFTP). HFTP provides professional resources for hospitality finance and technology leaders, including technology governance, data and operational considerations. https://www.hftp.org/

Chapter 6

Hospitality IT Ecosystem: IPTV, WiFi & Telephony

LEARNING OBJECTIVES

By the end of this chapter, you should be able to explain why guest-facing technology is part of the hospitality product rather than only a technical layer, and to connect WiFi, IPTV and telephony decisions to guest satisfaction, brand positioning and revenue protection. You should also be able to distinguish between a technical failure and a managerial failure in technology planning, understand the basic architecture of hotel WiFi, IPTV and telephony without unnecessary technical jargon, and identify the main sources of technology friction across the guest journey. Finally, you should be able to evaluate how poor connectivity can affect online reputation, ADR, RevPAR and corporate account retention, ask relevant executive questions when selecting vendors or setting service-level expectations, and apply a managerial diagnosis to a hotel case where bad WiFi reviews are damaging performance.

OPENING PERSPECTIVE

In earlier chapters, hospitality information technology was introduced as the backbone of hotel operations. The discussion then moved through architecture, cybersecurity, compliance and artificial intelligence. This chapter brings the topic back into the guest room, the lobby, the corridor, the meeting space and the everyday moments of a stay. WiFi, IPTV and telephony may sound like technical services. In reality, they are part of the guest experience architecture of a hotel.

A guest rarely thinks about access points, bandwidth allocation, middleware, PBX systems or network segmentation. A guest thinks in simpler and more emotional terms. Does the WiFi work? Can I join my video call? Can my children stream a film? Can I cast my own content to the room television? Can I call reception quickly? Can the hotel reach me in an emergency? Does the technology feel easy, elegant and aligned with the promise of the property?

Hospitality technology is successful when it disappears into the experience. When it works well, guests often do not notice the complexity behind it. When it fails, however, the failure becomes highly visible. A weak WiFi signal, a frozen television interface, a room phone that does not connect properly, or a casting system that requires repeated login attempts can turn a comfortable room into a source of irritation. The emotional impact is disproportionate because guests expect basic technology to work without effort.

For hospitality managers, this creates an important responsibility. WiFi, IPTV and telephony must not be managed as low-level technical utilities. They influence satisfaction scores, online reviews, repeat bookings, business traveler loyalty, meeting and event performance, staff coordination, safety procedures and the perceived modernity of the hotel. They also reveal the gap between the brand promise and the operational reality.

A hotel that claims to serve corporate travelers cannot tolerate unstable video-conference connectivity. A luxury hotel cannot deliver a premium room experience if the guest struggles with streaming, casting or basic network access. A lifestyle hotel cannot create fluid digital journeys if each touchpoint feels disconnected. A resort cannot rely on weak infrastructure when families, remote workers and leisure guests all expect multiple connected devices. In hospitality, technology is no longer backstage. It is part of the product.

TECHNOLOGY AS EXPERIENCE ARCHITECTURE

The phrase guest experience is often associated with design, service rituals, emotional intelligence, welcome gestures, food and beverage, spa, housekeeping and personalization. These elements remain central to hospitality. Yet the digital layer now shapes how many of those elements are discovered, accessed, delivered and remembered. Technology does not replace the human encounter. It structures the conditions under which the human encounter takes place.

Consider a simple arrival sequence. Before the guest enters the lobby, they may have received a pre-arrival message, completed online registration, selected preferences or requested an early check-in. At the front desk, the team may rely on the PMS, payment authorization, digital key tools and guest profile information. Once in the room, the guest may connect a phone, test the WiFi, open a streaming platform, scan a QR code, use the television to access room service, or call reception. Each step can feel seamless or fragmented.

This is why technology should be understood as experience architecture. It creates the invisible structure that allows the guest journey to flow. Good architecture is not simply a matter of having tools. It is the result of careful design, integration, vendor coordination, investment discipline, staff training and operational ownership. A hotel can buy an advanced IPTV platform, but if the content is outdated, the PMS integration is weak, or staff do not know how to support the guest, the investment will not create value.

The same logic applies to WiFi. Installing access points does not automatically mean delivering a reliable guest experience. The hotel must consider coverage, bandwidth, number of devices, peak demand, staff networks, conference spaces, guest segmentation, security, authentication, roaming and ongoing monitoring. Weak planning converts into frustration. Strong planning turns connectivity into an invisible service advantage.

Telephony follows a similar evolution. In-room telephone usage has declined for many guests, but voice communication has not disappeared from hospitality. Emergency calls, internal coordination, room-to-room communication, guest requests, back-of-house operations, call routing and integration with guest billing still matter. In some properties, the phone is less about revenue and more about safety, continuity and service tone. Decline in usage does not mean strategic irrelevance.

Managers must therefore avoid the trap of separating technology from hospitality. The guest does not experience a WiFi issue as a network design problem. The guest experiences it as inconvenience. The guest does not experience a frozen IPTV system as middleware failure. The guest experiences it as a room that does not feel premium. The guest does not experience telephony problems as routing errors. The guest experiences them as lack of access to service. In other words, technical friction becomes emotional friction.

FUTURE GUEST EXPECTATIONS

The expectations placed on hotel technology have changed because guests compare hotels not only with other hotels, but with the digital services they use every day. They compare the speed of hotel WiFi with their home fiber connection, their office network or mobile data. They compare the ease of in-room entertainment with Netflix,

YouTube, Disney+, Spotify and smart televisions at home. They compare digital check-in with airline boarding passes, ride-hailing applications and e-commerce platforms. This external benchmark is unforgiving.

The first major expectation is permanent connectivity. Guests arrive with more devices than before: smartphones, laptops, tablets, smartwatches, gaming devices, e-readers and sometimes work equipment. Families may connect multiple devices in the same room. Business travelers may require secure access to corporate systems through VPNs. Event guests may expect stable connectivity in meeting rooms, breakout areas and public spaces. Leisure travelers may use WiFi for video calls, streaming, social media, maps, translation and planning activities.

The second expectation is personalization. Guests increasingly expect technology to recognize them, or at least not force them to repeat information they have already provided. A returning guest may expect preferences to be remembered. A loyalty member may expect a smoother digital experience. A guest who has already completed online registration may not understand why the same information must be provided again at reception. Personalization is not only about luxury gestures. It is also about operational memory.

The third expectation is low tolerance for friction. Guests may forgive complexity in exceptional situations, but they rarely forgive basic failures. A complicated WiFi login page, repeated disconnections, slow speed, a television that cannot cast, a room phone that is confusing to use, or a digital service request that receives no response can create irritation quickly. This is especially true when the room rate is high. The higher the price positioning, the lower the tolerance for technical imperfection.

Different segments express these expectations differently. Luxury travelers often expect invisible technology. They do not want a room filled with gadgets that feel intrusive. They want flawless functionality that preserves calm, privacy and discretion. Business travelers expect reliability, speed and security. Their tolerance for connectivity failure is particularly low because poor WiFi can directly affect work. Lifestyle travelers may value digital ease, social sharing, casting and mobile-first interactions. Families may value simple access, multiple devices and safety controls. Long-stay guests may require work-from-room reliability and entertainment flexibility.

The managerial implication is clear: technology standards should be aligned with guest segmentation. A generic WiFi solution may satisfy no one. A hotel must ask who its guests are, what they do during the stay, what digital behaviors they bring with them, and which failures would damage the property's positioning most severely. Technology design begins with guest behavior, not with hardware specifications.

TECHNOLOGY AS PART OF THE BRAND

Brand promises in hospitality are not delivered only through logos, architecture, uniforms, menus or service language. They are also delivered through reliability. A brand that promises efficiency must remove friction. A brand that promises luxury must make technology discreet and effortless. A brand that promises lifestyle energy must make digital interaction fluid. A brand that promises corporate productivity must make connectivity stable. The technology ecosystem becomes a practical expression of the brand.

In a luxury hotel, technology should feel invisible, calm and supportive. Guests should not have to fight with passwords, complicated remotes or poor casting instructions. The television interface should not look cheap or outdated. The WiFi login should not feel like an airport portal filled with unnecessary steps. If technology appears, it should appear with elegance. A personalized welcome message on IPTV can reinforce recognition; a badly designed menu can do the opposite.

In a business hotel, the technology promise is speed and reliability. A guest may choose the property because of location, meeting facilities, brand familiarity and room comfort, but the ability to work effectively has become part of the value proposition. If the WiFi cannot support video calls, large file transfers or stable VPN connections, the hotel may lose corporate confidence. A business traveler who cannot work is unlikely to treat the problem as a minor inconvenience.

In a lifestyle hotel, technology may support identity and shareability. Guests may expect mobile check-in, social media-friendly spaces, casting, digital content, app-based service requests and flexible public-space connectivity. Here, technology can contribute to the brand atmosphere. It helps the hotel feel contemporary, connected and socially alive. However, lifestyle does not excuse unreliability. A playful brand still needs serious infrastructure.

In a resort, technology must support diverse behaviors. Some guests want to disconnect, but many still expect seamless access when they choose to connect. Families may use streaming platforms in rooms. Guests may book spa treatments, restaurants and activities digitally. Operations may rely on mobile communication across a large property. The challenge is to deliver connectivity without destroying the sense of escape.

Brand alignment also affects investment decisions. A hotel should not simply ask how much a WiFi upgrade costs. It should ask what the brand loses when connectivity fails. It should not ask whether IPTV is necessary in a narrow technical sense. It should ask whether the in-room digital experience reflects the room rate and positioning. It should not ask whether telephony is old-fashioned. It should ask what level of communication and safety the property must guarantee.

GUEST-FACING TECHNOLOGY ACROSS THE JOURNEY

The guest journey provides a useful way to understand the role of WiFi, IPTV and telephony. These systems do not appear only during the stay. They connect pre-stay communication, arrival, room access, in-room comfort, service delivery, check-out and post-stay feedback.

Before arrival, the guest may receive digital instructions about check-in, parking, transport, mobile key activation or room preferences. These communications depend on accurate systems and reliable integrations. A pre-arrival email that invites a guest to use online services raises expectations. If the digital experience later fails, the disappointment may be stronger because the hotel has promised convenience.

At check-in, connectivity supports the front desk, kiosks, mobile devices and payment terminals. Even when WiFi is discussed as a guest service, it often also supports operational mobility. Staff tablets, mobile check-in tools, luggage systems, guest messaging platforms and maintenance applications may depend on the same network environment. The guest may not know this, but they experience the consequences when staff systems are slow or disconnected.

In the room, WiFi and IPTV become central. The guest tests the internet, connects devices, checks the television, explores hotel information or uses the phone to contact reception. This is often the moment when the guest evaluates whether the room feels modern.

A beautiful room with weak connectivity creates cognitive dissonance: the physical product suggests quality, while the digital layer suggests neglect.

During the stay, technology supports service requests. A guest may order room service through the television, scan a QR code, call reception, message the hotel, stream content, join a meeting, control entertainment, review hotel information or access concierge recommendations. Each interaction is a chance to deliver ease or friction. A technology touchpoint that does not lead to a service response can be more damaging than having no digital touchpoint at all.

At check-out, billing accuracy, payment processing and communication depend on technology. Although this chapter focuses on WiFi, IPTV and telephony, these systems interact with the broader IT ecosystem. If the room television allows paid content or service ordering, billing integration matters. If telephony posts charges, PMS integration matters. If WiFi authentication links to loyalty tiers or room numbers, data quality matters.

After departure, the guest may mention technology in reviews. Connectivity failures appear frequently in online feedback because they are easy to describe and emotionally salient. A guest may not know how to evaluate the hotel's infrastructure, but they know whether the WiFi was slow. A review stating that the room was comfortable but the internet was unusable can influence future bookings, especially for business travelers.

THE BUSINESS IMPACT OF BAD TECHNOLOGY

Bad technology has a hidden cost. It rarely appears in the profit and loss statement as a line called poor WiFi loss or IPTV friction cost. Instead, it appears indirectly through lower satisfaction scores, negative reviews, reduced willingness to pay, lost repeat business, higher staff workload, compensation gestures, corporate account complaints, longer problem-resolution times and pressure on revenue performance.

The chain reaction can be simple. Bad WiFi creates guest frustration. Frustrated guests post negative reviews or mention the issue in satisfaction surveys. Repeated complaints damage the property's online reputation. A weaker reputation reduces pricing power or conversion. Lower pricing power affects ADR. If occupancy or rate performance declines, RevPAR is affected. The original issue may have been technical, but the business consequence is commercial.

The effect is not always immediate. A single connectivity complaint may not reduce revenue tomorrow. But repeated complaints create a pattern. Corporate travel managers may hear from travelers that the property is unreliable for work. Meeting planners may avoid the venue if delegates report poor conference connectivity. Remote workers may choose a competitor. Loyalty members may shift their stays to another brand. Over time, technology weakness becomes market weakness.

Staff productivity is also affected. When guest WiFi fails, front desk teams handle complaints. When IPTV does not work, engineering receives repeated calls. When telephony routing is poor, calls are transferred incorrectly or lost. When internal communication systems depend on an overloaded network, staff coordination slows down. The hotel may then spend labor time compensating for problems that should have been prevented through better planning.

Poor technology also creates brand inconsistency. A property may invest heavily in design, bedding, amenities, restaurants and service training, yet underinvest in connectivity. Guests then experience a mismatch. The physical product says premium; the digital product says basic. In a market where guests increasingly live through connected devices, this mismatch can undermine the entire positioning.

For owners and asset managers, technology investment should therefore be evaluated as revenue protection. A WiFi upgrade is not only a cost. It protects guest satisfaction, corporate relevance, online reputation and pricing power. An IPTV modernization is not only entertainment expenditure. It may support service access, upselling and room experience. A telephony upgrade is not only replacing old phones. It may protect safety, internal coordination and service continuity.

This does not mean every hotel should buy the most expensive solution. It means every hotel should evaluate the cost of underperformance. The cheapest technology choice may become expensive when it damages the guest experience. Conversely, a targeted investment may pay for itself through fewer complaints, stronger reviews, better event performance, higher upsell conversion and improved staff efficiency.

WIFI: NOT AN AMENITY, BUT A PROMISE

WiFi is often described as an amenity, but for many guests it has become closer to electricity, water or climate control. It is assumed. Guests do not feel grateful when it works; they feel frustrated when it does not. This asymmetry is important. WiFi rarely creates delight by itself unless it is exceptionally easy, fast and secure. But it can create disappointment very quickly.

The promise of WiFi is not only that internet access exists somewhere in the building. The promise is that guests can use their devices where and when they need them: in the room, at the desk, in bed, in the lobby, in meeting spaces, in restaurants, near the pool, in the fitness area, or in public zones. For business hotels, the promise includes stability for video calls and VPN access. For leisure hotels, it includes easy login and multi-device use. For luxury hotels, it includes invisibility and security.

A manager should avoid asking only whether the hotel has WiFi. The more useful question is whether the WiFi supports the actual behaviors of the target guests. How many devices per room are expected? How many guests stream video simultaneously? What happens during full occupancy? Does the network support conference demand? Are staff devices competing with guest devices? Are public spaces covered? Are there dead zones? Are complaints tracked by location and time of day?

The login experience matters as much as the technical speed. A network may be technically capable but frustrating to access. Guests dislike repeated logins, unclear instructions, weak passwords, portals that do not load, or systems that disconnect devices when they leave and re-enter the room. In luxury and business segments, simplicity is part of quality. A difficult login procedure communicates operational carelessness.

Security also matters. Guest WiFi should be separated from operational systems. A hotel must not allow guest traffic to interfere with PMS, POS, staff devices or back-office systems. Network separation protects both guest experience and operational resilience. Managers do not need to configure the network, but they must understand why segmentation is necessary. Convenience without security is not hospitality; it is exposure.

WiFi strategy should also address fairness and prioritization. Some hotels may offer tiered bandwidth for loyalty members, conference packages or premium needs. Others may decide that high-quality WiFi should be included for all guests. The right decision depends on brand positioning. Charging extra for acceptable WiFi may feel inconsistent in an upscale property. Offering enhanced bandwidth for event clients may make commercial sense. The key is coherence with the promise of the hotel.

WIFI ARCHITECTURE IN MANAGERIAL LANGUAGE

Hotel WiFi can be explained without technical complexity. The guest's device connects wirelessly to an access point. The access point connects to the hotel's core network. The core network connects to the internet service provider. The internet connection links the hotel to the outside world. Behind this simple chain are design decisions about bandwidth, coverage, security, authentication, monitoring and support.

The first element is internet capacity. The hotel must purchase enough bandwidth for expected demand. Underestimating demand is common because managers may think in terms of rooms rather than devices and behaviors. A 150-room hotel does not have 150 connections. It may have hundreds or thousands of simultaneous devices when staff systems, guest devices, meeting rooms, streaming, phones, tablets and operational applications are included.

The second element is the core network. This is the internal routing and switching environment that distributes connectivity across the property. Managers do not need to know the technical configuration, but they should understand that poor core design can create bottlenecks. If the core network is outdated, adding more access points may not solve the problem. The issue may be deeper than the visible WiFi signal.

The third element is access point placement. A hotel is not an open office. It has corridors, thick walls, bathrooms, mirrors, metal structures, doors, elevators, back-of-house areas and sometimes historical building constraints. Access points placed incorrectly may create dead zones, weak signals or uneven performance. WiFi design should be based on surveys, not assumptions. A manager should ask whether coverage has been measured in rooms, meeting spaces and public areas, not only in corridors.

The fourth element is device behavior. Guest devices move, sleep, reconnect and compete for capacity. A guest may connect a phone, laptop, tablet and streaming device. Families multiply this effect. Meeting spaces create sudden concentration of demand. Device overload can make a network feel slow even when coverage exists. Capacity planning must consider occupancy patterns and peak periods.

The fifth element is traffic separation. Guest traffic, staff devices, payment systems, back-office systems and IoT devices should not all live in the same uncontrolled environment. Separation reduces risk and improves performance. If guests stream video on the same network segment that supports operational applications, the hotel may harm both guest and staff experience. A good design protects critical operations while still offering strong guest connectivity.

The sixth element is monitoring and support. A network should not be managed only after complaints appear. Performance should be monitored proactively. Managers should be able to review recurring issues by zone, time, device type or demand level. If complaints are concentrated in certain rooms or floors, the problem is diagnosable. If failures occur during peak occupancy, capacity may be the issue. If only some devices fail, authentication or compatibility may be involved.

The essential managerial insight is that WiFi quality is not accidental. It is designed, funded, monitored and maintained. Most chronic WiFi problems are not mysterious. They reflect underinvestment, poor planning, weak vendor management, limited measurement or lack of operational ownership.

COMMON WIFI FAILURES AND THEIR MANAGERIAL MEANING

WiFi failures often appear technical, but they usually reveal managerial decisions. Four common problems illustrate this point: limited bandwidth, poor access point placement, device overload and lack of network separation.

Limited bandwidth means the hotel has not purchased or allocated enough internet capacity for actual usage. This may happen because the initial design was based on old assumptions. Ten years ago, guests may have checked email and browsed websites. Today they stream, work remotely, use video calls, upload content and connect multiple devices. Meeting spaces and hybrid events add further pressure. If the bandwidth contract has not evolved with guest behavior, the hotel has created a predictable problem.

Poor access point placement means coverage was not designed around the building and the guest journey. A signal that looks acceptable in the corridor may be weak inside rooms. Historical buildings, reinforced structures and decorative materials can complicate coverage. Managers should not accept generic statements such as the WiFi is fine. They should ask for measurement, heat maps, room-by-room testing and complaint analysis.

Device overload occurs when the number of connected devices exceeds the network's practical capacity. This is particularly relevant for full occupancy, conferences, resorts, family travel and long-stay environments. A network that works at 40 percent occupancy may fail at 95 percent. Testing must therefore consider peak conditions. Guests judge the hotel when it is busy, not when it is empty.

Lack of network separation occurs when guest traffic and operational traffic interfere. This is both a performance and security issue. Guest streaming should not slow down front desk operations. Staff applications should not be exposed through poorly separated networks. Smart televisions, thermostats, casting devices, access systems and other connected devices also require careful management. The more connected the property becomes, the more segmentation matters.

Each failure has a technical explanation, but also an executive lesson. Limited bandwidth may reveal poor forecasting. Bad access point placement may reveal weak project management. Device overload may reveal outdated assumptions about guest behavior. Lack of segmentation may reveal governance failure. The role of management is not to solve the technical configuration, but to ensure that the right questions are asked before guests experience the consequences.

A useful diagnostic question is: Is this an incident, or a pattern? A one-time network outage may be an incident. Repeated complaints about the same floor, meeting room or peak period indicate a pattern. Patterns require investment, redesign or vendor accountability. Treating a pattern as a series of isolated complaints is a managerial mistake.

IPTV: MORE THAN TELEVISION

IPTV is often misunderstood as simply the television in the guest room. In modern hospitality, it can be much more than that. IPTV can function as a welcome platform, information channel, service interface, upselling tool, content hub, brand expression and sometimes digital concierge. Its value depends on how well it is integrated into the guest experience.

At the simplest level, IPTV provides entertainment. Guests may access television channels, hotel information, music, films or casting options. But entertainment expectations have changed. Many guests no longer want only traditional channels. They want to stream their own subscriptions, cast from personal devices and continue the media habits they have at home. If the hotel television cannot support these behaviors, it may feel outdated.

A modern IPTV system can also personalize the welcome. A guest entering the room may see their name, loyalty status or language preference. This can support recognition, provided it is done tastefully and accurately. A wrong name or poorly timed message creates the opposite effect. Personalization requires data quality and sensitivity. It should feel elegant, not mechanical.

IPTV can provide access to hotel services. Guests may browse room service menus, restaurant information, spa offers, concierge recommendations, activity schedules, transport details, safety information or sustainability messages. This can reduce printed materials and make information easier to update. However, digital information must be maintained. An outdated digital menu is not more modern than a printed one. It is simply a visible failure.

IPTV can also generate revenue. Spa treatments, dining reservations, premium content, late check-out, upgrades or local experiences can be promoted through the in-room screen. The success of this depends on design and relevance. A luxury guest may reject aggressive promotion. A family resort guest may appreciate clear access to activities. A business traveler may value quick information rather than entertainment clutter. The platform must respect segment expectations.

Casting has become a particularly important feature. Guests increasingly prefer to watch their own content rather than learn a hotel's entertainment menu. A casting solution must be secure, simple and reset properly between guests. No guest should see the previous guest's account, device or viewing history. Privacy is part of the experience. A casting system that is difficult to use, insecure or unreliable can create more frustration than value.

For managers, IPTV should be evaluated through experience, integration and maintenance. Does it reflect the brand? Does it connect with PMS data when needed? Can it support service requests? Can it promote revenue without feeling intrusive? Can staff explain it? Is content updated? Does the vendor provide reliable support? Is guest data protected? These questions matter more than the number of channels listed in a technical proposal.

IPTV ARCHITECTURE IN MANAGERIAL LANGUAGE

IPTV architecture can be simplified into four elements: the content source, the network, the guest room display and the middleware. Understanding these elements helps managers evaluate reliability and integration without becoming technicians.

The content source, sometimes called the headend, receives and organizes television channels, digital content or other media sources. In the past, this may have been largely about channel distribution. Today, it may include streaming, casting, hotel information, branded content and service interfaces. The quality of the source affects what the guest can access.

The network delivers the content across the property. This is where IPTV connects to the broader infrastructure discussion. If the network is weak, IPTV performance suffers. If bandwidth is insufficient, streaming quality may decline. If the system is poorly designed, guests may experience delays, freezing or inconsistent service. IPTV cannot be separated from network quality.

The guest room display is the visible endpoint. It includes the television, remote control, user interface and casting instructions. Guests judge the system through this visible layer. A sophisticated backend is irrelevant if the interface feels confusing. The room television should be intuitive, responsive and aligned with the hotel's design language. The remote control, menu structure and instructions matter.

Middleware is the management layer that allows the system to control content, integrate with other systems and personalize the interface. Middleware may connect to the PMS for guest names, language preferences, billing or room status. It may also support service menus, analytics or content management. For executives, middleware is where experience, operations and data meet.

Integration is the main managerial issue. If IPTV is isolated, it remains entertainment. If integrated intelligently, it can support welcome, service, information, revenue and personalization. But integration also creates dependency and risk. If PMS data is wrong, the welcome message may be wrong. If billing integration fails, charges may be disputed. If content management is neglected, the system becomes outdated. Integration increases value when governed properly.

Managers should also consider lifecycle. Guest room televisions and IPTV platforms may have different replacement cycles. A hotel renovation may update rooms physically but leave digital systems behind. Conversely, a technology upgrade may require coordination with design, electrical infrastructure, network capacity and guest communication. IPTV should be part of room strategy, not an afterthought.

TELEPHONY: DECLINING USAGE, CONTINUING STRATEGIC VALUE

Telephony in hotels is sometimes dismissed because many guests use mobile phones. This is a mistake. Guest phone usage has declined, but telephony infrastructure continues to serve safety, service, internal coordination and operational continuity. The question is no longer whether guests make many paid calls from the room. The question is what communication capability the hotel must guarantee.

The first function is emergency and safety. Guests must be able to contact emergency services or hotel teams quickly. Regulations vary by country and property type, but the principle is universal: communication infrastructure must support guest safety. A hotel cannot treat phones as decorative objects. If a guest needs help, the communication path must work.

The second function is service access. Some guests still prefer to call reception, housekeeping, room service or concierge. This is especially true in luxury hospitality, among some older travelers, during urgent situations, or when digital channels are inconvenient. The way calls are answered reflects service culture. A phone call is not only a technical connection; it is a voice expression of the brand.

The third function is internal coordination. Back-of-house teams, security, engineering, housekeeping, front office, banqueting and management may use a mix of fixed phones, mobile devices, radios, softphones or integrated communication platforms. The goal is not to preserve old hardware, but to ensure reliable communication. A property with weak internal communication will struggle to deliver coordinated service.

The fourth function is integration. Telephony may connect to the PMS for room status, billing, wake-up calls, voicemail, guest names or call routing. Although revenue from guest calls has declined in many markets, integration still supports operational convenience. For example, call displays may identify the room, language preference or guest status. This can improve service response.

Telephony has also evolved from traditional PBX hardware to IP telephony, softphones and software-defined communication. Traditional PBX systems were hardware-based and often capital-intensive. IP telephony uses the data network to carry voice. Softphones allow calls through software on computers or mobile devices. Integrated platforms may combine voice, messaging and service workflows. This evolution can improve flexibility, but it also increases dependence on network reliability.

For managers, the key is to treat telephony as part of the communication architecture. Does the system support emergency requirements? Does it integrate with hotel operations? Is call routing clear? Are service teams trained? Are phones maintained? Is there a backup plan if network-based telephony fails? Does the tone of the call experience match the brand? These questions matter even if the volume of guest calls has declined.

DIAGNOSING TECHNICAL ISSUES AS BUSINESS ISSUES

One of the most important skills for hospitality executives is to translate technical issues into business language. Technical teams may speak about bandwidth, access points, latency, routers, middleware, PBX, SIP trunks, VLANs or codecs. Executives must understand the business consequences: guest friction, operational delay, brand inconsistency, risk, cost, revenue loss and owner confidence.

A WiFi complaint is not simply a WiFi complaint. It may indicate underinvestment, poor vendor performance, outdated infrastructure, lack of monitoring, insufficient bandwidth, weak segmentation, poor building survey or misalignment with guest expectations. A manager should ask whether the problem is local, recurring, segment-specific, occupancy-related, event-related or systemic.

An IPTV complaint may indicate poor user interface design, weak content management, lack of casting support, network instability, PMS integration failure or insufficient staff knowledge. If guests repeatedly call because they cannot use the system, the issue is not only technical. It is also a training and design problem.

A telephony issue may indicate outdated hardware, poor call routing, weak internal procedures, network dependency, lack of emergency planning or service culture weakness. If guests cannot reach the right department, the problem affects trust. If staff cannot coordinate quickly, the problem affects operational execution.

Managers should develop a diagnostic habit. First, define the guest impact. What does the guest experience? Delay, confusion, inability to work, lack of service access, privacy concern, safety issue or disappointment? Second, define the operational impact. Which teams are affected? How much labor is consumed? Are manual workarounds needed? Third, define the financial impact. Does this affect reviews, compensation, event revenue, corporate accounts or repeat business? Fourth, define the root cause category. Is it design, capacity, vendor support, training, governance or investment?

This diagnostic process prevents executives from accepting vague explanations. It also prevents overreacting to individual incidents.

The goal is not to blame IT. The goal is to understand dependencies and make decisions. A good executive does not say, fix the WiFi, and disappear. A good executive asks what is failing, why it is failing, how often it fails, who owns the issue, what investment is required, what risk remains if no action is taken, and how success will be measured after correction.

The same discipline applies to owner communication. Owners may resist technology investment if it is presented as cables, switches or televisions. They may understand it better when it is presented as RevPAR protection, corporate account retention, guest satisfaction improvement, event revenue support, complaint reduction and brand alignment. The manager's role is to translate technical need into strategic value.

VENDOR MANAGEMENT AND SERVICE-LEVEL EXPECTATIONS

WiFi, IPTV and telephony are often delivered with external vendors. Vendor management is therefore central to the hospitality IT ecosystem. Selecting a vendor is not only a procurement decision. It is a long-term service relationship that affects guest satisfaction and operational continuity.

A hotel should evaluate vendors through several lenses. The first is technical capability. Can the vendor design for the building, occupancy, device density and guest segments? Does the vendor understand hospitality use cases, not only generic networks? Does the vendor provide references from comparable properties? Can the solution scale? Does it support security and segmentation?

The second lens is integration. Does the vendor solution integrate with the PMS, guest authentication, loyalty tiers, IPTV, casting, telephony, billing or service platforms when needed? Integration promises should be tested carefully. A vendor that says integration is possible may mean that custom work, additional costs or operational complexity will be required. Managers should clarify responsibilities before signing.

The third lens is support. A hotel operates continuously. Vendor support must match hotel realities. What happens at midnight? What happens on weekends? Who responds during a major outage? What is the escalation path? Are there local technicians? Is remote monitoring available? Is there a service-level agreement? How are response times measured?

The fourth lens is lifecycle. Technology must be maintained, patched, upgraded and eventually replaced. A vendor proposal should not be evaluated only on installation cost. Managers should ask about maintenance fees, licensing, warranties, replacement cycles, software updates, cybersecurity patches, monitoring dashboards and future compatibility.

The fifth lens is data and security. Guest-facing systems may collect usage data, authentication information, device identifiers or service interactions. IPTV and casting systems may handle sensitive privacy issues. Telephony systems may record logs. Vendors must be subject to data protection obligations. Contracts should define responsibilities, access rights, breach notification processes and security requirements.

Service-level agreements should be written in business language as well as technical language. A technical uptime percentage is useful, but managers also need to understand operational consequences. If the WiFi fails during a conference, what support response is guaranteed? If IPTV fails across multiple floors, who communicates with operations? If telephony fails, what emergency procedures apply? The SLA should support the service promise, not simply list technical indicators.

Vendor management also requires internal ownership. A hotel cannot outsource accountability completely. Someone must review performance, track complaints, monitor service reports, coordinate upgrades, follow up on incidents and connect technology performance to guest feedback. Without internal ownership, vendor relationships become reactive. The hotel calls when something breaks, but no one manages the ecosystem strategically.

TECHNOLOGY INVESTMENT: COST, VALUE AND BRAND PROTECTION

Technology investment decisions are often difficult because the benefits of good guest-facing infrastructure are partly invisible. When WiFi works, guests may not mention it. When IPTV is intuitive, guests simply use it. When telephony supports safety, no crisis may occur. This can make investment feel less urgent than visible renovations. Yet the absence of problems is itself a form of value.

A manager defending investment should connect technology to measurable and strategic outcomes. WiFi investment can reduce complaints, improve online review sentiment, support conference business, retain corporate accounts, enable staff mobility and protect ADR. IPTV investment can improve in-room experience, promote hotel services, support upselling, reduce printed materials and reinforce brand perception. Telephony investment can improve safety, call handling, internal coordination and service reliability.

The cost of technology should also be compared to the cost of failure. A major conference with poor WiFi can damage event reputation and future group business. A corporate account that complains repeatedly about connectivity may shift room nights elsewhere. A luxury guest who cannot stream or access services may judge the room as outdated. A service failure that could have been prevented through better communication may generate compensation costs. These losses are not always easy to isolate, but they are real.

Investment prioritization should be based on risk and positioning. A hotel with frequent WiFi complaints should prioritize connectivity before adding flashy digital features. A property with outdated televisions and low service visibility may benefit from IPTV modernization. A hotel with emergency communication gaps must address telephony and safety quickly. A property preparing for renovation should integrate technology planning early rather than install systems after design decisions are complete.

Managers should also avoid overinvestment in technology that guests do not value. Not every property needs the most advanced room control system, robot service or complex application. The strongest investments are those that remove friction, strengthen the brand promise, support staff and create measurable value. Technology should be evaluated through readiness, adoption and maintenance, not novelty.

A useful question is: What failure would be most damaging for our target guests? For a corporate hotel, the answer may be WiFi instability. For a luxury resort, it may be intrusive technology or lack of privacy. For a conference property, it may be meeting-space bandwidth. For an airport hotel, it may be poor communication during disruption. For a lifestyle property, it may be a disconnected digital journey. Investment should address the most important promise first.

APPLIED CASE STUDY: BAD WIFI REVIEWS ARE DAMAGING REVPAR

Imagine a 220-room upscale business hotel located in a major European city. The property has strong location advantages, renovated rooms, a popular breakfast offer and several meeting spaces. For several years, it has performed well with corporate travelers and small conferences. Recently, however, online reviews have begun to mention WiFi problems more frequently. Guests describe unstable connections, slow speeds during evening hours, difficulty joining video calls and poor connectivity in meeting rooms.

At first, the hotel treats the problem as a technical irritation. The front desk apologizes. Engineering restarts equipment. The vendor is contacted occasionally. Guests receive explanations about temporary network congestion. Some are offered loyalty points or minor compensation. The issue does not immediately appear catastrophic, so no major investment is approved.

Over six months, the pattern becomes clearer. Corporate guests mention that they cannot work reliably from the room. Meeting planners ask whether the hotel can guarantee bandwidth for events. A regular corporate account reports negative feedback from travelers. Online review scores remain acceptable overall, but the technology comments become visible. The revenue team notices that the hotel is losing some rate confidence against a competitor known for strong business facilities.

The General Manager now faces a decision. Is this a technical problem, a service problem or a strategic underinvestment problem? The answer may be all three, but the most important shift is to recognize that repeated WiFi complaints are no longer isolated incidents. They are signs of a gap between the hotel's business positioning and its infrastructure capability.

The first managerial step is diagnosis. The hotel should collect data: complaint frequency, affected floors, time of day, occupancy levels, meeting-space usage, device counts, bandwidth consumption, vendor incident reports, online review patterns and staff feedback. This evidence prevents vague debate. If complaints peak during full occupancy and events, capacity may be insufficient. If certain rooms are affected, access point placement may be the issue. If staff systems slow down at the same time, network separation may be weak.

The second step is ownership. The issue should not remain only with IT or engineering. The GM, revenue manager, front office manager, sales director, IT vendor and possibly the owner's representative should understand the business impact. Sales can explain corporate account risk. Revenue can estimate pricing pressure. Front office can report complaint volume. IT can explain infrastructure constraints. Ownership creates a shared business case.

The third step is investment evaluation. The hotel may need a network survey, bandwidth upgrade, new access points, better segmentation, meeting-room dedicated capacity, vendor SLA revision or monitoring tools. The proposal should not be defended only as a technical upgrade. It should be positioned as protection of corporate business, meeting revenue, guest satisfaction and ADR.

The fourth step is communication and follow-up. Once improvements are made, staff should know what has changed. Sales should be able to reassure corporate clients. Front office should track whether complaints decline. Online reputation should be monitored. The hotel should measure success through fewer complaints, improved review sentiment, stronger event feedback and reduced guest compensation.

The final lesson is that technology failures become strategic when they contradict the hotel's market promise. A business hotel that cannot provide reliable WiFi undermines its own positioning. The problem may begin with access points, but it ends with revenue.

MANAGERIAL TAKEAWAYS

The first takeaway is that guest-facing technology is part of hospitality experience, not a separate technical category. Guests judge WiFi, IPTV and telephony through comfort, ease, trust and emotion. They do not separate the infrastructure from the brand.

The second takeaway is that invisible technology requires visible strategy. The goal is for networks and communication systems to feel effortless, but effortless experiences are designed. They require investment, governance, vendor management and operational ownership.

The third takeaway is that WiFi is now a core expectation. Hotels should treat connectivity as a baseline promise aligned with segment needs. Luxury, business, leisure, lifestyle and resort guests require different forms of excellence, but none of them accept careless design.

The fourth takeaway is that IPTV can become a service and revenue platform when integrated intelligently. It should not be reduced to television channels. It can support welcome, information, personalization, casting, upselling and brand expression.

The fifth takeaway is that telephony remains strategically relevant despite lower guest call volumes. Safety, internal coordination, service access and emergency communication still matter. A modern communication strategy may use fewer traditional phones, but it cannot abandon reliability.

The sixth takeaway is that poor technology affects revenue indirectly but powerfully. Bad WiFi, outdated in-room systems and weak communication can damage reviews, loyalty, corporate accounts, event business, ADR and RevPAR. The cost of failure is often larger than the visible technical invoice.

The seventh takeaway is that executives must translate technology into business outcomes. Owners and leadership teams do not need a lecture on cables. They need to understand risk, guest impact, revenue protection, brand alignment and return on investment.

The final takeaway is that technology should support hospitality rather than dominate it. The best systems create space for better service. They remove friction, protect trust, enable staff and make the guest journey feel coherent.

TO REVIEW THIS CHAPTER

KEY TERMS

Guest-Facing Technology: Technology directly or indirectly experienced by guests, including WiFi, IPTV, telephony, mobile access, casting and digital service interfaces.

WiFi: Wireless network access that allows guests and staff devices to connect to hotel systems or the internet.

IPTV: Internet Protocol Television; a system that delivers television, content, hotel information and sometimes service interfaces through an IP-based network.

Telephony: The hotel's voice communication infrastructure, including traditional PBX systems, IP telephony, softphones, call routing and emergency communication.

Access Point: A network device that provides wireless coverage to guest and staff devices in rooms, corridors or public spaces.

Bandwidth: The amount of data capacity available for internet or network use. Insufficient bandwidth can cause slow or unstable connections.

Network Segmentation: The separation of different types of network traffic, such as guest WiFi, staff systems, payment systems and IoT devices.

Casting: The ability for guests to stream content from their own devices to the guest room television.

Middleware: The management layer that allows IPTV or similar systems to integrate with hotel systems and control content or services.

PBX: Private Branch Exchange; a traditional telephone system used to manage internal and external calls within an organization.

IP Telephony: Voice communication delivered through internet protocol networks rather than traditional phone lines.

SLA - Service-Level Agreement: A contractual commitment defining the level of service, response time, uptime or support expected from a vendor.

RevPAR: Revenue per Available Room; a key hotel performance indicator affected by occupancy and ADR.

ADR: Average Daily Rate; the average room revenue earned per occupied room.

Technology Friction: Any digital or technical difficulty that creates inconvenience, frustration or interruption for the guest or staff.

Experience Architecture: The invisible structure of systems, processes and touchpoints that allows the guest journey to feel seamless.

REFLECTION QUESTIONS

- Why should WiFi be considered part of the hotel brand promise rather than only a technical amenity?
- How does a guest experience technology failure emotionally, and why does this matter for hotel managers?
- In what ways do luxury, business, leisure and lifestyle hotels require different technology strategies?
- Why can poor WiFi affect ADR and RevPAR even when the rooms and service are otherwise strong?

- How can IPTV be used as a service platform without becoming intrusive or overly commercial?
- Why does telephony remain important even when many guests use their own mobile phones?
- How should a General Manager distinguish between an isolated technical incident and a strategic infrastructure problem?
- What questions should an owner or asset manager ask before approving or refusing a WiFi upgrade?
- How can technology support hospitality without making the guest experience feel impersonal?
- What would be the most damaging technology failure for the type of hotel you know best?

REVIEW QUESTIONS

- Define guest-facing technology in a hotel context.
- Explain why WiFi is now a core guest expectation.
- Identify four common causes of poor hotel WiFi performance.
- Explain the difference between internet capacity and WiFi coverage.
- Describe how IPTV can support welcome, service and revenue generation.
- Name the main components of IPTV architecture in managerial language.
- Explain why telephony remains strategically relevant in hotels.
- Describe the business chain from bad WiFi to negative RevPAR impact.
- Explain what network segmentation means and why it matters in hospitality.
- List the key criteria managers should use when evaluating WiFi, IPTV or telephony vendors.

- Explain why technology investment should be connected to brand positioning.
- Describe how a manager should diagnose recurring WiFi complaints in a business hotel.

REFERENCES AND FURTHER READING

AHLA / HTNG. HTNG Technical Specifications. A useful resource for understanding hospitality technology standards, system integrations and technical guidance for hotel technology environments. https://www.ahla.com/htng-technical-specifications

Cisco. 5 Ways Wi-Fi 7 Elevates the Guest Experience with Smart Hospitality. This article discusses the increasing role of wireless connectivity in hospitality guest engagement, automation and personalization. https://blogs.cisco.com/networking/5-ways-wi-fi-7-elevates-the-guest-experience-with-smart-hospitality

Cisco Meraki. MR Hospitality Design Guide. A technical design reference for wireless network planning in hospitality environments, useful for understanding coverage, density and deployment considerations. https://documentation.meraki.com/MR/Deployment_Guides/MR_Hospitality_Design_Guide_%28CVD%29

Hotel Internet Services. Hotel Internet Services Hospitality Wi-Fi Resources. This industry resource discusses hotel WiFi, guest connectivity, streaming, casting and in-room technology expectations. https://www.hotel-online.com/industry-resources/hotel-internet-services

Hotel WiFi. Exceeding Guest Wi-Fi Expectations in the Hospitality Industry. A white paper focused on hotel guest connectivity expectations and the operational importance of reliable in-room WiFi. https://www.hotelwifi.com/wp-content/uploads/2022/06/2022-wifi-White-PaperV4.pdf

Oracle Hospitality. Hospitality Technology Solutions. Oracle's hospitality resources are useful for understanding how hotel systems connect guest rooms, management, event sales and POS systems to support integrated experiences. https://www.oracle.com/hospitality/

Wi-Fi Alliance. Wi-Fi CERTIFIED technologies and wireless standards resources. Useful for general understanding of WiFi technology evolution, certification and interoperability. https://www.wi-fi.org/

Chapter 7

IT Vocabulary, Governance & IT for Executives

Mastering Technology Leadership in Hospitality

LEARNING OBJECTIVES

By the end of this chapter, you should be able to explain why executive communication is a critical part of hospitality IT leadership; translate technical IT topics into business language; use essential technology vocabulary in a management context; understand the purpose of IT governance and steering committees; identify IT key performance indicators that matter to hotel executives; evaluate vendor dependency and service-level agreements; prepare a concise executive briefing on a technology decision; and frame IT investments as business choices linked to risk, revenue, guest satisfaction, operational continuity and brand value.

OPENING PERSPECTIVE

In hospitality, technology decisions are rarely blocked because the technology is impossible. They are often blocked because the business case is unclear, the language is too technical, the financial impact is poorly explained, or the decision-makers do not understand the risk of doing nothing.

A hotel executive does not buy a server, a router, a PMS migration, an endpoint protection tool, a cloud architecture or a dashboard. An executive buys operational continuity, faster openings, lower risk, better guest experience, stronger reporting, reduced dependency, more reliable payments, fewer complaints and a more resilient brand.

This distinction is essential. Technical teams often describe what a system does. Executives need to understand what the system protects, enables or improves. When an IT Director says, "We need to upgrade the network core," the General Manager, CFO or owner may hear only cost and complexity. When the same message becomes, "The current network creates a single point of failure for check-in, payment and guest WiFi; upgrading it protects revenue and reduces operational disruption," the discussion changes.

The purpose of this chapter is to help hospitality managers speak IT at executive level. This does not mean using more technical words. It means using fewer words, choosing clearer words, and connecting every technology topic to a business outcome.

THE EXECUTIVE CHALLENGE OF IT COMMUNICATION

Many hotel leaders are experienced operators. They understand guest satisfaction, staffing, service recovery, brand standards, owner expectations, pricing pressure and daily operational complexity. Yet when IT topics appear, the discussion often becomes uncomfortable. Technical vocabulary creates distance. Acronyms multiply. Vendors present impressive features. Internal teams refer to architecture, patches, interfaces, APIs, uptime, cloud migration, endpoint detection, VLANs, backup windows and dependencies. Executives may not want to admit that they do not fully understand the implications.

This communication gap creates three risks.

The first risk is underinvestment. If IT is perceived only as a cost center, projects that protect the business may be postponed. WiFi upgrades, cybersecurity controls, backup systems, integration work or PMS replacement may be delayed because the consequences are not visible until failure occurs. In hotels, delayed investment can appear financially prudent in the short term and become very expensive during a crisis.

The second risk is overinvestment in poorly understood solutions. A vendor may sell a fashionable system using attractive language: artificial intelligence, digital transformation, guest engagement, predictive intelligence, seamless experience or future-ready platform. Without executive-level IT literacy, managers may approve a project because it sounds strategic rather than because it solves a clearly defined business problem.

The third risk is political tension. IT teams may feel that executives do not listen. Executives may feel that IT teams do not explain. Operations may complain that systems do not support reality. Finance may challenge budgets. Vendors may exploit internal confusion. Instead of alignment, the hotel develops frustration around technology decisions.

Good IT governance begins with language. If people cannot explain the problem, they cannot prioritize the decision.

SPEAKING IT WITHOUT BECOMING TECHNICAL

A common misunderstanding is that hospitality executives need to become more technical. In reality, most executives need to become more precise. Precision is not the same as technical depth.

A General Manager does not need to know how to configure a firewall. But the GM should understand that the firewall is part of the protection between the hotel network and external threats. The GM should understand that weak configuration can expose guest data, payment systems and operational platforms. The GM should also know which executive questions to ask: Who monitors it? Who updates it? What happens if it fails? Is it covered by a support contract? Is there an incident response plan?

A CFO does not need to know how a PMS interface works. But the CFO should understand that poor integration between PMS, POS and ERP creates reconciliation issues, reporting delays and possible revenue leakage. The CFO should ask whether the investment reduces manual work, improves reporting reliability, supports auditability and protects margin.

A COO does not need to know the technical structure of a cloud environment. But the COO should understand whether cloud dependency affects business continuity, how properties will operate during internet disruption, what fallback procedures exist and how staff will be trained.

An asset manager does not need to troubleshoot WiFi coverage. But the asset manager should understand that repeated WiFi complaints weaken guest satisfaction, damage corporate account retention and reduce pricing power over time.

Executive IT literacy is therefore not about doing the work of IT. It is about knowing enough to lead, challenge and decide.

THE CORE TRANSLATION PRINCIPLE

Every IT topic must be translated into at least one executive concern. The strongest executive concerns in hospitality are usually risk reduction, revenue protection, guest satisfaction, operational efficiency, compliance, brand reputation, scalability and owner value.

Cybersecurity becomes reputation risk and business continuity.

PMS outage becomes operational paralysis and revenue loss.

WiFi complaints become guest dissatisfaction and weaker pricing power.

Cloud migration becomes scalability, resilience and future opening speed.

Vendor lock-in becomes strategic dependency and reduced negotiating power.

Poor data quality becomes unreliable reporting and weak decision-making.

A service-level agreement becomes contractual accountability.

This translation is not cosmetic. It changes the decision. A technical phrase describes the tool. An executive phrase explains why the tool matters.

For example, consider the sentence: "We need to migrate the PMS infrastructure to a cloud-based architecture." The sentence may be technically correct, but it does not explain the executive issue. A better version would be: "Moving the PMS to a cloud-based model will reduce local server dependency, support faster deployment across new properties, improve remote access for authorized teams and allow vendor-managed updates. The decision requires reliable connectivity, strong data protection terms and a clear continuity plan."

This version does three things. It explains value. It acknowledges risk. It prepares a decision.

IT AS A STRATEGIC ENABLER

IT becomes strategic when it enables the hotel to do something better, safer, faster, more consistently or more profitably. In hospitality, four impact areas are especially important: guest experience, operational efficiency, compliance and risk, and scalability.

Guest experience is often the most visible impact area. Technology shapes booking, pre-arrival communication, check-in, room access, WiFi, in-room entertainment, restaurant booking, service requests, billing, loyalty communication and review management. The guest may not see the technology architecture, but the guest feels the service result. A seamless stay is often supported by systems that work quietly in the background.

Operational efficiency is the second impact area. Hotels are labor-intensive environments. A technology decision may reduce duplicated work, eliminate manual re-entry, improve scheduling, support housekeeping prioritization, automate reporting or accelerate service response. Efficiency should not be confused with reducing hospitality. Good technology gives staff more time to be present with guests by removing unnecessary friction.

Compliance and risk form the third impact area. Hotels manage personal data, payment data, employee data, supplier data and sometimes sensitive guest preferences. They are exposed to cybersecurity threats, legal obligations, contractual commitments and operational continuity requirements. IT governance helps ensure that risk is not hidden inside daily convenience.

Scalability is the fourth impact area. A hotel group that wants to expand must think beyond one property. Systems must support additional hotels, new markets, consolidated reporting, consistent standards, multi-property access, vendor management and future integration. A solution that works for one independent property may not support a regional portfolio. Scalability is not only a technical concept. It is a growth concept.

THE EXECUTIVE TABLE: WHO DECIDES AND WHY

IT decisions are rarely made by IT alone. In hospitality organizations, technology governance often involves several stakeholders: the CEO or General Manager, CFO, COO or Operations Director, CIO or IT Director, Legal or Risk, Revenue Management, Sales and Marketing, Finance, Procurement and sometimes ownership or asset management.

Each actor brings a different logic.

The CEO or General Manager focuses on strategic alignment, brand impact, guest experience, operational feasibility and final accountability. The GM wants to know whether the investment supports the hotel's positioning and protects the operation.

The CFO focuses on cost, return on investment, cash flow, budget timing, contract exposure, total cost of ownership and financial risk. The CFO will often ask whether the project is urgent, whether it can be phased, whether the benefits are measurable and whether hidden costs have been considered.

The COO focuses on execution. Will the system disrupt operations during implementation? Will staff adopt it? Will processes need redesign? Will standards change? Will properties have enough support?

The CIO or IT Director focuses on technical feasibility, architecture, risk, integration, security, vendor capability and long-term sustainability. The best IT leaders do not speak only as technicians. They speak as business partners.

Legal and Risk focus on contracts, liability, data protection, compliance, insurance, auditability and incident obligations. In a hospitality environment, these concerns are especially important when guest data, payment flows or third-party processing are involved.

Owners and asset managers focus on asset value, investment discipline, brand positioning, operational risk and return. They may support technology when it protects long-term value, but they will challenge unclear or poorly justified spending.

A strong executive IT discussion recognizes these different perspectives before the meeting begins. Good preparation means anticipating what each stakeholder will care about.

ESSENTIAL IT VOCABULARY FOR HOSPITALITY EXECUTIVES

Executives do not need to master every technical term. They do need a working vocabulary that allows them to understand discussions, ask relevant questions and avoid being excluded from decisions.

OPEX and CAPEX are fundamental. CAPEX, or capital expenditure, usually refers to investments that create or improve long-term assets. In hotel IT, this may include infrastructure upgrades, servers, network equipment, cabling or major system implementation. OPEX, or operating expenditure, refers to recurring costs such as subscriptions, licenses, support contracts, cloud services, maintenance and managed services. The distinction matters because it affects budgeting, ownership expectations, cash flow and financial reporting.

SLA means Service Level Agreement. It defines the expected level of service between a provider and the hotel or hotel group. A strong SLA may specify uptime, response time, resolution time, support hours, escalation procedures, penalties and reporting obligations. For executives, the SLA is not paperwork. It is the contractual expression of reliability.

Downtime means that a system is unavailable or not functioning properly. In hospitality, downtime has immediate business consequences. PMS downtime blocks check-in and check-out. POS downtime affects billing. WiFi downtime affects guest satisfaction. Payment downtime affects revenue capture. Downtime should be discussed in business impact, not only in minutes.

Scalability is the ability of a system, process or architecture to grow without requiring a complete redesign. A scalable PMS, CRM, network or reporting solution can support more rooms, more properties, more users, more transactions or more integrations. Scalability is essential for hotel groups and for any property planning expansion.

Vendor lock-in describes a situation where it becomes difficult or expensive to change provider. Lock-in may happen because data is hard to export, integrations are proprietary, contracts are restrictive, staff are dependent on a system, or switching would disrupt operations. Vendor lock-in reduces future flexibility.

ROI, or Return on Investment, measures the financial value generated by an investment compared with its cost. In IT, ROI may be direct, such as labor savings or increased upsell revenue, or indirect, such as risk reduction, faster reporting, lower downtime or improved guest satisfaction. Executives must be careful not to reduce all technology value to immediate cost savings. Some IT investments protect revenue rather than visibly create it.

TCO, or Total Cost of Ownership, is broader than purchase price. It includes implementation, training, integrations, licenses, maintenance, support, upgrades, internal time, vendor management and eventual replacement or exit costs. A cheap system can become expensive if it requires heavy manual work, poor support or costly integrations.

API means Application Programming Interface. In simple terms, it allows systems to exchange data. In hospitality, APIs may allow PMS, POS, CRM, revenue management, booking engines, guest apps and finance systems to communicate. Executives do not need to understand API programming. They need to understand that poor integration creates operational friction.

Uptime is the percentage of time a system is available. A high uptime target matters when systems are essential to hotel operations. However, uptime is meaningful only when connected to service impact. A dashboard showing 99.9 percent uptime may still hide repeated guest-impacting incidents if the downtime occurs during peak check-in periods.

Cyber exposure refers to the level of risk created by systems, users, vendors, data and vulnerabilities. It should be discussed alongside business risk, not separately.

Business continuity refers to the hotel's ability to continue operating during disruption. It includes backup systems, manual procedures, crisis communication, recovery priorities and staff readiness.

Data governance refers to how data is collected, stored, accessed, protected, used, retained and deleted. In hotels, data governance affects guest trust, compliance, reporting and personalization.

The most important rule is simple: never use acronyms without explanation. Acronyms can make a speaker sound knowledgeable, but they can also exclude decision-makers. Executive communication must include people, not impress them.

KPIS THAT EXECUTIVES UNDERSTAND

IT KPIs are useful only when they help executives understand performance, risk or value. Some technical metrics are important for IT teams but weak for executive governance. Server CPU usage, number of lines of code, number of support tickets or storage utilization may matter operationally, but they do not automatically communicate business value.

Executives need IT KPIs that connect technology to outcomes.

System availability is a strong KPI when linked to business continuity. For example, a PMS availability target of 99.9 percent matters because the PMS supports check-in, check-out, billing and guest profiles. The metric should be accompanied by business interpretation: How many guest-impacting incidents occurred? During which periods? What revenue or satisfaction impact was observed?

Guest-impacting incidents are especially valuable in hospitality. A minor technical incident that affects no guests may be less urgent than a short WiFi outage during a corporate conference. The question is not only how many incidents occurred. The question is whom they affected and what business consequence followed.

Mean time to resolve, or MTTR, may be useful if explained clearly. It measures how quickly problems are resolved. For executives, the important point is service recovery: how long did guests, staff or revenue processes remain affected?

Cost per room, cost per occupied room or technology cost per booking can help executives understand unit economics. These indicators are especially useful when comparing properties, evaluating vendor contracts or assessing technology efficiency across a portfolio.

Cybersecurity indicators should be framed carefully. "Number of attacks blocked" may sound impressive but may not explain risk. More meaningful executive indicators include critical vulnerabilities remediated within target time, phishing training completion, privileged accounts reviewed, backup tests completed, incident response exercises performed and audit findings closed.

Project delivery KPIs are also important: budget variance, timeline variance, adoption rate, training completion, stabilization period and post-implementation issues. A technology project should not be considered complete when the system goes live. It is complete when the business can use it reliably.

A good executive IT dashboard should therefore avoid excessive detail. It should show availability, incidents, risks, major projects, budget status, vendor performance and key decisions required.

DASHBOARDS, NOT REPORTS

Executives do not need long IT reports full of technical detail. They need dashboards that support decisions. A good executive dashboard has three characteristics: it is short, visual and action-oriented.

Short means that the dashboard fits on one page or one screen. If everything is important, nothing is important. The dashboard should show only the indicators that help executives understand status, risk and required decisions.

Visual means that status is easy to interpret. Traffic light logic can be effective: green for on track, yellow for watch, red for action required. Trends are often more useful than isolated numbers. A single month of higher support tickets may not matter; a three-month trend of guest-impacting WiFi complaints may require investment.

Action-oriented means that the dashboard identifies what decision is needed. A dashboard that only reports problems can create frustration. A stronger dashboard states: "Issue: guest WiFi incidents increased in three properties. Risk: corporate guest satisfaction and online reviews. Options: increase bandwidth, redesign access point coverage, segment guest and operational traffic. Decision needed: approve diagnostic audit and budget envelope."

The executive dashboard should reduce cognitive load. Its purpose is not to display how much IT knows. Its purpose is to help leadership decide.

VENDOR MANAGEMENT AS STRATEGIC CONTROL

Hotels depend heavily on vendors: PMS providers, POS providers, network suppliers, cybersecurity partners, payment gateways, IPTV providers, telecom operators, CRM systems, revenue management platforms, cloud services and managed service providers. Vendor management is therefore not an administrative task. It is a form of strategic control.

Executives should care about four vendor issues: dependency risk, contract duration, exit strategy and SLA enforcement.

Dependency risk asks how much the hotel depends on one provider. If one vendor controls the PMS, guest data, interfaces and reporting environment, switching may be difficult. This dependency may be acceptable if the vendor is excellent and contract terms are fair, but the risk must be understood.

Contract duration creates a trade-off between price and flexibility. A long contract may reduce cost, but it may also limit the hotel's ability to adapt. A short contract may preserve flexibility but increase price or reduce vendor commitment. The right answer depends on strategic context.

Exit strategy is often neglected. Before signing a contract, executives should ask how data can be exported, how long transition support will be provided, what fees apply, whether integrations can be reused and what happens if the vendor is acquired, fails to perform or changes pricing.

SLA penalties create accountability. Without penalties or escalation mechanisms, an SLA may become symbolic. However, penalties should not be the only focus. The goal is not to punish vendors; it is to ensure service reliability. Strong vendor relationships combine clear obligations, regular reviews, transparent communication and escalation discipline.

Vendor management also has a political dimension. Vendors may develop relationships with different departments. Sales may prefer a CRM tool. Operations may prefer a housekeeping platform. Finance may prefer a reporting system. IT may prefer architectural consistency. Procurement may push cost savings. Governance helps align these preferences before fragmented decisions create long-term complexity.

IT STEERING COMMITTEES

An IT steering committee is a structured forum where technology meets business strategy. It is not a technical troubleshooting meeting. It is a governance mechanism used to align priorities, control budgets, supervise risk and make trade-offs between competing initiatives.

A strong IT steering committee usually reviews major projects, investment requests, risk indicators, vendor performance, cybersecurity posture, system performance, compliance issues, data governance and upcoming decisions. It should include the right stakeholders, use clear language and focus on business outcomes.

The committee's purpose is not to approve everything. Its purpose is to prioritize. In hotels, many technology needs compete for attention: PMS modernization, WiFi upgrades, cybersecurity investment, guest app development, CRM enhancement, energy management, data dashboards, payment security, digital keys, IPTV renewal, HR systems and back-office automation. Not all can be funded at the same time.

Steering committees help leadership decide what matters most now.

For example, a property may want a guest app, but cybersecurity risks may be urgent. A hotel group may want a new CRM, but PMS data quality may be too weak to support it. A resort may want IPTV upgrades, but WiFi coverage may be the more important guest issue. A board may want AI, but the organization may still lack basic data governance.

The steering committee should ask five questions for each major initiative.

What business problem are we solving?

What happens if we do nothing?

What options do we have?

What is the recommended option and why?

What decision is required today?

These questions create discipline. They prevent IT governance from becoming either too technical or too vague.

HOW DECISIONS ARE REALLY MADE

Executive decisions are not always purely rational. A technically strong proposal can fail because it arrives at the wrong time, lacks political support, threatens another department, appears too risky, exceeds the budget cycle or is poorly presented. A weaker proposal can succeed because it is simple, well-framed and linked to a visible business problem.

Budget pressure is one factor. Even when an IT project is justified, there may be limited cash, competing renovation needs, staffing pressure or owner resistance. The executive presenter must be ready to explain phasing, risk of delay and minimum viable investment.

Personal agendas also matter. A department may support a system that increases its influence. Another may resist a project that exposes performance weaknesses. A vendor may have a strong relationship with one executive. A property may resist a group standard. Governance must manage these dynamics without becoming political theater.

Fear of failure is another factor. Executives may have experienced past IT projects that exceeded budget, disrupted operations or failed adoption. A new proposal must therefore address implementation risk, training, change management and contingency planning.

Timing can determine success. A WiFi investment after a wave of negative reviews may receive approval quickly. The same proposal six months earlier may have been rejected. Cybersecurity investment after an industry breach may feel urgent. Before the breach, it may feel abstract.

Good IT leaders anticipate these realities. They do not only prepare technical arguments. They prepare decision psychology.

THE FIVE-MINUTE EXECUTIVE BRIEFING

Technology briefings should be concise. A practical structure is the five-minute rule: context, risk or opportunity, options, recommendation and decision needed.

Context should take about thirty seconds. It answers the question: why does this matter now? The context must be specific. "Our WiFi is old" is weak. "Corporate guest complaints about WiFi have increased for three consecutive months, and two key accounts have raised connectivity as a renewal concern" is stronger.

Risk or opportunity should take about one minute. It explains what is at stake. This may include revenue, guest satisfaction, operational continuity, compliance, cost, staff productivity or brand reputation.

Options should take about two minutes. Executives should not be given ten alternatives. Three options are usually enough: do nothing or postpone, partial investment, full investment. Each option should include benefits, costs, risks and consequences.

Recommendation should take about one minute. The presenter must take a position. Executives do not want a neutral list of possibilities. They want a clear recommendation supported by reasoning.

Decision needed should take about thirty seconds. The ask must be explicit: approve the budget, authorize vendor negotiation, launch a diagnostic audit, approve phase one, accept a risk, or defer with consequences.

The five-minute structure works because it respects executive attention. It also forces the presenter to think clearly.

WHAT NOT TO DO IN EXECUTIVE IT COMMUNICATION

Several habits destroy credibility in executive IT discussions.

The first is the technical deep dive. Architecture diagrams, configuration details and system specifications may be useful in technical workshops, but they should not dominate executive meetings. If executives ask for detail, provide it. Do not lead with it.

The second is the twenty-slide deck. Long presentations often hide weak thinking. An executive meeting should not be used to educate the room on every technical aspect of the project. It should be used to obtain a decision.

The third is the unclear ask. If the presenter does not state what decision is needed, the meeting may end with polite discussion and no action. Ambiguity delays decisions.

The fourth is excessive hedging. Of course, IT decisions involve uncertainty. But constant use of "it depends" can weaken confidence. A better approach is: "It depends on the risk tolerance and budget timing. Based on the current guest-impact data and the age of the infrastructure, my recommendation is to approve phase one now and schedule phase two for the next budget cycle."

The fifth is hiding bad news. Executives can accept problems when they are informed early and presented with mitigation options. Surprises destroy trust.

EXECUTIVE TRUST AND CREDIBILITY

Trust is one of the most important assets in IT governance. Executives trust IT when IT speaks their language, communicates risk transparently, avoids surprises and follows through on commitments.

Speaking the executive language means leading with business outcomes. A cybersecurity project protects brand trust. A network investment protects guest satisfaction and operational continuity. A

PMS replacement enables future growth and reduces manual work. A dashboard improves decision speed and reporting consistency.

Transparent risk communication means explaining problems early. If a project is behind schedule, the steering committee should know before the go-live date is threatened. If a vendor is underperforming, leadership should know before guest impact occurs. If cybersecurity risk is rising, executives need a clear mitigation plan.

No surprises means that IT governance should create visibility. Executives do not want to discover a major issue through guest complaints, media exposure, owner escalation or audit findings. They expect internal systems to surface risk before it becomes crisis.

Credibility also depends on delivery. If IT repeatedly overpromises, trust declines. If IT explains trade-offs honestly, provides realistic timelines and delivers stable improvements, trust grows.

In hospitality, trust between IT and operations is especially important because technology is experienced through service. A system may be technically stable, but if staff find it unusable, the business result is weak. Executive credibility requires listening to both technical teams and operational users.

CASE STUDY: THE GRANDSTAY HOTELS

Consider a rapidly expanding European hotel chain with fifteen premium properties. The group has grown quickly through acquisitions and management contracts. Some hotels are recently renovated. Others operate with legacy systems. The brand wants to position itself as modern, reliable and guest-focused, but technology weaknesses are becoming visible.

Three critical issues have reached the Executive Committee.

First, guest WiFi complaints are increasing. Business travelers complain about unstable connections during video calls. Leisure guests complain about slow streaming. Meeting planners have raised concerns about conference connectivity. Online reviews mention WiFi more often than before. The operations team argues that WiFi is now affecting satisfaction scores.

Second, the PMS infrastructure is aging. Some properties use outdated versions. Interfaces with POS, CRM and reporting systems are inconsistent. Staff rely on manual workarounds. New guest services are difficult to deploy because the core system is not flexible enough. The IT Director warns that modernization is necessary for future growth.

Third, cyber risk is rising. Legacy systems, inconsistent access controls, older operating environments and fragmented vendor support create exposure. The Legal and Risk team worries about guest data, payment flows and incident readiness. Recent industry breaches have increased owner concern.

The Executive Committee has a budget of 500,000 euros. It cannot fully solve all three problems at once. The question is simple and difficult: what should be done first?

A weak response would choose based on personal preference. The GM may choose WiFi because complaints are visible. The IT Director may choose PMS because architecture is foundational. Legal may choose cybersecurity because risk is serious. The CFO may delay everything because the budget is limited.

A stronger response uses executive decision criteria.

Guest impact asks which issue is already affecting the customer. WiFi has visible guest impact and may affect reviews, corporate retention and brand perception.

Operational impact asks which issue affects internal efficiency. PMS limitations may create manual work, integration issues and future deployment constraints.

Risk exposure asks which issue could create severe downside. Cybersecurity may not generate daily complaints, but a major incident could damage the brand, trigger legal obligations and disrupt operations.

Strategic scalability asks which investment supports future growth. PMS modernization may enable expansion, consistent reporting and group standards.

Financial logic asks which investment has measurable return, which risk is unacceptable and whether phasing is possible.

A strong recommendation might be phased. For example, the Executive Committee could approve an immediate cybersecurity baseline program across all properties to address critical vulnerabilities, allocate a focused WiFi upgrade to the highest-risk properties affecting corporate accounts, and launch a PMS modernization assessment with vendor selection for the next investment cycle. Another committee might prioritize WiFi first if guest dissatisfaction is directly threatening revenue, while approving minimum cybersecurity controls as non-negotiable. A third might prioritize PMS if growth strategy depends on standardization.

There is no universal answer. The quality of the decision depends on the quality of the reasoning.

PREPARING AN EXECUTIVE RECOMMENDATION

When preparing a recommendation for GrandStay Hotels, the presenter should avoid technical overload. The briefing should be clear, structured and decisive.

A possible opening context might be: "GrandStay is facing three technology issues that affect guest satisfaction, operational scalability and cyber exposure. With 500,000 euros available, we cannot solve all three fully. We need a phased decision that protects the brand now while preparing the group for growth."

The risk explanation might be: "WiFi complaints are already visible in reviews and corporate feedback. PMS limitations are slowing integration and future service innovation. Cybersecurity gaps create low-frequency but high-severity exposure. The risk of doing nothing is not neutral; it means accepting continued guest dissatisfaction, operational workarounds and increasing cyber vulnerability."

The options might be: "Option one is to prioritize guest-facing WiFi upgrades. This has immediate satisfaction impact but leaves PMS and cyber risk partly unresolved. Option two is to prioritize PMS modernization. This supports long-term scalability but may not solve immediate WiFi complaints. Option three is a balanced phased approach: fix critical cyber gaps, upgrade WiFi in the highest-impact properties and prepare PMS replacement through a structured roadmap."

The recommendation might be: "I recommend option three. It protects the business against severe cyber risk, addresses the most visible guest pain points and avoids rushing a PMS replacement without proper vendor selection. This is the best balance between risk, guest impact and strategic readiness."

The decision needed might be: "We ask the committee to approve the 500,000 euro phase-one envelope, authorize vendor negotiations for WiFi upgrades and cybersecurity remediation, and approve a PMS roadmap to be presented in the next budget cycle."

This is executive language. It gives context, options, recommendation and decision.

THE ROLE OF POSTURE IN IT LEADERSHIP

Executive communication is not only content. It is also posture. Posture means the way a manager carries the discussion: calm, clear, prepared, concise and responsible.

A strong posture does not mean pretending to know everything. It means knowing what decision is required, what evidence supports the recommendation, what risks remain and who must be involved.

In hospitality, posture matters because technology decisions often affect multiple departments. A Front Office Manager may resist a PMS change because it disrupts routines. Finance may worry about reporting. Housekeeping may worry about room-status workflows. Sales may worry about CRM integration. Owners may worry about capital expenditure. The executive communicator must hold these perspectives together.

A credible presenter does not attack other departments. They frame shared business outcomes. Instead of saying, "Operations does not understand the system," they say, "The success of this project depends on operational adoption, so training and process redesign must be included in the budget." Instead of saying, "Finance blocks IT," they say, "The financial concern is valid, so we propose a phased investment with measurable checkpoints."

Posture turns technology into leadership.

Hospitality Applications Across Departments

Executive IT vocabulary becomes useful when it is applied to the departments that actually run a hotel. A hotel is not a single process. It is a collection of service moments, commercial decisions, financial controls and operational dependencies. Each department experiences technology differently, and each department needs a different translation of IT value.

For Front Office, technology is about arrival quality, guest recognition, room assignment, payment authorization and issue resolution. A PMS delay is not a technical inconvenience for the front desk. It is a lobby problem. It creates waiting, pressure, apologies and emotional friction. When briefing executives, a Front Office technology issue should be described in terms of queue time, guest satisfaction, room readiness, service recovery and brand first impression.

For Housekeeping, technology is about room status, prioritization, productivity, inspection, maintenance alerts and communication. A housekeeping application is not simply a tablet system. It is a coordination mechanism between occupancy, arrivals, departures, VIP priorities and labor deployment. If it works well, rooms are released faster and staff coordination improves. If it works poorly, the hotel may have clean rooms that are not visible in the PMS, guests waiting for rooms that are physically ready, or supervisors manually chasing updates.

For Food and Beverage, technology is about POS reliability, menu management, room-charge posting, revenue control, inventory, kitchen communication and guest billing accuracy. If POS and PMS do not communicate reliably, the impact appears as wrong invoices, delayed checkout, manual corrections and potential revenue leakage.

The executive language is not "interface issue." It is "billing accuracy and revenue integrity."

For Sales and Marketing, technology is about CRM quality, segmentation, campaign execution, lead tracking, corporate account management and loyalty communication. If data is duplicated, outdated or fragmented, marketing personalization becomes weak and sales reporting becomes unreliable. The executive language is not "data hygiene." It is "commercial relevance and account intelligence."

For Revenue Management, technology is about demand signals, rate accuracy, distribution control, channel cost and forecasting. Poor integrations between PMS, CRS, channel manager and revenue management system can result in wrong availability, rate parity issues or missed pricing opportunities. The executive language is "revenue optimization and distribution control."

For Finance, technology is about reconciliations, audit trails, revenue recognition, cost control, payment flows, invoice accuracy and reporting deadlines. Finance does not only need systems that work. It needs systems that produce reliable evidence. The executive language is "financial control and management confidence."

For Human Resources, technology is about scheduling, payroll, onboarding, training, access rights and employee lifecycle management. When an employee leaves, their system access must be removed. When a new employee starts, their access must match their role. Weak HR-IT coordination becomes a security risk. The executive language is "people risk and access governance."

For Engineering and Maintenance, technology is about work orders, asset management, preventive maintenance, energy systems, guest-room equipment and critical alarms. A maintenance platform is not only a tool for technicians. It supports asset protection and guest comfort. The executive language is "asset reliability and service continuity."

The strongest hospitality IT leaders can translate the same technology issue differently depending on the audience, while keeping one consistent business message.

Governance Maturity in Hotel Groups

A single independent hotel and a multi-property hotel group do not need exactly the same governance model. However, both need maturity. Governance maturity refers to the organization's ability to make technology decisions deliberately rather than reactively.

At a low maturity level, technology decisions are often informal. A property buys systems when problems become urgent. Vendor selection may depend on personal relationships or immediate price. Documentation is limited. Access rights are not reviewed regularly. Dashboards are weak. Projects depend on individuals rather than process. This model may function while the hotel is small, but it becomes fragile as complexity grows.

At an intermediate maturity level, the hotel has clearer responsibilities. Major systems are documented. Support contracts exist. Budgets are reviewed annually. Vendors are evaluated. Cybersecurity is discussed. Data protection is better understood. However, decisions may still be fragmented across departments.

At a higher maturity level, technology is governed strategically. The organization has a technology roadmap, a steering committee, a vendor portfolio, data governance standards, cybersecurity oversight, project prioritization criteria, change management processes and executive dashboards. Technology decisions are linked to brand positioning, expansion strategy, guest experience and financial planning.

Hotel groups need this maturity because inconsistency multiplies across properties. If each hotel selects its own tools without shared standards, the group may face incompatible systems, inconsistent reporting, duplicated contracts, weak negotiating power and uneven guest experience. At the same time, excessive central control may ignore local operating realities. Mature governance does not mean centralizing everything. It means defining which decisions belong at group level and which belong at property level.

For example, cybersecurity standards, data protection requirements, core PMS strategy and reporting definitions may need strong central governance. Local service workflows, training details, guest-facing configurations or property-specific enhancements may allow more flexibility. Governance maturity is the art of knowing the difference.

The Owner and Asset Manager Perspective

Hospitality executives must also understand how owners and asset managers hear IT proposals. Owners may not be interested in the technical elegance of a system. They want to know how the decision protects asset value, supports brand positioning, reduces risk, improves profitability or prepares the property for future transactions.

An owner may ask: Will this investment increase revenue? Will it reduce operating cost? Will it protect the brand agreement? Will it reduce insurance or legal exposure? Will it help retain corporate accounts? Will it extend the useful life of the asset? Will it be obsolete in three years? Is the operator asking for a necessary investment or simply a preferred system?

Asset managers often evaluate technology through performance and risk. A WiFi upgrade may be justified if it protects business traveler satisfaction and meeting revenue. A PMS replacement may be justified if it improves reporting, reduces manual work and supports revenue management. A cybersecurity investment may be justified if the downside risk is severe even when the direct financial return is hard to calculate.

This perspective matters because many hotel technology decisions involve ownership approval. A General Manager who can speak only from operational frustration may struggle to obtain funding. A General Manager who can connect technology to RevPAR, GOP, guest satisfaction, risk exposure, brand standards and asset value will be more persuasive.

Change Management and Adoption

Even the best technology decision can fail if people do not adopt it. This is one of the most underestimated aspects of IT governance in hospitality. Hotels are human organizations. Systems are used under pressure, during service peaks, by employees with different levels of digital confidence, across departments that may not interpret the same process in the same way.

A PMS replacement, a new housekeeping platform, a CRM upgrade or a digital payment process can change routines that employees have used for years. Resistance is not always irrational. Staff may fear slower service, loss of control, additional reporting, poor training or being blamed for system issues. Managers must therefore treat technology implementation as organizational change.

Good change management begins before go-live. It includes stakeholder consultation, process mapping, training, super-users, communication, realistic timelines, fallback procedures and post-launch support. It also includes listening to operational feedback. If a system creates more work than it removes, adoption will suffer.

Executive governance should therefore ask not only, "Is the system ready?" but also, "Is the organization ready?" A technically ready system can still fail if the hotel is not ready to absorb it.

This is especially true in luxury hospitality, where service flow and emotional intelligence matter. Technology should not make staff look less confident in front of guests. If employees struggle with a tool during service, the guest does not blame the software. The guest perceives the hotel as disorganized.

From Information to Decision

The final skill of executive IT leadership is converting information into decision. Many meetings fail because they stop at information. Participants know the problem, discuss the options and agree that something must be done, but no decision is made.

A decision-ready IT proposal should include the issue, the business impact, the options, the recommendation, the cost, the risk of delay, the implementation approach and the exact approval requested. It should also state what will be measured after approval.

For example, a WiFi proposal should not simply request funding for access points. It should explain the guest problem, review data, conference impact, bandwidth usage, coverage audit, investment options, implementation timeline, expected improvement, disruption plan and post-implementation KPIs.

A cybersecurity proposal should not simply list tools. It should explain exposure, likelihood, potential impact, minimum controls, insurance implications, compliance concerns, incident readiness and executive accountability.

A PMS proposal should not simply present vendor features. It should explain operational limitations, reporting weaknesses, integration needs, scalability requirements, training implications, migration risk and future growth value.

Executives respect clarity because clarity reduces perceived risk. When a proposal is clear, the committee may still say no. But the discussion becomes strategic rather than confused.

MANAGERIAL TAKEAWAYS

The first takeaway is that executives want decisions, not technology lectures. Technical information is useful only when it supports a business choice.

The second takeaway is that language can make or break an IT project. A good idea explained poorly may fail. A complex project explained clearly may gain support.

The third takeaway is that governance is not bureaucracy. It is a decision system. It helps the organization prioritize, allocate resources, manage risk and maintain accountability.

The fourth takeaway is that vendor management is strategic. Hotels depend on external providers, but dependency must be controlled through contracts, SLAs, exit strategies, performance reviews and data portability.

The fifth takeaway is that executive trust is built through transparency. Bad news should travel early, accompanied by options. Hidden risk becomes crisis.

The sixth takeaway is that hospitality IT must always connect back to the guest, the employee, the owner and the brand. Technology that cannot be connected to these dimensions may not deserve executive attention.

The final takeaway is that future hospitality leaders do not need to speak like technicians. They need to speak clearly enough to make technology decisions responsibly.

TO REVIEW THIS CHAPTER

KEY TERMS

IT Governance : The system of roles, forums, policies, processes and decision rules used to align technology with business objectives, manage risk, control budgets and ensure accountability.

Executive Communication : The ability to translate technical information into concise business language focused on outcomes, risks, options and decisions.

Steering Committee : A cross-functional governance forum where leadership reviews technology priorities, budgets, risks, projects, vendor performance and required decisions.

OPEX : Operating expenditure. Recurring costs such as subscriptions, licenses, support contracts, maintenance, cloud services and managed services.

CAPEX : Capital expenditure. Long-term investment in assets such as infrastructure, equipment, major implementation projects or property-level technology upgrades.

SLA - Service Level Agreement : A contractual agreement defining expected service performance, such as uptime, response time, resolution time, escalation procedures and penalties.

Downtime : A period during which a system is unavailable or not functioning properly. In hotels, downtime may affect check-in, billing, payments, reporting, guest WiFi or operations.

Scalability : The ability of a system or architecture to grow with business needs without major redesign or disruption.

Vendor Lock-in : A dependency situation where switching providers becomes difficult, expensive or operationally risky.

ROI - Return on Investment : A measure of the value generated by an investment compared with its cost. In IT, ROI may include revenue gains, cost savings, risk reduction and improved efficiency.

TCO - Total Cost of Ownership : The full cost of a system over time, including purchase, implementation, licenses, training, integration, support, maintenance, upgrades and exit costs.

API - Application Programming Interface : A mechanism that allows systems to exchange data. In hotels, APIs often support communication between PMS, POS, CRM, booking engines and reporting systems.

Business Continuity : The ability of the hotel to continue operating during or after disruption, using backup systems, manual procedures, crisis roles and recovery plans.

Data Governance : The way data is collected, stored, accessed, protected, used, retained and deleted across the organization.

Executive Dashboard : A concise visual tool showing key indicators, risks, trends and decisions required for leadership oversight.

REFLECTION QUESTIONS

- Why do many executives struggle with IT topics even when they are strong business leaders?
- How can a technical issue such as server uptime be translated into business language?

- Why should IT projects be framed around business outcomes rather than system features?
- Which IT KPIs would be most useful to a General Manager? Which would be less useful?
- Why is vendor lock-in a strategic risk for hotel groups?
- How can a steering committee help prevent fragmented technology decisions across properties?
- Why is "it depends" often a weak answer in executive presentations, even when the situation is complex?
- What makes a technology dashboard useful for executives?
- How can IT leaders build trust with Operations, Finance and ownership?
- In the GrandStay Hotels case, which investment would you prioritize first and why?

REVIEW QUESTIONS

- Define IT governance in a hospitality context.
- Explain the difference between technical language and executive language.
- Give three examples of translating IT issues into business outcomes.
- Identify five essential IT vocabulary terms that hotel executives should understand.
- Explain the difference between OPEX and CAPEX.
- What is an SLA and why does it matter in hotel technology management?
- What are the main purposes of an IT steering committee?
- Name four IT KPIs that executives can understand and use.
- Explain why vendor management is a strategic responsibility.

- Describe the five-minute executive briefing structure.

REFERENCES AND FURTHER READING

ISACA. COBIT 2019 Framework: Governance and Management Objectives. A widely used framework for governance and management of enterprise information and technology, useful for understanding how IT aligns with business goals, value delivery and risk management.

PeopleCert. ITIL 4 Foundation and ITIL 4 Service Level Management resources. These resources explain service management, value, outcomes, service levels and the role of service-level agreements in managing digital services.

Hospitality Financial and Technology Professionals (HFTP). Professional resources for hospitality finance and technology leaders, useful for understanding the intersection of technology, financial discipline and hospitality management.

American Hotel & Lodging Association / HTNG. HTNG Technology Resources and Technical Specifications. These resources support hospitality technology standards, interoperability and industry-specific technology practices.

National Institute of Standards and Technology. Cybersecurity Framework 2.0. A useful reference for linking technology governance, risk management, cybersecurity oversight and executive accountability.

Oracle Hospitality. Hospitality technology resources on PMS, cloud platforms and operational systems. These materials support understanding of hotel systems, integration needs and technology value in hotel operations.

Chapter 8

IT Financial Management: OPEX, CAPEX & ROI

Why IT Decisions Are Never Just Technical

LEARNING OBJECTIVES

By the end of this chapter, you should be able to explain why hospitality IT has become a major financial management topic; distinguish between CAPEX and OPEX in technology decisions; evaluate SaaS and cloud proposals with financial discipline; identify visible and hidden IT costs; assess the complexity of ROI in hotel technology investments; include risk, guest experience, staff adoption and business continuity in an IT business case; understand how General Managers, CFOs, owners, asset managers and IT leaders view the same investment differently; and prepare a clear executive recommendation on whether to invest, postpone, phase or redesign a major hospitality IT project.

OPENING PERSPECTIVE

Technology decisions in hotels are often presented as technical questions. Should the property replace its PMS? Should the hotel move to a cloud-based system? Should WiFi infrastructure be upgraded now or next year? Should cybersecurity spending be increased? Should the property accept a SaaS proposal from a vendor? Should the current POS be integrated with the accounting system? Should a regional office standardize systems across all hotels?

These questions may sound technical, but they are financial and strategic questions first. Each one affects cash flow, profit and loss, EBITDA, owner expectations, asset value, guest satisfaction, staff productivity, operational risk and brand reputation. A technology investment can protect revenue, reduce manual work, support growth, improve guest experience and lower risk. It can also create long-term subscription dependency, implementation disruption, training costs, integration complexity and vendor lock-in.

In hospitality, IT financial management is not about choosing the cheapest option. It is about understanding the full cost of a decision and the full cost of not deciding. A hotel can lose money by investing too early in a poorly prepared system. It can also lose money by postponing a necessary upgrade until the cost of failure becomes much higher than the cost of prevention.

The strongest hospitality executives do not ask only, "How much does it cost?" They ask, "What value does it create? What risk does it reduce? What operational problem does it solve? What hidden cost are we not seeing? What happens if we wait?"

This chapter develops the financial logic required to answer those questions.

HOW IT BECAME A FINANCIAL MANAGEMENT TOPIC

For many years, hotel IT was treated as a support function. Technology was often associated with hardware, back-office systems, telephones, servers, cabling, printers, terminals and technical maintenance. Budgets were relatively limited and many decisions could remain within the property or the IT department.

That world has changed. Modern hotels depend on technology for reservations, distribution, revenue management, payments, guest communication, loyalty, cybersecurity, cloud platforms, WiFi, IPTV, telephony, data analytics, housekeeping systems, finance systems, procurement, HR, compliance and reporting. Technology now affects almost every part of hotel performance.

This means that IT is no longer a marginal cost. It has become one of the major investment and operating expense areas for hospitality organizations. The financial question is not only whether the hotel can afford technology. The question is whether the hotel can afford weak technology, fragmented systems, poor data, vulnerable infrastructure or delayed modernization.

The shift from on-premise systems to cloud-based and subscription-based systems has also changed the financial conversation. In the past, many hotel technology investments were structured as capital expenditure: the hotel purchased hardware, installed servers, bought perpetual licenses and depreciated assets over time. Today, many systems are sold as subscriptions: the hotel pays monthly or annually for access, hosting, support and updates. This creates a shift from CAPEX to OPEX.

That shift has advantages. It reduces upfront investment, accelerates deployment, transfers some technical responsibility to vendors and gives hotels access to modern systems without owning the full infrastructure. It also creates new risks. Subscriptions accumulate over time. Pricing can increase. The hotel may become dependent on a vendor. Integrations may cost extra. Exit fees may be high. Data migration may be difficult. What looked cheaper in year one may become more expensive across five or seven years.

Hospitality executives therefore need to understand IT finance at the same level as they understand payroll, rooms revenue, F&B margins, distribution cost, maintenance capex or brand standards. Technology is now part of the economics of the hotel.

WHERE IT COSTS SIT IN A HOTEL P&L

One reason IT spending is difficult to manage is that it is often fragmented. It does not always appear in one clean budget line. Some costs are visible, while others are hidden across departments, projects and contracts.

OPEX may include software subscriptions, cloud hosting, support contracts, managed services, cybersecurity monitoring, internet connectivity, payment processing fees, licensing, help desk support and vendor maintenance.

CAPEX may include network infrastructure, cabling, switches, WiFi access points, servers, in-room technology, telephony equipment, IPTV systems, hardware replacement, major implementation projects and large system migrations.

Hidden costs may include staff training, temporary productivity loss, integration work, data cleaning, vendor workshops, project management, parallel running, consulting, internal meetings, downtime during transition, additional modules, customization, legal review, procurement time and change management.

The financial danger is that each cost may appear reasonable in isolation. A monthly subscription looks manageable. A small integration fee looks acceptable. A training day looks minor. A support contract appears routine. But when all costs are added together, the total technology cost may be much higher than expected.

This is why executives must examine total cost, not only purchase price. A hotel may approve a SaaS platform because the monthly subscription is attractive, then discover that interfaces, data migration, staff training, additional users, premium support and reporting modules significantly increase the real cost.

A second challenge is that IT spending may be split between property-level budgets, regional budgets, brand-level budgets and owner-funded capital projects. The General Manager may see some expenses. The CFO may see others. Corporate IT may negotiate contracts. Owners may approve capital expenditure. Departments may purchase tools independently. Without governance, the organization loses visibility.

A hotel that does not know its true IT cost cannot manage its technology strategy.

WHO DECIDES IT INVESTMENTS?

IT investment decisions involve multiple stakeholders because each stakeholder sees a different part of the value and risk.

The General Manager is concerned with guest experience, operational continuity, staff productivity, service reputation and property performance. For the GM, a PMS replacement is not only a system decision. It affects check-in, billing, reporting, room assignment, staff morale and complaints. A WiFi upgrade is not only a network decision. It affects reviews, meetings, corporate accounts and guest trust.

The CFO is concerned with cash flow, EBITDA, budget classification, ROI, contract commitments, depreciation, recurring costs and financial risk. The CFO will ask whether the investment is CAPEX or OPEX, whether savings are realistic, whether the contract creates long-term obligations and whether the payback is credible.

The owner or asset manager is concerned with asset value, long-term competitiveness, brand compliance, investment horizon, capital allocation and return on invested capital. Owners may be willing to fund technology that protects the asset, supports repositioning, improves market share or reduces operational risk. They may resist investments that appear fashionable, poorly justified or disconnected from financial performance.

The IT leader is concerned with technical feasibility, architecture, cybersecurity, vendor quality, integration, resilience, user support and future scalability. A good IT leader must translate these concerns into financial language. The best IT leaders do not only say, "This system is outdated." They explain what the outdated system is costing the business and what risk it creates.

Operations leaders are concerned with implementation reality. They ask whether staff can absorb the change, whether training is sufficient, whether the timing conflicts with peak season, whether workflows will improve and whether the guest will benefit.

Legal and procurement teams may focus on contracts, data processing, liability, service levels, termination clauses, insurance and compliance obligations.

Because every stakeholder has a different lens, IT financial management requires alignment. A strong business case must speak to all these perspectives.

TYPICAL IT FINANCIAL MISTAKES IN HOTELS

Several financial mistakes appear frequently in hospitality technology decisions.

The first mistake is assuming that SaaS is always cheaper. SaaS can reduce upfront cost, but it does not automatically reduce total cost. A subscription of a few thousand euros per month may appear modest, yet over five years it can exceed the cost of a traditional solution. The true comparison must include implementation, integrations, support, user licenses, price escalation, data migration and exit costs.

The second mistake is ignoring integration costs. Hotels rarely operate one system alone. A PMS may need to connect with POS, CRS, channel manager, payment gateway, CRM, revenue management, accounting, housekeeping, key card, IPTV, guest app and reporting tools. Each interface may create cost, testing, support dependency and maintenance. A system that is inexpensive but difficult to integrate can become financially dangerous.

The third mistake is underestimating change management. Hotels are human organizations. Staff must learn new workflows, managers must adapt reporting, supervisors must support adoption and guests must not feel disruption. Training, communication and stabilization time are not optional. If they are excluded from the financial plan, the project may look profitable on paper and fail in reality.

The fourth mistake is postponing critical decisions. Delaying investment may protect cash in the short term, but it can create technical debt. Technical debt is the accumulation of outdated systems, manual workarounds, unsupported software, weak interfaces, security exposure and operational inefficiency. Like financial debt, it grows quietly until it becomes expensive.

The fifth mistake is approving projects based on vendor promises rather than internal readiness. A vendor may present strong features and attractive return estimates, but the hotel must ask whether its data is clean, whether staff are prepared, whether interfaces exist, whether governance is strong and whether the operating model can absorb the change.

The sixth mistake is measuring ROI too narrowly. Some technology investments do not directly create new revenue, yet they protect revenue, reduce risk, preserve guest trust or avoid operational disruption. Cybersecurity, compliance, backup systems and business continuity may not produce visible daily income, but their absence can create catastrophic losses.

Good IT finance requires seeing beyond the invoice.

CAPEX EXPLAINED FOR HOSPITALITY MANAGERS

CAPEX means capital expenditure. It refers to spending on assets that create value over several years. In hotels, CAPEX is often associated with renovations, furniture, equipment, building systems and major technology infrastructure. In IT, CAPEX may include network infrastructure, servers, cabling, access points, telephony equipment, IPTV hardware, major implementations, large system migrations and sometimes perpetual software licenses.

The key feature of CAPEX is that it is usually an upfront investment. The hotel or owner pays a significant amount at the beginning, and the asset is then depreciated over its useful life. This means the expense is not fully recognized in the P&L immediately; it appears over time through depreciation.

From an owner or asset management perspective, CAPEX can be attractive when it improves asset quality, extends useful life, supports brand compliance, protects competitiveness or reduces future operating risk. A network upgrade, for example, may not generate revenue directly, but it may protect guest satisfaction, meetings business, employee productivity and cloud system reliability.

CAPEX also has disadvantages. It requires cash availability and often a higher approval threshold. Owners may compare technology CAPEX with other capital needs such as rooms renovation, bathroom upgrades, F&B concepts, spa improvements, energy systems or building repairs. Technology projects must compete for capital against visible guest-facing improvements.

This creates a challenge for IT leaders. A renovated lobby is visible. A stronger network core is invisible until it fails. A new suite design is easier to photograph than a cybersecurity upgrade. Yet invisible technology may protect the visible experience.

A good CAPEX business case must therefore explain the operational and financial consequences of underinvestment. It should show what the investment protects, what it enables and what risk it reduces.

OPEX EXPLAINED FOR HOSPITALITY MANAGERS

OPEX means operating expenditure. It refers to recurring expenses that are recognized in the profit and loss statement as they occur. In hospitality IT, OPEX commonly includes SaaS subscriptions, cloud hosting, software licenses, support contracts, managed services, cybersecurity monitoring, internet service, telecom services, vendor maintenance and per-transaction fees.

The main advantage of OPEX is lower initial cash impact. A hotel can access modern technology without buying servers, installing major infrastructure or paying a large license fee upfront. This can be especially attractive for independent hotels, management companies, fast-growing groups and properties with limited capital reserves.

OPEX can also improve predictability. Monthly or annual fees make budgeting easier. Vendor-managed systems reduce the need for internal technical talent. Updates and maintenance may be included. Deployment may be faster. For cloud systems, authorized users can access the platform from multiple locations, which helps regional offices and multi-property management.

However, OPEX can become a long-term financial drain. Subscriptions continue every year. Fees may increase when the hotel adds rooms, users, features or integrations. Transaction-based pricing may grow with business volume. A system that is easy to approve initially may become difficult to remove once staff, data and workflows depend on it.

The financial trap is psychological. A large CAPEX amount triggers scrutiny because it looks expensive. A monthly OPEX amount may seem harmless. Yet the total cost over a contract term may be higher than expected.

Executives should therefore ask: What is the annual cost? What is the three-year cost? What is the five-year cost? What is included? What is excluded? What happens if we add users? What happens if prices increase? What is the exit cost? What internal work is required?

OPEX increases agility, but it can also create dependency.

CAPEX VS OPEX: THE EXECUTIVE COMPARISON

The CAPEX versus OPEX decision is not a simple question of old versus modern. It is a question of cash, control, flexibility, accounting treatment, risk and strategy.

CAPEX usually creates a higher upfront cash requirement. It may be harder to approve because it competes with other capital projects. It may give the hotel more control over assets and infrastructure, but it can also expose the property to obsolescence if the technology becomes outdated before the investment is fully useful.

OPEX usually reduces the initial barrier to adoption. It supports speed, scalability and vendor-managed delivery. Yet it creates recurring P&L impact and may increase dependency on vendors. It may appear flexible, but contract terms, data migration and operational dependency can make exit difficult.

From a cash flow perspective, OPEX preserves capital at the beginning but creates continuous drain. CAPEX consumes capital upfront but may have lower ongoing operating cost.

From a risk perspective, CAPEX may expose the hotel to ownership of aging technology. OPEX may expose the hotel to vendor dependency, price increases, service outages and contract limitations.

From a strategic perspective, the right choice depends on context. A single independent hotel with limited cash may prefer SaaS for speed and lower initial investment. A hotel group with many properties may prefer standardized cloud platforms for scalability and reporting. A resort in a location with unreliable internet may require stronger local fallback capabilities. A luxury hotel may prioritize resilience and guest experience over the lowest cost model.

The best executives do not ask whether CAPEX or OPEX is better in general. They ask which model fits the asset, the brand, the risk profile, the ownership strategy and the operational reality.

SAAS MODELS IN HOSPITALITY

SaaS means Software as a Service. Instead of buying and installing software locally, the hotel subscribes to software hosted and maintained by the provider. SaaS is now common across hospitality: PMS, revenue management systems, CRM, POS, channel management, reputation management, HR, finance, procurement, housekeeping, maintenance and guest messaging.

SaaS pricing varies. Some vendors charge per room. Others charge per user, per property, per transaction, per booking, per module or by feature tier. Some pricing combines a base subscription with additional fees for implementation, integrations, support, reporting, premium modules, onboarding or storage.

The phrase "all inclusive" should always be examined carefully. In hospitality technology, all inclusive rarely means everything the hotel will need. Interfaces may be extra. Data migration may be extra. Training may be extra. Custom reports may be extra. Premium support may be extra. Payment integrations may be extra. API access may be extra. Multi-property consolidation may be extra.

This does not mean SaaS is bad. SaaS often makes sense. It can provide faster updates, access from anywhere, vendor-managed infrastructure, lower internal IT burden, scalability, standardization and improved innovation cycles. Many hotel groups adopt SaaS because they lack internal technical talent, want predictable budgeting, need faster deployment and prefer vendors to carry infrastructure responsibility.

But SaaS must be evaluated with rigor. The hotel must understand not only the subscription but the full relationship. What service levels are guaranteed? Where is the data hosted? Who owns the data? How can data be exported? What happens if the vendor is acquired? How are price increases handled? What is the minimum term? What penalties apply? What happens during an outage? What support is available during peak hotel operations?

SaaS is not simply a technology model. It is a financial and contractual model.

THE REAL ROI PROBLEM IN HOSPITALITY IT

ROI means return on investment. In simple terms, it asks whether the value generated by an investment justifies its cost. In hotel technology, ROI is often harder to calculate than in other investments because the benefits are not always direct, immediate or easy to isolate.

Some IT investments generate direct financial return. A revenue management system may improve pricing decisions. A pre-arrival upsell platform may increase ancillary revenue. A channel management tool may reduce distribution errors. A payment automation tool may reduce administrative work. These projects may produce measurable gains.

Other IT investments produce indirect value. A WiFi upgrade may improve reviews and corporate guest satisfaction. A PMS replacement may reduce staff frustration and manual work. A CRM enhancement may improve guest recognition and repeat stays. A cybersecurity project may prevent losses that never appear because the incident never occurs.

This creates a problem: prevention is difficult to prove. If a cybersecurity investment prevents a ransomware incident, the hotel may never see the avoided loss. If a backup system prevents a long outage, the success is invisible. If a compliance project avoids penalties, the value is the absence of failure.

Hospitality executives must therefore use several ROI categories, not just one.

Financial ROI includes direct cost reduction, labor savings, revenue gains, upsell revenue, fewer errors, lower maintenance cost or reduced support hours.

Operational ROI includes time saved, smoother workflows, faster check-in, reduced manual reconciliation, fewer workarounds, better reporting and improved coordination between departments.

Guest experience ROI includes higher satisfaction, better reviews, repeat bookings, loyalty, stronger corporate account retention, fewer complaints and improved perceived value.

Risk mitigation ROI includes cybersecurity protection, compliance, business continuity, reduced downtime, insurance alignment, data protection and avoidance of regulatory or reputational damage.

A credible IT business case should identify which type of ROI is being claimed. Not every project must generate immediate revenue. But every project must have a clear value logic.

HIDDEN COSTS EXECUTIVES MUST CONSIDER

The visible cost of a technology project is usually the easiest cost to understand. The hidden costs are the ones that damage budgets and credibility.

Integration complexity is often the largest hidden cost. A new PMS may require interfaces with POS, CRS, channel manager, payment gateway, accounting, CRM, housekeeping, key card system, revenue management and reporting tools. Each interface requires configuration, testing, vendor coordination and future maintenance. Legacy systems may not connect easily. Integration can double or triple the implementation effort.

Training and adoption are another major hidden cost. Staff need time to learn new workflows. Supervisors need to support adoption. Some employees may resist the change. Productivity may drop during the transition. Mistakes may increase temporarily. Training must be budgeted as a serious operational requirement, not as a small final step.

Vendor lock-in creates long-term cost. Once the hotel depends on a platform, switching may be difficult. Data export may be complicated. Staff may be trained on one system. Interfaces may be specific to one vendor. Contracts may include minimum terms or termination penalties. The cost of exit must be considered before signing.

Contract exit penalties can trap the hotel in underperforming relationships. Early termination fees, data extraction charges, transition support costs and integration rebuilds may make switching financially painful.

Migration downtime can affect guest experience and revenue. A system change during peak season can disrupt operations. Even if the vendor performs well, the hotel must plan for parallel running, cutover windows, emergency fallback and support during stabilization.

Internal time is also a cost. Managers attend workshops. Department heads validate workflows. Finance checks reports. Front office tests scenarios. IT coordinates vendors. Procurement reviews contracts. Legal reviews terms. These hours may not appear on vendor invoices, but they are real.

A project budget that excludes hidden costs is not conservative. It is incomplete.

INVESTMENT ARBITRATION WHEN BUDGET IS LIMITED

Hotels rarely have unlimited budgets. IT investments must compete with rooms renovation, F&B concepts, energy projects, payroll pressure, debt service, marketing, maintenance and owner distributions. When budget is limited, executives need a clear arbitration logic.

The first question is whether the investment is mandatory. Mandatory projects include compliance, cybersecurity, business continuity, payment security, legal requirements, system support end-of-life or operational survival. If a system no longer receives security updates and handles guest data, postponement may be unacceptable even if the financial return is difficult to quantify.

The second question is whether the investment protects revenue. A PMS, CRS, payment platform, channel manager, WiFi network or POS system may directly affect bookings, billing, guest spend or service delivery. If failure would stop revenue, the investment deserves priority.

The third question is whether the investment improves the guest journey in a measurable way. Not every guest-facing technology is strategic. A tool should solve a real friction point, support the brand promise or strengthen satisfaction. A luxury hotel may prioritize discreet personalization. A business hotel may prioritize connectivity and speed. A resort may prioritize mobile service requests and family-friendly access.

The fourth question is whether the investment can wait. Some projects are useful but not urgent. A project that does not reduce risk, protect revenue, improve guest experience or support a strategic plan may be phased or delayed.

This framework helps managers avoid two extremes: approving every technology request because it sounds modern, or rejecting every technology request because it costs money.

IT investment arbitration is the art of saying yes to the right project at the right time, and no to attractive distractions.

THE THREE-SENTENCE EXECUTIVE FRAMEWORK

A strong IT business case should be explainable in three clear sentences.

The first sentence defines the problem: What breaks, fails or remains exposed without this investment?

The second sentence defines the solution: How does the proposed investment fix the issue measurably?

The third sentence defines the return: What financial, operational, strategic or risk-based value will the hotel obtain?

For example: "Our current PMS is 12 years old, creates manual workarounds, slows check-in and no longer supports the integrations required for modern guest service. Replacing it with a cloud-based PMS will reduce manual reconciliation, improve front-office workflows, strengthen system support and enable future integrations. The investment requires a higher first-year cost but reduces operational risk, protects guest satisfaction and supports long-term asset competitiveness."

This structure forces clarity. If an investment cannot be explained this way, either the project is not ready or the business case is weak.

Complexity often hides uncertainty. Clarity demonstrates mastery.

CASE STUDY: PMS REPLACEMENT DECISION

Imagine a 180-room, four-star independent urban hotel. The property runs at an average occupancy of 75 percent. Its current PMS is 12 years old. The system still functions, but limitations are becoming visible. Guest complaints about slow check-in have increased. Staff rely on manual workarounds. Interfaces are unstable. Reports require corrections. The front desk team feels frustrated. The IT support team spends more time maintaining the old system. The hotel's online rating has dropped from 4.2 to 3.8, and some reviews mention slow arrival experience and billing delays.

The executive team must decide whether to replace the PMS now or postpone for 12 months.

A vendor proposes a new SaaS PMS. The monthly subscription is EUR 3,600, calculated at EUR 20 per room. The annual subscription cost is therefore EUR 43,200. The contract requires a three-year minimum commitment. Implementation costs EUR 65,000. Data migration costs EUR 18,000. Staff training costs EUR 12,000. Integration with existing systems costs EUR 22,000. The first-year investment totals EUR 160,200.

The current PMS costs EUR 15,000 per year in maintenance. Additional IT support hours are estimated at EUR 8,000 per year. Manual workarounds create approximately EUR 25,000 per year in labor cost. The visible annual cost of the status quo is therefore about EUR 48,000.

At first glance, postponing looks cheaper. The new PMS costs EUR 112,200 more in year one than the status quo. A CFO under cash pressure may ask why the hotel should spend more now. The owner may prefer to protect EBITDA. The GM may worry about disruption. Staff may resist another system change, especially if previous IT projects failed.

However, the decision cannot be made only by comparing year-one cost. The old PMS creates operational risk, guest experience risk, cyber and compliance risk, staff productivity loss and competitive disadvantage. If security updates are no longer provided, the risk becomes more serious. If the system cannot integrate with modern tools, the hotel may fall behind competitors. If slow check-in continues to damage reviews, pricing power may weaken.

The decision therefore requires a broader financial logic.

READING THE PMS CASE LIKE AN EXECUTIVE

An executive analysis should begin with the problem, not the solution. The problem is not simply that the PMS is old. Many old systems work. The problem is that the system is creating measurable business friction: slow check-in, staff frustration, manual workarounds, unreliable integrations, rising support needs, guest complaints and potential security exposure.

The second step is to separate visible costs from hidden costs. The current system appears to cost EUR 48,000 per year, but this may exclude lost productivity, reputation damage, review impact, missed upsell opportunities, reporting delays, employee frustration and cyber risk. The new system appears to cost EUR 160,200 in year one, but some of that is non-recurring implementation cost. The longer-term comparison should examine annual subscription and support costs, not only first-year transition cost.

The third step is to consider timing. Postponing by 12 months may save cash this year, but it may also increase the cost of future implementation. Staff frustration may grow. Data quality may deteriorate. Security exposure may increase. Vendor support for the old system may weaken. The hotel may face a forced migration later under worse conditions.

The fourth step is to consider change management. Even if the executive team decides to invest, success is not automatic. The hotel must budget training, identify super-users, prepare front desk scenarios, clean data, test integrations, communicate to staff, avoid peak periods for migration and plan stabilization support.

The fifth step is to identify risks accepted and risks avoided. Investing now accepts cash flow pressure, implementation disruption and adoption risk. It avoids growing technical debt, security exposure, guest experience decline and operational inefficiency. Postponing accepts the risk of further complaints, higher manual work, greater cyber exposure and emergency migration. It avoids immediate cash outflow and change fatigue.

There is no perfect answer. But there is a more professional answer: the decision must be justified by numbers, risk and operational reality together.

BUILDING A FINANCIAL RATIONALE

A weak PMS business case might say, "We need a modern PMS because the current one is outdated." This is not enough.

A stronger business case would calculate visible savings and strategic value. For example, if the new PMS reduces manual workaround labor by EUR 25,000 per year and lowers IT support hours by EUR 8,000 per year, it creates EUR 33,000 of identifiable annual benefit. If faster check-in and better guest experience help recover part of the lost rating impact, the indirect revenue upside could be higher. If the system reduces billing errors, accelerates reporting and enables future upsell or CRM integration, the value increases further.

However, executives must avoid unrealistic assumptions. It is dangerous to claim that the new PMS will immediately solve all guest satisfaction problems or generate large revenue gains without evidence. The business case should be credible. It should include conservative assumptions, implementation risk and sensitivity.

A useful structure is to present three scenarios.

A conservative scenario includes only confirmed savings: lower support, reduced manual work and avoided maintenance. This may show a longer payback period.

A realistic scenario adds moderate guest experience improvement, fewer errors and improved staff productivity.

An upside scenario includes successful integration with CRM, upselling tools, mobile check-in or revenue management, creating additional value.

This approach builds trust because it does not oversell the project.

THE ROLE OF TECHNICAL DEBT

Technical debt is one of the most important financial concepts in hospitality IT. It describes the cost of accumulated shortcuts, delays, outdated systems and unresolved weaknesses.

In a hotel, technical debt may appear as unsupported software, old network equipment, manual data exports, duplicate data entry, shared passwords, unstable interfaces, outdated PMS infrastructure, inconsistent reporting, weak cybersecurity controls or systems that cannot support new guest expectations.

Technical debt is dangerous because it often remains invisible. Operations find workarounds. Staff adapt. Managers accept delays. Finance reconciles manually. Guests tolerate friction until they stop tolerating it. By the time the issue becomes urgent, the cost of correction is higher.

Postponement is sometimes wise. Not every project should be approved immediately. But postponement should be a conscious decision with a known risk, not a default reaction to cost.

A professional executive should ask: If we wait 12 months, what will deteriorate? What risk will increase? What cost may become unavoidable? What guest impact may accumulate? What future project will become harder?

Delay has a price, even when no invoice arrives.

PEOPLE, ADOPTION AND ROI

Technology ROI depends heavily on people. A system does not create value simply because it is installed. It creates value when employees use it properly, managers adapt processes, data quality improves and the organization changes behavior.

This is especially true in hotels because many systems are used under pressure. Front desk agents use PMS during arrivals and departures. F&B teams use POS during service peaks. Housekeeping uses room-status tools during tight turnaround windows. Finance uses reports under deadline. Revenue managers use systems in fast-changing demand conditions. If the system is difficult to use or poorly introduced, the value collapses.

Training should therefore be treated as an investment, not an accessory. The hotel needs role-based training, practice scenarios, super-users, floor support during go-live, escalation channels and post-launch feedback. Managers must explain why the change matters, not only how to use the screens.

Staff resistance also has financial consequences. If employees do not trust the system, they create shadow processes. They keep manual lists. They export data to Excel. They bypass workflows. They call colleagues instead of using the tool. These behaviors reduce ROI and increase risk.

A business case that ignores people is incomplete.

VENDOR PROPOSALS AND EXECUTIVE CHALLENGE

Vendors are essential partners, but their proposals must be challenged. A polished presentation may emphasize benefits while minimizing complexity. Hospitality executives should ask disciplined questions.

What problem does this solution solve for our hotel? Which current cost or risk will disappear? Which new cost or dependency will appear? Which systems must integrate? What is included in the price? What is excluded? How long is implementation? What internal resources are required? What happens if the project runs late? How will staff be trained? What support is available after go-live? What service levels are guaranteed? What are the exit conditions? How do we retrieve our data? What happens if the vendor increases prices? What references can we verify from comparable hotels?

The goal is not to distrust vendors. The goal is to build a professional relationship based on clarity. Strong vendors should welcome precise questions because they reduce future conflict.

Executives should also distinguish between vendor ROI and hotel ROI. A vendor may calculate savings based on ideal usage, perfect data, full adoption and immediate efficiency. The hotel must adjust assumptions to its own reality.

A vendor can provide the tool. The hotel must create the value.

FROM COST CONTROL TO VALUE PROTECTION

A common weakness in hotel technology discussions is that IT is framed mainly as a cost to be reduced. Cost discipline matters, but cost reduction is not the same as value protection. A hotel can reduce IT spending in a way that increases operational risk, damages guest experience, weakens cybersecurity or creates future capital pressure.

For example, reducing WiFi investment may save money in the short term, but if the hotel serves corporate travelers, groups, consultants, airline crews or digital nomads, unreliable connectivity may damage repeat demand. Cutting cybersecurity monitoring may reduce monthly OPEX, but it may increase exposure to ransomware or data breach. Postponing PMS integration may avoid implementation cost, but it may preserve manual reconciliation and reporting errors.

Value protection means asking what the technology is protecting. A payment platform protects revenue collection. A secure network protects data and continuity. A PMS protects operational coordination. A backup solution protects recovery. A WiFi infrastructure protects guest satisfaction and meeting business. A reporting dashboard protects decision quality. A staff scheduling system protects labor efficiency and employee experience.

This does not mean every IT request should be approved. It means that every rejection should also be financially understood. The cost of saying no may be lower cash spending today and higher risk tomorrow.

A mature executive discussion therefore separates waste from protection. Waste is spending that does not solve a business problem, reduce risk, improve guest experience, support compliance or enable strategy. Protection is spending that preserves the hotel's ability to operate, compete and earn.

In financial leadership, the goal is not to spend less on technology. The goal is to spend intelligently on the technologies that matter.

OWNER AND ASSET MANAGER PERSPECTIVE

Hotel owners and asset managers often view IT through a different lens from operators. Operators experience daily friction. Owners focus on asset performance, capital allocation, value creation and investment horizon. Both views are legitimate, but they must be connected.

An owner may ask whether a PMS replacement increases asset value. The operator may answer that it reduces front desk frustration. That answer may be true, but it is not enough. The stronger answer is that the PMS improves operational reliability, supports brand compliance, reduces manual inefficiency, improves reporting quality, enables future guest-facing tools and lowers cyber exposure linked to unsupported systems. This connects operational pain to asset protection.

An asset manager may compare IT investment with rooms renovation. A renovated room may directly support ADR improvement, while a PMS project may feel less visible. The IT business case must therefore explain how technology supports the revenue strategy behind the physical asset. If the hotel invests in renovated rooms but keeps a weak booking engine, poor WiFi or slow check-in, the guest may not experience the full value of the renovation. Technology can either reinforce or undermine physical capital investment.

Owners also care about timing. If the investment horizon is short, they may be reluctant to approve major systems with long payback. If the asset is being repositioned, rebranded or prepared for sale, technology quality can influence due diligence, brand requirements, operational credibility and buyer confidence. A property with weak systems, security gaps and poor data can carry hidden liabilities.

For this reason, technology should be part of asset planning. It should not be treated as a last-minute operating request. The property improvement plan, brand standards, distribution strategy, cybersecurity posture and technology roadmap should speak to each other.

PHASING, POSTPONING OR REDESIGNING AN INVESTMENT

Executive decision-making is not limited to yes or no. Many IT decisions have at least four possible outcomes: invest now, postpone, phase the project or redesign the proposal.

Investing now is appropriate when the risk is immediate, the business case is clear, the organization is ready and delay would increase exposure. Examples include unsupported systems handling sensitive data, cybersecurity vulnerabilities, payment compliance issues, network failures affecting guests, or a PMS that blocks essential operations.

Postponing may be appropriate when the project is useful but not urgent, when data readiness is weak, when staff cannot absorb the change, when vendor terms are unclear, or when the business case depends on unrealistic assumptions. Postponement should not be passive. It should include a date for reassessment, risk monitoring and actions to improve readiness.

Phasing is often the best option for complex projects. A hotel may begin with data cleaning, interface mapping and staff training before full migration. A hotel group may roll out a new PMS to one pilot property before all properties. A cybersecurity program may prioritize identity access management and backups before advanced analytics. Phasing reduces risk and allows learning.

Redesigning the proposal may be necessary when the original scope is too large, too expensive or too dependent on uncertain benefits. A vendor may propose a full suite, while the hotel may only need three critical modules. A regional office may want complete standardization, while a hybrid model may better fit property diversity. A project should be shaped around business need, not vendor catalogue.

The executive question is therefore not simply, "Do we approve this?" It is, "What is the smartest way to create value while controlling risk, cash impact and organizational absorption?"

PRESENTING IT FINANCE TO A BOARD

A board or ownership presentation requires a different style from an operational meeting. The speaker must be concise, financially clear and explicit about trade-offs. The objective is not to prove technical knowledge. The objective is to make a decision possible.

A strong board presentation begins with the business problem. For example: "Our current PMS is creating increasing check-in delays, manual workarounds and security exposure." This immediately frames the issue as performance and risk.

The second step is to present options. Option one may be to maintain the current system for another year. Option two may be to replace it immediately. Option three may be to phase replacement over a defined timeline. Each option should include cost, risk, operational impact and management recommendation.

The third step is to quantify what can be quantified and qualify what cannot. Labor savings, maintenance cost, implementation cost and subscription cost can often be estimated. Reputation impact, guest satisfaction improvement and risk avoidance may require proxy indicators such as reviews, complaint trends, incident likelihood or audit findings. Executives should be honest about uncertainty without becoming vague.

The fourth step is to state the recommendation clearly. A board does not need a list of technical possibilities. It needs a position: "We recommend investing now, with a phased implementation after peak season, because the incremental year-one cost is justified by reduced operational risk, security exposure and guest satisfaction decline."

The fifth step is to explain governance. Who owns the project? What is the timeline? What are the risk controls? What are the success metrics? When will the board receive an update? How will benefits be measured after implementation?

This discipline builds credibility. It shows that technology leadership is not about enthusiasm for systems. It is about responsible business management.

MANAGERIAL TAKEAWAYS

The first takeaway is that IT finance is strategic leadership. Technology investments affect cash flow, operations, guest experience, risk, compliance and asset value. They must be treated with the same seriousness as any major business decision.

The second takeaway is that SaaS is not cheaper by default. It may be faster, more scalable and easier to adopt, but total cost depends on contract length, integrations, modules, support, price escalation and exit conditions.

The third takeaway is that ROI must include risk and people. A narrow financial calculation may miss cybersecurity exposure, compliance risk, business continuity, staff adoption and guest experience.

The fourth takeaway is that hidden costs determine success. Integration, training, migration, downtime, vendor dependency and internal time must be budgeted realistically.

The fifth takeaway is that delay has a cost. Postponing a decision may preserve cash today while accumulating technical debt and competitive disadvantage tomorrow.

The sixth takeaway is that executives must communicate IT value clearly. A strong technology recommendation should explain the problem, the solution and the return in simple business language.

In hospitality, IT decisions are never just technical. They are choices about the kind of hotel the organization wants to operate, the risks it is willing to accept and the value it is prepared to protect.

TO REVIEW THIS CHAPTER

KEY TERMS

CAPEX : Capital expenditure. Spending on long-term assets that create value over several years, often requiring higher approval and usually depreciated over time.

OPEX : Operating expenditure. Recurring expense recognized in the profit and loss statement, such as SaaS subscriptions, support contracts, cloud hosting or managed services.

SaaS : Software as a Service. A subscription-based model in which software is hosted and maintained by the vendor rather than installed and fully managed on the hotel property.

ROI : Return on Investment. A measure of the value generated by an investment compared with its cost. In IT, ROI may be financial, operational, guest-experience related or risk-based.

TCO : Total Cost of Ownership. The full cost of a technology solution, including purchase or subscription, implementation, integration, training, support, maintenance, internal time and exit costs.

EBITDA : Earnings Before Interest, Taxes, Depreciation and Amortization. A key profitability measure often used by owners and asset managers to assess operating performance.

Technical Debt : The accumulated cost and risk created by outdated systems, workarounds, unsupported software, weak integrations or postponed technology decisions.

Vendor Lock-In : A situation in which the hotel becomes dependent on a provider and changing vendor becomes difficult, expensive or operationally risky.

Integration Cost : The cost of connecting one system to another, including configuration, testing, vendor coordination, interface maintenance and troubleshooting.

Implementation Cost : The cost required to deploy a new system, including project management, configuration, data migration, testing, training and go-live support.

Data Migration : The process of transferring information from an old system to a new system. It often requires cleaning, mapping, testing and validation.

Change Management : The structured process of helping employees and the organization adopt a new system, workflow or operating model.

Payback Period : The time required for an investment to recover its cost through savings, revenue gains or measurable value creation.

Risk Mitigation ROI : The value created by reducing exposure to cybersecurity incidents, compliance failures, downtime, business interruption or reputational damage.

Asset Value : The long-term value of the hotel as an investment asset. Technology can influence asset value by supporting competitiveness, operational reliability and brand standards.

REFLECTION QUESTIONS

- Why is it misleading to evaluate a hotel technology project only by its initial purchase price?

- How can a SaaS model be financially attractive in the short term but risky in the long term?
- Which hidden IT costs are most likely to be underestimated by hotel executives?
- Why is ROI difficult to calculate for cybersecurity, compliance and business continuity investments?
- How can poor technology investment decisions affect guest satisfaction and online reputation?
- What is the difference between postponing a project strategically and accumulating technical debt?
- How should a General Manager, CFO, owner and IT leader each evaluate a PMS replacement decision?
- Why should training and change management be included in the financial business case for IT projects?
- How can vendor lock-in affect future hotel strategy and negotiating power?
- What makes an IT investment recommendation credible at executive or board level?

REVIEW QUESTIONS

- Define CAPEX and give three examples of hospitality IT CAPEX.
- Define OPEX and give three examples of hospitality IT OPEX.
- Explain why SaaS is not automatically cheaper than traditional technology ownership.
- What is Total Cost of Ownership and why is it important in IT investment decisions?
- Name five hidden costs that should be included in a technology business case.

- Explain the difference between financial ROI, operational ROI, guest experience ROI and risk mitigation ROI.
- What is technical debt and how can it appear in hotel operations?
- In a PMS replacement case, why is the status quo not necessarily the cheapest option?
- What questions should executives ask before approving a SaaS contract?
- Explain the Three-Sentence Executive Framework for IT investment decisions.

REFERENCES AND FURTHER READING

HFTP and AHLA. Uniform System of Accounts for the Lodging Industry, 12th Revised Edition. The USALI is a key hospitality financial reporting reference, with the 12th revised edition announced for adoption from January 1, 2026. https://usali.hftp.org/

American Hotel & Lodging Association. HFTP, AHLA and GFC Unveil 12th Revised Edition of the Uniform System of Accounts for the Lodging Industry. This source is useful for understanding the role of standardized lodging financial reporting. https://www.ahla.com/news/hftp-ahla-and-gfc-unveil-groundbreaking-12th-revised-edition-uniform-system-accounts-lodging

Oracle Hospitality. Hotel Cloud Property Management System. This resource introduces cloud PMS capabilities, integrated operations, open architecture and hotel technology scalability.

https://www.oracle.com/hospitality/hotel-property-management/hotel-pms-software/

ISACA. COBIT. COBIT provides a governance framework for enterprise information and technology, useful for connecting IT investment decisions to business objectives, risk and accountability. https://www.isaca.org/resources/cobit

National Institute of Standards and Technology. The NIST Cybersecurity Framework 2.0. This framework helps organizations understand, assess, prioritize and communicate cybersecurity risk, which is essential when valuing risk mitigation investments. https://csrc.nist.gov/pubs/cswp/29/the-nist-cybersecurity-framework-csf-20/final

Cloud Security Alliance. SaaS Security Capability Framework. This resource helps organizations evaluate SaaS security controls and vendor responsibilities, supporting better cloud and subscription-based technology governance.
https://cloudsecurityalliance.org/artifacts/saas-security-capability-framework

Conclusion

Technology Serves Hospitality

The central lesson of this book is simple: technology should serve hospitality, not replace it. A hotel is not valuable because it has systems, applications, networks, dashboards, artificial intelligence or digital tools. A hotel is valuable because it welcomes people, protects trust, creates comfort, supports meaningful service and delivers a coherent experience. Technology matters because it has become one of the main infrastructures through which that experience is prepared, delivered, secured and measured.

In modern hospitality, IT can no longer be treated as a back-office topic reserved for technical teams. Reservations, check-in, room assignment, housekeeping, payment, restaurant operations, WiFi, IPTV, telephony, guest profiles, cybersecurity, data protection, AI, vendor management and financial reporting all depend on technology. When those systems work, hospitality feels fluid. When they fail, the failure becomes visible at the front desk, in the guest room, in online reviews, in finance reports and in executive meetings.

The role of the hospitality leader is therefore not to become a technician. The General Manager, asset manager, owner representative or consultant does not need to configure routers, code interfaces, build AI models or audit PCI-DSS controls personally. However, the leader must understand the business consequences of technology decisions. A PMS outage is not only a system outage. It is a guest experience issue, an operational continuity issue, a revenue issue and a reputation issue. Bad WiFi is not only weak connectivity. It can become a brand promise failure, especially for business and luxury guests. A poorly governed AI initiative is not only a digital experiment. It can create ethical, privacy, service and investment risks.

This is why hospitality IT must be discussed in executive language. The most important questions are not only technical: What does this system allow the hotel to do better? What guest friction does it remove? What operational risk does it reduce? What revenue does it protect? What data does it collect? What compliance exposure does it create? Which vendor will support it? What happens if it fails? How will success be measured? These questions connect technology to leadership.

The chapters of this book have followed a deliberate progression. The first chapter positioned IT as a strategic function in hospitality. The second chapter revealed the architecture and network design behind the hotel operation. The third chapter showed that cybersecurity is a leadership and business continuity issue. The fourth chapter linked GDPR and PCI-DSS to guest trust, payment security and operational discipline. The fifth chapter demystified artificial intelligence and insisted on data readiness, ethics and human oversight. The sixth chapter brought technology back into the guest journey through WiFi, IPTV and telephony. The seventh chapter focused on executive vocabulary, governance, KPIs, dashboards and vendor management. The eighth chapter explained that IT investment decisions are financial decisions involving OPEX, CAPEX, ROI, hidden costs, technical debt and strategic arbitration.

Taken together, these themes show that hotel technology is not a separate discipline floating above hospitality. It is embedded in the way hotels operate, compete and protect their promise. A hotel that ignores technology risks becoming operationally fragile. A hotel that worships technology risks becoming impersonal. The right path is neither rejection nor fascination. The right path is disciplined integration.

Hospitality remains a human industry. Guests remember how they were welcomed, helped, recognized, reassured and respected. Employees remain the ones who interpret situations, repair emotions, read subtle signals and embody the brand. Technology can provide information, speed, reliability and memory, but it cannot replace empathy, judgment, culture or leadership. The future of hospitality will not belong to hotels that automate everything. It will belong to hotels that know what should be automated, what should be supported by data, and what must remain deeply human.

For students and future executives, the ambition is clear. You do not need to speak like an engineer, but you must no longer be silent when technology is discussed. You should be able to question vendors, challenge assumptions, understand risk, defend investment, interpret dashboards, protect data, evaluate AI and explain why a technical decision matters to the guest and to the business. This is not technical expertise. It is hospitality leadership in a digital operating environment.

Technology is now part of the grammar of hotel management. It shapes the invisible conditions of service. It protects trust. It enables continuity. It supports revenue. It reveals performance. It also creates new responsibilities. The stronger the technology, the more important the leadership behind it becomes.

Final Executive Framework — The Hospitality IT Decision Checklist

The purpose of this framework is to help hospitality leaders evaluate any technology decision with executive discipline. It can be used before approving a new system, renewing a vendor contract, replacing a PMS, launching an AI tool, upgrading WiFi, redesigning payment flows, or presenting an IT investment to ownership.

THE CORE PRINCIPLE

Every hospitality IT decision should be evaluated through four lenses: guest experience, operational reliability, risk management and financial value. A decision that looks attractive technically may still be weak if it damages the guest experience, increases compliance exposure, creates vendor dependency or cannot be financially justified. A decision that looks expensive may be necessary if it protects revenue, continuity, safety or trust.

THE EXECUTIVE CHECKLIST

Use the following checklist before approving, postponing or rejecting a hospitality technology decision. The questions are designed to translate technical proposals into business consequences, so that executives can evaluate guest impact, operational reliability, risk exposure and financial value before committing resources.

- Guest Impact: What guest problem does this technology solve? Does it remove friction, improve recognition, support comfort, strengthen safety or make the journey more seamless?

- Operational Impact: Which departments will be affected? Will the solution improve workflows, reduce manual work, improve accuracy or create new complexity?
- Revenue and Cost Impact: Does the decision protect ADR, RevPAR, direct bookings, corporate accounts, food and beverage revenue, event revenue or labor productivity? What cost does it create over time?
- Risk Reduction: Does the solution reduce cybersecurity, compliance, payment, operational or business continuity risk? What risk remains if the investment is postponed?
- Data and Privacy: What data will the system collect, process, store or share? Is the data necessary? Who can access it? How long will it be retained?
- Integration: Which systems must communicate with this solution? Does it connect to PMS, POS, CRS, CRM, ERP, payment gateways, loyalty platforms or reporting tools?
- Vendor Dependency: How dependent will the hotel become on the vendor? What are the contract length, exit conditions, data portability rules and service-level commitments?
- Support and Continuity: Who supports the solution during normal operations, at night, on weekends and during crises? What happens if it fails?
- People and Adoption: Who must use the system? What training, communication and change management will be required? Will employees trust and adopt the solution?
- Measurement of Success: Which KPIs will prove that the investment worked? Will success be measured through guest satisfaction, revenue, cost reduction, reduced incidents, speed, adoption or risk reduction?

THE THREE-SENTENCE TEST

Before approving a major IT investment, the executive sponsor should be able to explain the decision in three clear sentences:

The problem: what breaks, weakens or remains exposed if the hotel does nothing.

The solution: how the proposed technology solves the problem in practical and measurable terms.

The return: what financial, operational, guest experience or risk-reduction value the decision creates.

If the value cannot be explained clearly, the business case is not ready. Complexity often hides weak justification.

MANDATORY, STRATEGIC OR OPTIONAL?

When budgets are limited, IT investments should be classified according to urgency and business impact.

- Mandatory investments protect compliance, cybersecurity, payment continuity, safety or critical operations.
- Strategic investments protect competitiveness, brand positioning, guest satisfaction, revenue or scalability.
- Optional investments may create convenience or differentiation but can be postponed without immediate business risk.

Executive Translation Examples

- The AI tool is innovative. Executive translation: The tool should be approved only if the hotel has the data readiness, governance and measurable business case to absorb it responsibly.

- We should move to cloud. Executive translation: A cloud model may improve scalability and support, but it must be evaluated against dependency, cost, data location and continuity risks.
- We need cybersecurity investment. Executive translation: The current risk exposure could interrupt operations, expose guest data and damage brand trust.
- The PMS is outdated. Executive translation: Our core operating system is increasing manual work, slowing check-in and limiting future service improvements.
- We need more bandwidth. Executive translation: Current connectivity cannot support guest and meeting-room demand, creating satisfaction risk and potential corporate account loss.

FINAL FRAMEWORK STATEMENT

A hospitality executive should not approve technology because it is fashionable, nor reject it because it is technical. The right decision is the one that protects the hotel promise, supports employees, reduces risk, creates measurable value and remains aligned with the brand and the asset strategy.

Final Capstone Case Study

The Valmont Meridian Technology Transformation

This final case is designed as an integrative exercise. It connects the main themes of the book: hotel IT functions, architecture, cybersecurity, compliance, AI, guest-facing technology, governance and financial decision-making. It should be read as a professional decision scenario rather than a technical problem.

SCENARIO

The Valmont Meridian is a 210-room upscale independent hotel located in a major European capital. The hotel has a strong location, a loyal base of corporate travelers, two restaurants, a bar, a spa, five meeting rooms and a growing leisure segment during weekends. The property was renovated six years ago, but its technology environment has evolved unevenly. Some systems are modern and cloud-based. Others are aging, locally managed or poorly integrated.

The hotel has historically performed well, but several warning signs have appeared over the last twelve months. Guest reviews increasingly mention unstable WiFi, especially in meeting rooms and on higher floors. Corporate accounts have complained that travelers struggle to join video calls from guest rooms. The PMS is eleven years old and requires manual workarounds at check-in, billing and reporting. The POS does not always post charges correctly to the PMS, creating reconciliation issues. The marketing team wants to launch a more personalized loyalty campaign, but guest data is spread across PMS, CRM exports and email marketing tools.

At the same time, the owner is pressuring the General Manager to protect EBITDA. The CFO is concerned about rising SaaS subscription proposals. The IT provider warns that the current infrastructure is becoming fragile. The Revenue Manager wants to test an AI revenue management tool. The Front Office Manager wants the PMS replaced as soon as possible. The Sales Director argues that WiFi must be fixed first because meeting clients are becoming dissatisfied. The Legal Advisor has raised concerns about guest data exports and payment practices.

CURRENT ISSUES

The PMS is outdated, difficult to integrate and no longer supports modern guest-service workflows effectively.

WiFi complaints are increasing and have begun to affect corporate traveler perception and meeting-room sales.

There are shared user accounts in some operational systems, making accountability weak.

Guest data is exported into spreadsheets for marketing and VIP preparation, creating GDPR and governance risk.

Payment processes vary between front office, restaurant, spa and events, making PCI-DSS scope unclear.

The hotel has no formal IT steering committee and technology decisions are handled reactively.

The owner has approved a maximum technology envelope of EUR 450,000 for the next twelve months, but expects clear financial logic.

Several vendors are proposing cloud-based and AI-enabled solutions, but the executive team is unsure how to compare them.

EXECUTIVE DECISION CHALLENGE

The General Manager must present a twelve-month technology roadmap to the owner and executive committee. The roadmap must prioritize investments, explain risks, define governance, protect guest experience and remain financially realistic.

AVAILABLE INVESTMENT OPTIONS

IPTV modernization: estimated cost EUR 95,000. Main benefit: Improves in-room experience and upsell potential. Main risk: Lower urgency if WiFi and PMS issues remain unresolved.

AI revenue management pilot: estimated cost EUR 70,000. Main benefit: May improve pricing, forecasting and channel decisions. Main risk: Requires clean historical data and human oversight.

CRM and data governance cleanup: estimated cost EUR 60,000. Main benefit: Improves personalization and GDPR readiness. Main risk: Marketing impact may take time to materialize.

Payment-flow and PCI-DSS remediation: estimated cost EUR 45,000. Main benefit: Clarifies payment scope and reduces card-data exposure. Main risk: Requires operational discipline across departments.

Cybersecurity and access management program: estimated cost EUR 75,000. Main benefit: Reduces risk, improves accountability and supports compliance. Main risk: Benefits may feel invisible until an incident is avoided.

WiFi infrastructure upgrade: estimated cost EUR 120,000. Main benefit: Protects guest satisfaction, meetings and corporate accounts. Main risk: May not solve all issues if core network is also weak.

PMS replacement: estimated cost EUR 185,000 first year. Main benefit: Improves core operations, integrations and reporting. Main risk: High change-management effort and staff resistance.

QUESTIONS FOR ANALYSIS

Which issues are mandatory, strategic or optional? Explain your classification.

What should be prioritized in the first three months, and why?

Which investment protects the guest experience most directly?

Which investment protects the hotel from the highest operational or legal risk?

How should the hotel evaluate the PMS replacement against the WiFi upgrade?

What governance structure should be created before approving additional technology projects?

Which vendor questions should the executive team ask before signing any SaaS or AI contract?

How should the hotel reduce GDPR and PCI-DSS exposure in its current practices?

Should the hotel launch the AI revenue management pilot immediately or postpone it? Explain using data readiness and ROI logic.

Prepare a five-minute executive recommendation for the owner, using business language rather than technical language.

EXPECTED EXECUTIVE LOGIC

A strong answer should not simply choose the most visible or fashionable investment. It should identify mandatory risk areas, protect immediate guest and revenue impact, and build a realistic roadmap. A possible approach would be to begin with WiFi diagnosis and upgrade where urgent, cybersecurity and access control remediation, payment-flow clarification, and governance creation. The PMS replacement may be phased if the business case is strong and change management is realistic. The AI pilot should probably be postponed until data quality and system integration are better understood. IPTV modernization may remain valuable, but only after the foundation is stabilized.

The strongest recommendation is the one that connects technology to guest satisfaction, revenue protection, compliance, operational continuity and asset value. The weakest recommendation is the one that lists tools without explaining why the hotel should invest in them now.

Complete Glossary of Hospitality IT Terms

Access Control: The process of limiting system access according to user roles, business need and security requirements.

Access Point: A network device that provides wireless coverage to guest and staff devices.

ADR: Average Daily Rate, the average room revenue earned per occupied room.

AI Governance: The policies and controls used to ensure that AI is safe, ethical, reliable and aligned with business goals.

Analytics: The analysis of past or current data to explain performance, reveal patterns and support decisions.

API: Application Programming Interface, a structured method that allows software systems to exchange data.

Artificial Intelligence: Technologies that identify patterns, make predictions, generate outputs or recommend actions based on data.

Attack Surface: The collection of systems, users, devices, vendors and access points through which an attacker could compromise an organization.

Automation: A rules-based process that performs predefined tasks without necessarily learning from data.

Bandwidth: The amount of data capacity available for internet or network use.

Business Continuity: The ability of the hotel to continue essential operations during and after a disruption.

CAPEX: Capital expenditure, usually used for long-term assets or major projects that are depreciated over time.

Cardholder Data: Payment card information protected under PCI-DSS.

Cloud-Based System: A system hosted remotely by a vendor or service provider and accessed through the internet.

Compliance Culture: Shared behaviors and leadership expectations that make data protection and payment security part of daily operations.

CRM: Customer Relationship Management, a system or approach used to manage guest profiles, preferences, loyalty and communication.

CRS: Central Reservation System, a system used to manage reservations, availability and distribution.

Cyber Risk: The possibility that a digital threat will create operational, financial, legal or reputational consequences.

Cybersecurity: The practices and controls used to protect systems, networks and data from unauthorized access or disruption.

Data Breach: Unauthorized access, disclosure, alteration, loss or exposure of personal, payment or confidential information.

Data Minimization: The principle that organizations should collect only the data necessary for the intended purpose.

Data Processing Agreement: A contract defining how a processor handles personal data on behalf of a controller.

Data Readiness: The degree to which an organization has clean, reliable, accessible and integrated data for analysis or AI use.

Downtime: A period during which a system is unavailable or cannot support normal operations.

ERP: Enterprise Resource Planning, a business system supporting finance, HR, procurement, accounting and reporting.

Firewall: A security gateway that helps control and protect traffic between networks.

GDPR: General Data Protection Regulation, the European legal framework governing personal data processing.

Guest-Facing Technology: Technology directly or indirectly experienced by guests, including WiFi, IPTV, casting and digital service tools.

Hybrid Model: A technology model combining cloud-based and on-premise components.

Incident Response: The structured process of preparing for, detecting, managing and recovering from cybersecurity incidents.

Integration: The ability of different systems to communicate and exchange data reliably.

IP Telephony: Voice communication delivered through internet protocol networks rather than traditional phone lines.

IPTV: Internet Protocol Television, a system delivering TV, content, hotel information and service interfaces through an IP-based network.

IT Governance: The framework defining who makes IT decisions, how risks are controlled and how technology aligns with business objectives.

LAN: Local Area Network, the internal network connecting devices within one physical location such as a hotel.

Middleware: A management layer that allows systems such as IPTV to control content and integrate with hotel systems.

Network Segmentation: The separation of different types of network traffic, such as guest WiFi, payment systems and staff systems.

On-Premise System: A system hosted locally on servers physically controlled by the hotel or organization.

OPEX: Operating expense, recurring costs that affect the profit and loss statement directly.

PBX: Private Branch Exchange, a telephone system used to manage internal and external calls.

PCI-DSS: Payment Card Industry Data Security Standard, a global security standard for organizations handling cardholder data.

Phishing: A fraudulent attempt to trick people into revealing credentials or opening malicious links or attachments.

PMS: Property Management System, the core hotel system supporting reservations, check-in, room assignment, billing and profiles.

POS: Point of Sale, a system used to record and process transactions in hotel revenue centers.

Purpose Limitation: The principle that data should be used only for the specific purposes for which it was collected.

Ransomware: A cyberattack that makes systems or data unavailable and demands payment for restoration or non-disclosure.

Redundancy: Backup systems, alternative connections or contingency procedures used to reduce the impact of failure.

RevPAR: Revenue per Available Room, a key hotel performance indicator combining occupancy and ADR.

ROI: Return on Investment, the value created in relation to the cost of an investment.

SaaS: Software as a Service, a subscription-based software delivery model usually hosted in the cloud.

Scalability: The ability of a technology solution to grow with the needs of the business.

Service-Level Agreement: A contractual commitment defining service availability, response time, uptime or support expectations.

Single Point of Failure: A component or connection whose failure can disrupt an entire process or system.

Technical Debt: The accumulated cost and risk created by delaying needed upgrades, fixes or modernization.

Tokenization: A payment security technique that replaces sensitive card data with a non-sensitive token.

Vendor Lock-In: Dependency on a vendor that makes switching providers difficult or costly.

WAN: Wide Area Network, the connection linking the hotel to external networks, cloud platforms, vendors and corporate systems.

WiFi: Wireless network access used by guests, staff devices and operational tools across the property.

Final Reflection Questions

These questions are designed to help readers connect the whole book and develop executive judgment. They are not simple memory questions. They invite reflection on how technology, hospitality, risk, finance and leadership now intersect in hotel management.

- How has your understanding of hospitality IT changed after reading this book?
- Why can technology no longer be considered only a back-office function in hotels?
- Which chapter topic do you consider most urgent for the future of hospitality leadership, and why?
- In what ways does IT now shape the emotional quality of the guest experience?
- What kind of technology failure would most seriously damage the brand promise of a luxury hotel?
- How should a General Manager balance innovation, cybersecurity, compliance and financial discipline?
- Why is data protection connected to the traditional hospitality value of discretion?
- What does it mean to say that AI should support human judgment rather than replace hospitality leadership?
- How can a hotel avoid confusing technology novelty with strategic value?
- If you had to defend one IT investment to an owner, what would it be and how would you frame the business case?
- How should hotel leaders decide whether a technology decision is mandatory, strategic or optional?

- What questions should executives ask vendors before trusting their promises?
- How can poor IT governance create operational problems even when individual systems appear strong?
- Why should ROI analysis include risk reduction, guest satisfaction and employee adoption, not only direct revenue?
- What role should employees play in technology adoption and digital transformation?
- How can hospitality leaders preserve warmth, empathy and discretion in a more digital operating environment?
- What is the difference between being technologically modern and being strategically mature?
- Which IT decision in a hotel would you personally feel least comfortable making today, and what knowledge would you need to improve?
- How can technology help hotels become more reliable without becoming less human?
- What kind of hospitality leader do you want to become in relation to technology?

Final Consolidated References and Further Reading

The following resources provide useful professional and institutional foundations for readers who wish to continue exploring hospitality IT, cybersecurity, compliance, artificial intelligence, governance and financial decision-making.

Hospitality Technology and Hotel Systems
Oracle Hospitality. What Is a Hotel Property Management System. https://www.oracle.com/hospitality/what-is-hotel-pms/

Oracle Hospitality. Hospitality Technology Solutions. https://www.oracle.com/hospitality/

AHLA / HTNG. HTNG Technical Specifications. https://www.ahla.com/htng-technical-specifications

Hospitality Financial and Technology Professionals (HFTP). https://www.hftp.org/

Network, Cloud and Infrastructure
Cisco. What Is a LAN? Local Area Network. https://www.cisco.com/site/us/en/learn/topics/networking/what-is-a-lan-local-area-network.html

Cisco. What Is a Wireless LAN? https://www.cisco.com/site/us/en/learn/topics/networking/what-is-a-wireless-lan.html

Mell, P., and Grance, T. The NIST Definition of Cloud Computing. NIST Special Publication 800-145. https://csrc.nist.gov/pubs/sp/800/145/final

Cisco Meraki. MR Hospitality Design Guide. https://documentation.meraki.com/

Cybersecurity and Risk

National Institute of Standards and Technology. The NIST Cybersecurity Framework 2.0. https://www.nist.gov/cyberframework

CISA. StopRansomware Guide. https://www.cisa.gov/stopransomware/ransomware-guide

Verizon. Data Breach Investigations Report. https://www.verizon.com/business/resources/reports/dbir/

GDPR and PCI-DSS

European Parliament and Council of the European Union. Regulation (EU) 2016/679, General Data Protection Regulation.

European Data Protection Board. Guidelines and resources on GDPR. https://www.edpb.europa.eu/

Information Commissioner's Office. Guide to the GDPR and lawful basis resources. https://ico.org.uk/

PCI Security Standards Council. PCI DSS standards and documentation. https://www.pcisecuritystandards.org/

Artificial Intelligence and Governance

European Commission. AI Act. https://digital-strategy.ec.europa.eu/en/policies/regulatory-framework-ai

National Institute of Standards and Technology. Artificial Intelligence Risk Management Framework. https://www.nist.gov/itl/ai-risk-management-framework

OECD. OECD AI Principles. https://oecd.ai/en/ai-principles

McKinsey & Company. The State of AI. https://www.mckinsey.com/capabilities/quantumblack/our-insights/the-state-of-ai

IT Governance and Finance

ISACA. COBIT resources. https://www.isaca.org/resources/cobit

PeopleCert. ITIL resources. https://www.peoplecert.org/

AHLA and HFTP. Uniform System of Accounts for the Lodging Industry resources. https://www.ahla.com/

Cloud Security Alliance. Cloud security guidance and resources. https://cloudsecurityalliance.org/

About the Author

Eric Bouf is a hospitality management professor and international hotel management professional with more than thirty years of experience across Asia, America, Europe, Dubai and North Africa among major hospitality brands such as Hilton, The Ritz, Disney, Marriott and others.

He teaches hospitality management to Master's students at AIM and Ferrandi in Paris and Bordeaux. His teaching work focuses on preparing future hospitality leaders to connect operational reality, executive judgment and strategic decision-making. Through his educational projects, he develops applied learning materials, case studies and executive-oriented frameworks for students and professionals in hospitality and tourism.

This book reflects his conviction that technology has become an essential management language for hospitality leaders. Hotel executives do not need to become IT specialists, but they must understand how digital systems affect service, trust, revenue, compliance, risk and long-term value. His approach is practical, hospitality-centered and designed to bridge the classroom, the hotel floor and the executive meeting room.